Kelly Gallagher • Penny Kittle

180 Days

Two Teachers and the Quest to Engage and Empower Adolescents

HEINEMANN
Portsmouth, NH

Heinemann
361 Hanover Street
Portsmouth, NH 03801–3912
www.heinemann.com

Offices and agents throughout the world

The authors and publisher wish to thank those who have generously given permission to reprint borrowed material:

Figure 1.1: "In my first year of college, I will be expected to complete" chart by reDesign. Copyright © 2014 by reDesign. Published by reDesign. Reprinted by permission of the publisher.

Acknowledgments for borrowed material continue on page xxii.

Cataloging-in-Publication Data is on file at the Library of Congress.
ISBN: 978-0-325-08113-7

Editor: Katie Wood Ray
Production: Vicki Kasabian
Cover and interior designs: Suzanne Heiser
Typesetter: Kim Arney
Manufacturing: Steve Bernier

Printed in the United States of America on acid-free paper
22 21 20 19 18   VP   2 3 4 5

180 Days

Content**s**

We are grateful to poets and writers
who inspire our students to read
and write with determination and joy.
We dedicate this book to you.

Video Access

Visit http://hein.pub/180days-login to access the online videos and online resources. [QR code]

Enter your email address and password (or click "Create an Account" to set up an account). Once you have logged in, enter keycode **one80** and click "Register."

There is only one URL, which leads you to a landing page that contains all the video clips. The landing page has the video listed by chapter and by category.

We've included the QR code at the first instance in each chapter for ease of use, along with an icon ([icon] or [icon]) that indicates there's accompanying video.

Video Contents

Introduction

Teaching is a complex act. Charlotte Danielson (1996) estimates that a teacher makes more than three thousand nontrivial decisions every day. No list can capture the extraordinary subtlety involved in making instant decisions about which student to call on, how to frame an impromptu question, or how to respond to an interruption. The late Madeline Hunter compared teaching to surgery, "where you think fast on your feet and do the best you can with the information you have. You must be very skilled, very knowledgeable, and exquisitely well trained, because neither the teacher nor the surgeon can say, 'Everybody sit still until I figure out what in the heck we're gonna do next.'" (Hunter quoted in Goldberg 1990, 43)

A new school year approaches, and we will soon meet our students.

We cannot wait to get started.

We already know a few things about our students: too many will arrive with a pronounced lack of interest in reading and writing; some will have very low skills; and a few will have read all summer and will be excited for what lies ahead. We know that engaging all of our students will be a challenge every day. And we also know there's a lot we just don't know yet.

We expect the usual hurdles that emanate from outside our classrooms. Our instruction will no doubt be interrupted by messages sent by the office, by emergency evacuation drills, by assemblies. We will be asked to attend unproductive meetings. We will be given budgets that are laughable, given the challenges in front of us. And we will be handed mandates by public school bureaucracies that are at odds with what we are trying to accomplish. Sometimes it will feel as if the world outside our rooms is hell-bent on getting in our way.

But despite these obstacles, let us repeat: we cannot wait to get started. We believe that the teaching of literacy can be life changing. Literally. We know that after years of mind-numbing worksheets and packet work, too many of our students have come to see reading and writing as mundane chores. Many of them have parents who are not readers and writers, and because of this, many have never seen a person write something personal and powerful. We want something different for our students. We want to show them the beauty reading and writing can bring to their lives. We do not want them to be indifferent; we want them to be empowered and independent, curious and passionate. We feel an urgency that goes far beyond the standards. And because so much is at stake, we are willing to fight through all that stands in our way. We know the work is vitally important, and we will not be deterred.

Because the stakes are so high, we believe that every moment spent with our students matters—that time is a precious commodity. This, of course, leads us to a simple truth known to all English teachers: there is simply too much to do and not enough time to do it. When we conduct workshops, teachers often say hello or share ideas and resources with us. But more often than not, the teachers who approach ask what we've come to call The Question: *How do you fit everything into one school year?* Sometimes we can even tell The Question is coming before the teacher says a word, because it is written in the teacher's face—an expression that roughly translates as follows: "I like what you shared today, but what you are proposing does not fit in my curriculum. *How do you fit it all in?*"

In response, we often have been guilty of giving a very flippant two-word answer: "We don't." And because there really is not enough time to answer The Question standing in the hallways after a workshop, we have suggested that teachers begin by prioritizing what their students need most and to start their planning process by first addressing those needs and moving outward from there. This, of course, is surface-level, shallow advice, and it does little to help anyone arrive at deeper, more authentic answers. Having been asked The Question untold times, we had become adept at answering it without really answering it.

But then a funny thing happened. One day, while having lunch together, we were marveling at how often we get asked The Question. This, in turn, *led us to ask each other* The Question. This high-level discussion went something like this:

> **Penny:** So, Kelly, how *do you* fit everything into a single school year?
>
> **Kelly** (*Long pause*): Hmm . . . well . . . I don't. (*Another long pause*) How do *you* fit everything into one school year?
>
> **Penny:** I . . . um . . . well, I don't try to . . . it's complicated.

It *is* complicated. But since all teachers struggle with The Question, we felt compelled to explore it. *How do you fit it all in?* is hard because there are many layers to the answer. Instead of starting with the district-mandated curriculum guide or a list of required texts, we first ask, "What are the most pressing needs of the students who sit before us?" This leads us to ask,

"What then are the essential things we must teach them?" And then, "*When* during the school year should those things be taught, and *how* should we teach them?" Answering one question leads us to the next, which, in turn, leads us to other questions.

✦ A Year of Teaching Dangerously

This book began as an earnest attempt to share the decisions we make when determining what will fit into a single school year. To move beyond the surface-level responses we had grown accustomed to giving, we decided that the best way to get to the answer was to first plan a year together, and to then teach a year together. This book captures that year, but it has evolved into much more than simply sharing what we did.

At its heart, this book is about *why* we did what we did. Creating a classroom conducive to raising engaged readers, writers, listeners, speakers, and thinkers continually led us back to closely examining our decision-making process. And teaching the units we designed meant paying attention throughout the unit to what our students were learning. That led to unforeseen lessons that had to be taught (or retaught). This created tension in our year plan since extending time during one unit constricted time for something else. The bottom line: *it didn't all fit.*

Given the demands of the modern-day classroom, we were forced to make critical additions and deletions. We began making these decisions in the summer before we met our students, and we continued to make them as the year unfolded. Often, we found ourselves making decisions while standing in front of a room full of adolescents. In this book, it is our intention to capture as many of these decisions as possible and to share our thinking behind them.

Truth be told, both of us are feeling a sense of unease in opening up our classrooms to this level of public scrutiny. Writing a book that attempts to show why we do what we do— and exposing all that we didn't get to in a year of teaching, even with our best intentions—is very different from writing a book that simply shares what we would *like* to do. It feels risky to have to account for sometimes painful decisions. Why does this stay in? Why does this get cut? Why are we teaching it this way? Why did this work? Why did this not work? What should we do next?

We think about this work constantly—our spouses would say obsessively—and we still don't have all the answers we're seeking. But we know this: teaching is seductive simply because of its complexity. We want our love of English to be present in the lives of our students this year, and we want our lessons and units to be clearly organized in order to effectively teach well, day in and day out. We invite you to share the journey with us in this book as well as online, where you will see videos of our team-teaching, conferences with our readers and writers, and planning discussions we held throughout the year.

✈ Our Two Schools

When Kelly first walked into Penny's classroom, he scanned the six round tables with four chairs each and asked, "Where do all of the rest of the students sit?" Classes are small or "just right" in Penny's school—a product of declining enrollment and administrative determination to provide excellent conditions for learning. Ten years ago Penny taught thirty-four seniors squeezed into a portable on the back lot behind an overcrowded, crumbling 1923 building. In 2007 a new high school was built, creating new opportunities for the use of space.

Penny has almost two thousand books organized into categories (like a bookstore) in tall shelves that rim her classroom. Her walls are painted with bright colors. Her classroom is a warm and inviting place. Penny's school has a vibrant Career and Technical Center, and the Little Eagles Preschool playground is outside the windows along one wall. When the weather cooperates, Penny's students work next to the squeals and giggles of four- and five-year-olds. The school is built on a hill one mile from the center of a small collection of towns and is surrounded by forest. Black bears occasionally wander through the parking lot.

When Penny first stepped from the blazing California heat into the dark of Kelly's classroom, the first thing she noticed was books and the annoying buzz of the air conditioner. Kelly also has an extensive classroom library, organized by categories. The second thing Penny noticed was lots and lots of students (thirty-eight of them in his ninth-grade class). Students are jammed into desks from one side of the classroom to the other, which is why Kelly strongly encourages the regular use of deodorant.

Kelly's portable classroom is wedged into the back of the school. Unlike Kennett High School, Magnolia High School has received only superficial facelifts over the years, and it shows. Kelly's portable has drab, beige walls made of clothlike material, thus making them impossible to paint. The school, located in the center of urban sprawl, has mostly concrete grounds, with little vegetation. There is zero chance that a black bear will wander through the parking lot, though stray dogs are not uncommon.

Figure I.1 describes a more detailed comparison between our two schools.

	Kelly's School	Penny's School
Location	Kelly teaches at Magnolia High School, an urban school in the Anaheim Union High School District, in Southern California.	Penny teaches at Kennett High School, a rural school in the White Mountains of New Hampshire that draws students from eight communities covering more than 1,000 square miles.
School history	Magnolia High School was built in 1963. It is the smallest of eight high schools in the Anaheim Union High School District.	The new Kennett High School was built in 2007 but was first established in 1923. It is the only high school in the valley on the New Hampshire side of the border with Maine.
Teaching history	Kelly has taught at Magnolia for 29 of his 33 years of teaching. He has taught all but one of his years at the high school level.	Penny has taught at Kennett for 20 of her 33 years in teaching. She started as an elementary teacher, then moved to middle school, college teaching, and then back to middle school before settling in high school.
School enrollment	1,854 students	749 students
Demographics	The ethnic breakdown of the student population is as follows: White: 10 percent African American: 3 percent Latino: 67 percent Asian: 8 percent Native Hawaiian / Pacific Islander: 1 percent Filipino: 3 percent Two or more races: 8 percent	The ethnic breakdown of the student population is: White: 95 percent African American: 2 percent Alaskan native: 0.5 percent Latino: 1.2 percent Asian: 1.2 percent
Language learners	English language learners constitute 29 percent of the students. There are over 30 languages spoken on the campus.	English language learners constitute 3 percent of the students. There are 3 languages spoken on campus.
Free and reduced lunch	Magnolia offers free and reduced lunches to 85 percent of its students. The school has the highest percentage of homeless students in the district's sixteen schools.	Kennett offers free and reduced lunches to 28 percent of its students.
Dropout rate	Magnolia has a dropout rate of 8.4 percent.	In 2006, Kennett had the highest dropout rate in the state. Since 2013, the dropout rate has been less than 0.2 percent.
College attendance	In 2015, 67 percent of Magnolia's graduates went on to two- and four-year colleges.	In 2015, 84 percent of Kennett graduates went on to two- and four-year colleges.
School schedule	Magnolia is on a traditional schedule, so Kelly sees his students every day. The class periods are 53 minutes. Kelly has 9,360 instructional minutes in a school year.	Kennett is on an A/B block schedule of 80-minute classes. Penny sees ninth-grade students every other day for 80 minutes. Penny has 7,200 instructional minutes in a school year.
Class sizes	Kelly's ninth-grade class has 38 students (21 girls and 17 boys). Students in the class are heterogeneously mixed, so there are general-level, college prep, and honors students in each class.	Penny's ninth-grade classes average 17 students (12 girls and 23 boys in two classes). Students in both classes are heterogeneously mixed, so there are general-level, college prep, and honors students in each class.

Figure I.1 Comparison of Our Two High Schools

After our initial visits to each other's classrooms, we were intrigued by our different teaching worlds, and these visits led us to consider some interesting questions:

- In what ways would a ninth-grade year in New Hampshire look the same as a ninth-grade year in California? In what ways would they look different?

- What is common no matter where you teach?

- How will our very different environments shape our decision-making?

- How will the difference in the hours we have to teach students affect our decision-making?

- What kind of cross-country collaboration might occur between our students? How might our kids benefit from this collaboration?

We knew it would be easier to continue to do what we have done for years, but after visiting each other's classrooms, we could see that a collaboration would challenge our thinking and our practices. The Question would push us both to new understandings of teaching and learning.

✈ How This Book Is Framed

This book is divided into two sections. Section 1, "Planning Decisions," takes you through the process we used—and you might consider—to plan a year of teaching. The section includes five chapters:

1: Start with Beliefs

2: Establish Daily Practices

3: Map a Year of Reading

4: Map a Year of Writing

5: Balance Feedback and Evaluation.

Section 2, "Teaching Essential Discourses," begins with an introduction that explains the general framework for planning a unit of study in a specific writing discourse. Then, in the four chapters that follow, we detail the decisions we made in four discourse studies: narrative, informational, argument, and multigenre. Our hope is that by reading about the decisions we made as we planned together, you will be inspired to reimagine the beautiful possibilities for your teaching.

We know that the choices we make about how to spend time show students what we value. Our choices determine what our students will do and what they will learn. This responsibility is daunting, and it is exhilarating. We are already making choices about what fits, but in August time feels expansive. The year is filled with possibility: We will discover books that will keep us up late at night. We will learn new technologies to lead our students. We will live as readers and writers in a community with fascinating, complex young people. We are ready to lead and to follow them. We can't wait to get started.

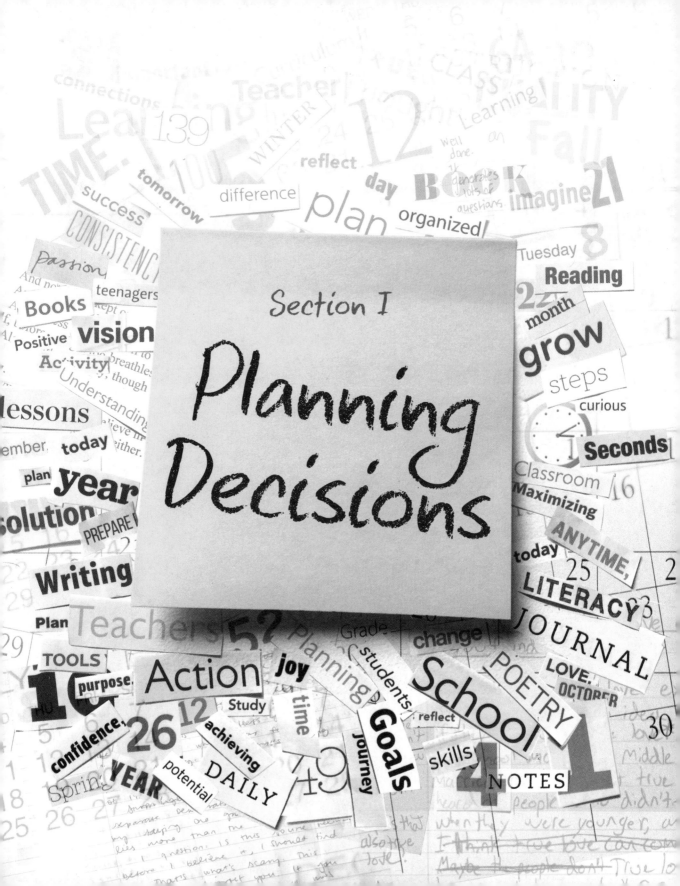

Section I

Planning Decisions

A... ...pt on the fridge.
And ... ...ys you had crushes on.
And ... ...at got worn to a dance at which you danced by
yourself, befo... you got too breathless to dance.
Along with, probably, though this isn't worthy of huge thinking, a
soul or
something.
Anyway, adults don't believe in Santa Claus. They try hard not to
believe in Santa Claus in Reverse either.

plan Create

Choice

Start with BELIEFS

We both began our careers patching together activities to fill time.

When Penny started teaching, the work felt possible and impossible at the same time. She loved her third graders, so bringing joy and energy to her classroom each day was easy. She thought that it would not take long before she had the units, the lessons, and the smooth management of a classroom figured out. She stayed at school until dark almost every night, climbing a chain-link fence to get to her car. She placed her lesson plans in orderly files and imagined gliding from September to June the next year. She even imagined teaching third grade for thirty years, eventually earning a Superteacher cape she would snap into place at the start of each new year. She had no idea what she didn't know. She was surprised that over the next five years teaching did not get easier. She moved among three states and five different grade levels, and each year became another first year. She also began to recognize gaps between the complex needs of each of her students and her ability to address them. She began to sense that filling time and teaching well were not the same thing.

When Kelly began his teaching career, he was thrown into a high school English classroom without much support, and he really struggled to fill 180 days. Kelly recalls getting to May and wondering, "What the heck am I going to do with these kids for the last month of school?" He was inventing on the fly, staying a day ahead of his students. Panic was never far away. Over time, however, Kelly finally created enough lessons to take his students through an entire year. Once these lesson plans were in "the can," Kelly, like Penny, thought he had turned a corner and that the job would soon become a lot easier. He, too, was wrong. Kelly was surprised to find that over time the job did not get any easier. On the contrary, it kept getting *harder*.

In our sixty-six combined years of teaching experience, we moved from filling time to spending time. What's the difference? A year of filling time is focused on lessons. A year of spending time is focused on students. We've learned to start each year by asking, "How will *these students* be empowered as readers, writers, listeners, and speakers after a year under our care?" This question makes us realize that everything matters: what we plan, how we refine our plans while teaching, how we reflect, and how we decide what comes next. Crafting engaging and relevant learning experiences, combined with the decisions teachers have to make in the moment, defines good teaching.

We know how to connect lessons and units so that students become inquisitive readers, writers, listeners, and speakers, but every year, of course, we are introduced to students we've never met. We are always teaching new students in a world rich with evolving stories and ideas. We learn from moments we can't anticipate but must react to. We learn from lessons that seem smart but fall flat. We sketch out the year before we begin, and we detail our plans weeks ahead, but we are also constantly watching and shifting to meet students where they are.

Of course, we sift through previous lessons, looking for what might interest and engage our new students. But we also start over every year looking for how teaching possibilities unique to this moment in history can enliven genre study. For example, the year we taught together, our students wrote argument pieces on who to vote for in the last presidential election. They wrote about this because *it was happening*. The immediacy of the argument elevated our students' interest in a way it never would have the year before. Finding resources to support new lessons brings an intensity to our work. We recognize that teaching is a live performance that takes place in an inconstant world. We create our teaching; what power lies in those four words.

Unfortunately, this professionalism of teaching—the expectation that teachers create their work—is not popular. English teachers often have a herd mentality; in many schools, teachers and administrators have traded the art of teaching for common ground. The meaningful reflection that should drive key teaching decisions is often buried in unmanageable curriculum and pacing guides. We have both seen whole-class instruction of a novel occur simply because this novel "has always been taught at this school." We have both sat in professional learning communities (PLCs) where teachers are not philosophically aligned yet are charged with designing common assessments and structuring units along timelines that frustrate all involved. And we have both seen school districts where teachers have been required to walk their students lockstep through scripted curricula. We reject these approaches and their cost to the developing expertise we need in our profession. If teachers never practice making instructional decisions, they will never get good at making them. When we strip teachers of agency in designing curricula, they stop thinking critically about the design of their instruction.

We recognize it is hard to break out of the herd. Adam Grant says in *Originals* (2017), "Although America is a land of individuality and unique self-expression, in search of excellence and in fear of failure, most of us opt to fit in rather than stand out . . . We find surface ways of appearing original—donning a bow tie, wearing bright red shoes—without taking the risk of actually being original. When it comes to the powerful ideas in our heads and the core values in our hearts, we censor ourselves" (13). We know that teachers in public schools must make compromises. We have made many throughout our careers, but questioning those compromises is important and necessary. We were drawn to teaching because it is imaginative, original work. We believe teacher agency fights off stagnation and is fundamental to both teacher growth and student investment. We will show you how our creative collaboration improved our teaching and our students' learning in this one school year.

Every moment matters. We begin anew every year with too many students who do not know the power of reading and writing. We continue to see how the pedagogy in most English classes consistently fails to create passionate readers and writers. Reading and writing in school is rarely practiced as the life-sustaining force it is. Students leave one year after another having missed the personal joy, the satisfaction, and the power of creating their own canon of books they love and pieces of writing they cherish.

We listen and learn from the students we are currently teaching and design instruction that will move *them*. We start with contagious enthusiasm for both reading and writing. Joy is an intentional stance. We seek life-sustaining, mind-expanding experiences with books and writing that will resonate with our current students. We believe in redesigning our units of study each year, considering the alignment between our aspirations and our new students' needs and interests. We seize the moment: a poem we've just discovered, breaking news that invites comment, or photographs that compel our students to write with passion. Likewise, we adjust daily plans when we find gaps in what we thought students would know. The continual reimagination of our curriculum increases our energy and brings an immediacy to our work each day.

When we reframe planning as figuring out how to *spend* time with *these* students in *this* moment in history, the reason teaching is still so damn hard becomes clear: we have limited time. One hundred eighty days. This is clearly not enough time, especially when you consider (1) the issues that come attached to our students (poverty, lack of motivation, high and low skills mixed in the same classroom) and (2) all the things that impede time—minutes stolen by testing, assemblies, earthquake drills (Kelly), snow days (Penny), interruptions, field trips, and chronic absenteeism.

✎ The Demands of Time

The pressure of planning a year is real, especially given the unrealistic expectations placed on ELA teachers. This was readily apparent at Penny's school when members of her department received a 101-page model curriculum document outlining a long list of objectives, as well as the skills and outcomes for teachers to address over the course of a single school year. The demands are subdivided and broken down unit by unit, in a prescribed scope and sequence. Your school or district probably has similar prescribed goals and expectations. Just reading these guides induces stress. Spend some serious time studying them and there is a good chance you will find yourself suddenly enrolling in regular yoga classes.

Length is not the only problem with documents like these; they were written by well-meaning people who have never met your students. There is too much to do, and no expectation that you will adjust the district curriculum to meet the needs of the students sitting in your classroom right now. Your decision-making is not expected or respected in a standardized curriculum, yet a one-size-fits-all approach is problematic in a world of diverse students. Our experience has taught us what is essential in any English classroom at any grade level: a curriculum that is responsive to the needs of the students. This means a foundation of daily practice in meaningful reading that is engaging, sometimes difficult, and most often pleasurable, and in daily writing that invites individuality and helps students gain confidence and independence in their decisions about crafting their ideas and experiences for audiences within and outside school. Achieving this is difficult, if not impossible, when you strictly adhere to someone else's vision of what's best for your students.

To make matters even harder for teachers, there is a bigger picture beyond our curriculum maps. Penny's 101-page curriculum guide, for example, certainly covers the ELA standards, but it doesn't cover what we call the "missing standards." Nowhere in Penny's curriculum guide, for example, does it say that one of our primary goals is to raise kids who find joy in reading. Nowhere in the guide does it say we should raise kids who look forward to their next book club meeting. Nowhere in the guide does it say we should raise kids who read dozens of books a year. And these are just the hidden standards for reading. There are hidden standards for writing, listening, and speaking as well.

With so much to do and so little time, we can't help but wonder how any teachers approach a new school year without getting tangled in skills and strategies and outcomes—lost within the very map they've been given. As we've wondered about this together, we've come to realize that The Question to ask is not "How do you fit it all in?" The question is "How do you *decide* how to spend your time in a classroom?" We can't do everything. We take time for *this*, which decreases time for *that*. Planning is ultimately about deciding how we will spend the limited time we are given with our students.

✈ What Are We Planning *For*?

Planning in any facet of life begins with a desired outcome or destination in mind, and the same is true for teaching. If we don't have a clear picture in mind of what we're planning for, it's hard to imagine how we'll make good planning decisions.

What guides us in our planning for young readers and writers? We believe all students should develop the reading and writing habits needed for success outside school: in college, work, and in their personal lives. We know all of our students will not attend college, but we believe it is our responsibility to prepare all of them for the reading and writing expectations at the postsecondary level in case they decide to attend later in life. Because of this belief, we have to think about the expectations summarized in a graphic like Figure 1.1 from reDesign.†

As this figure makes clear, the tangible demands of college in the twenty-first century are extensive. Are our students ready to meet these demands? That's the question the *Framework for*

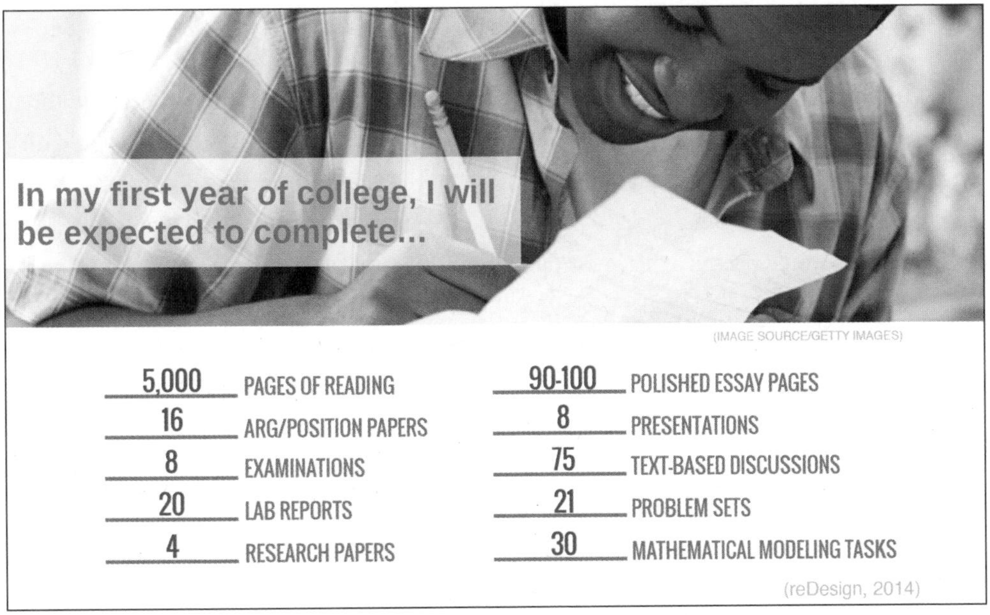

In my first year of college, I will be expected to complete...

(IMAGE SOURCE/GETTY IMAGES)

5,000	PAGES OF READING	90-100	POLISHED ESSAY PAGES
16	ARG/POSITION PAPERS	8	PRESENTATIONS
8	EXAMINATIONS	75	TEXT-BASED DISCUSSIONS
20	LAB REPORTS	21	PROBLEM SETS
4	RESEARCH PAPERS	30	MATHEMATICAL MODELING TASKS

(reDesign, 2014)

Figure 1.1 Expectations for First-Year College Students   *Source:* reDesign 2014

† The information displayed in Figure 1.1 is a summary of a small-scale, informal study of the syllabi of college freshmen courses. While the graphic resonates with many college graduates, reDesign is clear that this is not the result of a formalized analysis of a representative set of syllabi.

Success in Postsecondary Writing seeks to answer. Developed jointly by the Council of Writing Program Administrators, the National Council of Teachers of English, and the National Writing Project (2011), the document describes, among other things, eight habits of mind that are critical for college success. These eight habits are ways of approaching learning that are both intellectual and practical and that will support students' success in a variety of fields and disciplines:

- *Curiosity.* The desire to know more about the world.

- *Openness.* The willingness to consider new ways of being and thinking in the world.

- *Engagement.* A sense of investment and involvement in learning.

- *Creativity.* The ability to use novel approaches for generating, investigating, and representing ideas.

- *Persistence.* The ability to sustain interest in and attention to short- and long-term projects.

- *Responsibility.* The ability to take ownership of one's actions and understand the consequences of those actions for oneself and others.

- *Flexibility.* The ability to adapt to situations, expectations, or demands.

- *Metacognition.* The ability to reflect on one's own thinking as well as on the individual and cultural processes used to structure knowledge. (4–5)

We have both spent hours thinking about how these eight habits of mind intersect with experiences in our English classrooms. For example, we made "How do others see the world differently than I do?" an essential question for the school year after considering how critical it is to develop *openness* in our students. (We had no idea in September how the rhetoric of the presidential election would magnify this question.) Likewise, to model *flexibility*, we committed to composing with digital technologies even though our lack of experience in creating digital texts made us vulnerable when leading students. *Metacognition* was front and center as we modeled the navigation through struggle and failure that is necessary to wrestle with a new skill.

More than anything, though, we considered how *engagement* is a necessary habit of mind. To cultivate engagement, students need interesting texts to read and respond to: literature, yes, but also charts, infographics, campaign ads, photographs, editorials, and poems. Lots of poems. To develop expertise through a volume of practice—the kind of volume required for college—we knew we had to make room for our students to read, write, and talk every day.

It seemed so simple.

We had set aside a few hours to begin planning our first three weeks of school together. Four hours later, we adjourned, having planned a grand total of two days. Four hours to plan two days of instruction! Why was it so difficult? Because every time we started to plan a lesson, we found we had to back up and discuss our thinking behind it. Before we could discuss *what*, we realized that we first needed long conversations about *why*. Kelly asked, "When you say *unit*, what do you mean by that?" Penny asked, "Have you always had students write stories as the first unit of the year? Why?" Our conversation went back and forth between *How do you do that?* and *Why do you do that?*

We came to understand that to plan a year of instruction together, we first had to come to terms with our shared values and beliefs. Having a destination in mind was not enough. We first needed to come to terms with what mattered.

✈ What Do We Believe About Teaching and Learning?

Planning doesn't start with *what* and *how* questions. Planning starts with *why*. All the chapters that follow this one will tell you what we did to plan a year of instruction, but all those plans start here, with these ten core beliefs. As you read them, we invite you to consider the philosophical underpinnings of your own teaching. What are the values and beliefs that guide your actions?

We Believe Each Academic Year Is a Unique, Living Mosaic

Every year is its own story, coauthored with dozens of students we meet for the first time each fall. As Chris Lehmann wrote in the foreword to *Reading Wellness* (Burkins and Yaris 2014), "Our best work happens when we align our instructional decisions to their strengths . . . when our children become our curriculum, their actions our data, their potential our standards" (x). We believe in Nancie Atwell's vision as described in *In the Middle* (2015), where she encourages teachers to pay close attention to the choices, intentions, and needs of students so that we will be better equipped "to respond to them, lead them, and show them how to grow" (5).

(Every year, we believe we must rewrite curriculum so it is responsive to the mosaic of our students and our changing world.) Students are at the center of our work. We teach them, not curriculum. Even though we plan ahead for a year, our day-to-day teaching will vary as we respond to the learning of our students. (We do not microplan very far ahead. Instead, we teach with urgency—deciding daily how best to lead our students to engage deeply and to sustain energy for learning.)

Conversation Clip

See multiple
planning
conversations in
the online video

We are excited by both knowing and not knowing what will happen each day in class. Some teachers believe planning is deciding ahead of time how things will go, which is true, but we believe it is also *planning* for what we can't yet know (Glover and Berry 2012). We plan for the inevitable variation in unit design that occurs when we study students' work so that we can then respond with better teaching. It is the alchemy of our ongoing active thinking about our students' progress and our goals that drives our instruction in class—that tells us what to cut and what to keep when a schoolwide lockdown expands second period an extra thirty minutes and shrinks fourth period to half its size.

We map each year with careful planning, but we're always aware that if we keep our heads down studying a map, we miss our most alive teaching—responsive, dynamic, and exhilarating. A map shouldn't be so specific that it prevents us from using current texts. A malleable curriculum map encourages a hidden standard—relevancy—to be central in our practice. We want our content to matter *now*, and helping students see this relevancy increases their engagement and thus their achievement.

At the center of our practice is conferring—the heart of responsive teaching. We center our thinking on Don Murray's college writing workshop, which was originally called the "Conference Model" because of the importance of daily conversations with students. When we confer, we pay attention to what students are coming to know as readers and writers and seek ways to nudge them toward more independence and power. Conferring creates opportunities for us to guide and support students while they are in the creative process. Helping our students begins with knowing our students, and we craft the responsive classroom practices of a rich reading and writing workshop for them. We believe each classroom is its own mosaic, influenced by our thinking about the unique challenges of our students in this moment in time.

We Believe There Is Beauty in Our Content

In *The Courage to Teach* (1997), Parker Palmer talks about the "great things" that are found at the center of any subject matter, such as "the symbols and referents of philosophy and theology," "the shapes and colors of music and art," or "the archetypes of betrayal and forgiving and loving and loss that are the stuff of literature" (107). We are at our best, Palmer writes, when we gather around these great things, as their greatness will propel us to be knowers, teachers, and learners.

We believe there is greatness to be found when we gather around literature and poetry, but students do not discover this greatness through lectures, quizzes, worksheets, or poster projects. Students discover beauty when given the opportunity to wrestle with the greatness of literature on their own terms. We personalize reading and writing, seeking the deep connection that happens when you trust students to choose what they read and write and then teach into their developing understandings.)

We believe in the value of reading and writing for their own sake, and we know there is a wide range of novels that will create an urgency to read. Likewise, writing is more than its parts, and the complex craft of composition is worthy of study. Students have stories to tell, and when they work to write them, they feel the power of creation as poets, storytellers, and artists of words and ideas. We strive to create classroom conditions that support discovery, persistence, and connection with writers in the room and writers they meet in the books they read.

We Believe in the Power of Models

We believe that as English teachers we must be readers and writers because it is the heart of our content area. Just like those of our students, our reading and writing lives are being shaped by the evolving world and the new tools available to us. All of Penny's writing starts, lives, and breathes by a window in her office. She works in the dark before dawn, writing mostly by hand in her notebook with her dog, Cody, beside her. Kelly writes early, as well, usually between 4:00 and 5:30 A.M. in an office lined with wooden bookshelves. He turns off his phone and email and tries to write at least five hundred words a day. His dog, Scout, sleeps beside him as Kelly pecks away on his laptop.

To both of us, momentum matters, and though we are not always successful, we try to write every morning. When we begin the day by writing, we often find that our ideas continue to dance at the edge of our consciousness even while we teach, or as we plow through eight inches of powder in the deep of the woods or swim laps in the pool at dusk. What we wrote one morning often helps us when we sit down to write on the next. Conversely, it is always hard to start writing again after we've been away for a few days. The increased distance between moments spent writing increases its difficulty.

We are also both active readers, constantly looking for books and passages that call to something deep inside of us—that answer questions we didn't even know we were asking. We seek the words that we can't let go of and we seek the books that will connect with our students. We believe we must be active, engaged readers in order to create a contagious passion for reading in our classrooms.

Recognizing the importance momentum plays in our reading and writing lives reinforces the importance of developing momentum in our students, so we make time for both reading and writing every day in our classrooms. This predictable time affects our students' thinking as well as their confidence. Our units and lessons are designed to create daily reading and writing habits.

Reading and writing with our students is also demonstration teaching; it's show-not-tell teaching, and it establishes our credibility. We live as mentors for our students amidst the complexity of reading and writing. What matters most to this teaching? Authenticity. We share what we are reading with students, and when we read difficult texts, we do some of that reading in front of them, thinking aloud to model moves that readers make. We write in front of students to model engagement with words and ideas, revision, rereading, and problem-solving. We write whatever our students are writing, developing our own drafts throughout each unit of study.

We model the value of talk and collaboration, and we model in nontraditional ways as well: punctuality, curiosity, inquisitiveness, kindness, open-mindedness, professionalism, patience, and the ability to listen.

Conversation Clip
See "Writing to Understand What You're Asking Students to Do"

We Believe Choice Drives Engagement

We agree with Carol Ann Tomlinson and Susan Demirsky Allan (2000) that students should have choice in (at least) one of these factors with every assignment: content, process, product, or conditions for learning. We know adolescents are more likely to invest in the deep thinking needed for intellectual growth when given choice, and our units are designed to give students choices.

Across the year, we plan for a balance between independent reading, book clubs, and core texts, so that students have choice in what they read 75 percent of the time. The order of these experiences matters. Many of our students come to us as dormant readers after a summer, or in too many cases, after years of reading only excerpts and short texts, not books. We also know that when teachers make all or most of the choices about what is read, students do not read enough. We believe the "Hey kids, I know you don't like to read so let's get started by reading *Romeo and Juliet*!" approach is counterproductive.

We want our students to establish significant reading traction, so we begin our school year by inviting them to find books *they* are interested in reading. Right from the start, we battle resistance, apathy, and disinterest in reading by providing students with interesting books and time to read them at their own pace and by establishing regular reading conferences where we listen more than we talk. It takes time—weeks of time—to establish regular independent reading both inside and outside class in students' increasingly distracted and busy lives.

Across the year, students will select books to read with others in book clubs, and they will read two core texts chosen for the entire class to read together. The balance we try to maintain that privileges choice over whole-class, assigned reading is grounded in both research (Reeves 2006) and our own experience motivating disengaged readers.

We also privilege choice in writing instruction, in which we seek a better balance between task writing and having students generate writing from their own ideas and experiences. Across the year, our students will have both wide-open choices (self-selected writing topics and/or genres) and limited choices (writing in genre units of study). Students will also write (rarely) for district-mandated assessments in which the topic and form are chosen for them.

We want to create classrooms where students feel their lives are worthy of study and reflection. We find our students are more likely to engage in their literacy development when given the opportunity to explore their own lives. There is a voice, a liveliness, that arises when Maria writes of the time immigration officials stormed into her house and dragged her undocumented father out the front door. There is an intimacy, an intensity, that occurs when Jacqueline writes of her last moments with her fatally ill aunt. Our students have stories to tell. Encouraging them to write them builds an investment in school that does not occur when the only writing done is to answer the teacher's questions.

We Believe Reading Identity Matters

It seems obvious to say this, but readers are people who read. Often, and a lot. We are both active readers. Kelly has hosted a faculty book club on his campus for twenty-four years, and as a member has read over two hundred books in this club alone. Penny piles books in towers in every room of her house, often balancing the reading of four or more books at once.

We believe success in reading is built on engagement, which leads to a volume of reading—a necessary foundation for tackling complex texts. Unfortunately, too many adolescent readers suffer from an unhealthy school reading diet in which they fake or skim-read one whole-class novel, then another, then another. This agonizingly slow crawl through texts is continued month after month, year after year. Many give up believing that reading will offer them anything except meaningless work. We believe in the value of challenging books, but when students *only* read core texts chosen by their teachers, readicide (Gallagher 2009) occurs.

Because it leads to a volume of reading, we care more about our students' active engagement than we care about any particular literary work. To nurture reading identities, we believe that the diversity of students and their experiences must be represented in the reading in our

Conversation Clip
See "Aligning
Students with
Authors and Genres
They Love"

classrooms.)We seek students who will read without being asked to by the teacher and who will eagerly discuss their thinking with others.

We begin the year with three major goals for our young readers:

1. Students will increase the volume of their reading.
2. Students will increase the complexity of their reading.
3. Students will develop allegiances to authors and genres.

None of these goals will be reached without engagement, but engagement occurs only when kids have interesting books to read and time to read them. We set goals for independent reading both inside and outside school and regularly support them, and we will occasionally ask students to write as a means to more deeply understand what they are reading. Momentum matters. We make time for reading in class each day because it affects our students' confidence and engagement. Our reading lives have made us better teachers, and we know regular reading will make our students better citizens of the world.

When kids have interesting books to read and time to read them, they read more, and *more* matters. Students who read regularly grow as readers, they acquire more vocabulary, and they become better writers. They develop the stamina to engage with complex ideas or characters over hundreds of pages (stamina many of them will need for college). They sometimes experience that breathless feeling we get when we surface from the depths of a book. Increasing the volume of reading helps prepare students to navigate a changing world as well as to develop empathy and understanding. Readers are important in a democracy.

We Believe Writing Identity Matters

We want our students to live as writers. Writing creates an opportunity to understand life better and to navigate its challenges and opportunities. Writing is for life, not just for school.

We feel the pedagogical tension, as defined by Henry Widdowson (2003), between approaches to teaching writing that are designed to train for specific tasks (e.g., report writing) and those designed to position students to be creative in a world with unpredictable writing tasks. We feel conflicted by how much time we ourselves spend on the necessary, often mind-numbing writing tasks to explain, provide information, or answer emails. We see this experience echoed in our students, who must prove that they remember or know something that has been told to them—in orderly, complete sentences that can be outlined into paragraphs and turned into coherent essays. Unfortunately, crafting beautiful writing is not important for most writing tasks in school; functional, clear writing is "good enough" for tests and assignments. But when this is the only writing our students do, they lose the opportunity to explore the beauty and conflict that is coursing through each of their lives.

Teachers are making a critical error when they focus on writing for tasks only.

There is another kind of writing altogether, of course. It is the writing we read. It is the writing in memoirs and poetry and commentaries that leaves us stunned in the wake of lovely sentences. It is the writing that takes an unlikely rowing team from the University of Washington in the midst of the start of World War II (*The Boys in the Boat*) and makes those years so alive we cannot turn away. It is writing that follows a boy from the gritty, dangerous streets of Newark to the campus of Yale (*The Short and Tragic Life of Robert Peace*). This is writing that reaches *inside* us—writing that clarifies, refines, and allows us to explore and consider our own lives, our passions, our pasts, our futures. When we see this writing in the work of others, we often find the boldness to try this in our own writing. This writing cannot be drafted once and set aside; these are drafts that invite a second reading, a tenth. This is writing that deserves refinement. When students find this writing, the writing process becomes a living thing.

We both write what is difficult, what is only for us, because when we write for ourselves we learn how to seek ideas and how to find them, how to nurture them, how to question them, how to seek answers to bigger questions. Most of the writing in our notebooks will never be seen by anyone: the endless pondering and re-creating of moments we have lived both in our teaching and in our lives outside our classrooms. This writing leads to thinking that makes us better parents, friends, spouses, and teachers. This writing helps us forgive people and come to terms with moments from our past. This writing makes us hum inside with the challenge of getting it "right" and the delight when we almost do. This is the kind of writing that is most meaningful to us, and it's the experience with writing we want for our students.

Similarly, we feel the tension brought about by the overemphasis of traditional text types. It's hard to say which type has more power in classrooms today, argument or informational writing. Unfortunately, the literary analysis essay remains front and center in many ELA classrooms. As a result, narrative writing has been marginalized. Students are too often denied the opportunity to write from their own experiences, a paradox since writing what is personally meaningful is where writers invest the most. Curriculum that is narrowly focused on traditional genres stunts the creativity and flexibility we want our students to acquire. When young writers are required to repeatedly write the same essays as their peers, their unique writing identities do not emerge.

Conversation Clip

See "Modeling with Personally Authentic Topics"

We Believe in the Value of Talk

Learning is social. When you go to the theater on Friday night to see a complex film, what is the first thing you want to do immediately following the movie? Talk about it. We are both in book clubs with other adults, and we participate in these book clubs because we know that the conversations will deepen our understanding. When either of us hit a roadblock while writing sections of this book, what did we do? We talked through the problem.

Talk deepens thinking and learning. Yes, there are moments when we seek deep, reflective silence in our classrooms, but these moments are balanced by the frequent buzz that occurs when students share interesting thinking with each other. As Dennie Palmer Wolf (2015) writes, "Listening and speaking have to come back into the heart of the curriculum, out from under the dominance of reading and writing. For inquiry to flourish, young people have to grow up in discussion, public speaking, interviewing, debating, and spoken word and oral performance" (190). We agree, and so we work to place talk in the center of our classrooms.

Every day, across every unit of study in both reading and writing, we plan opportunities for students to

- talk to us (one-to-one)
- talk to one another
- talk to bigger audiences
- practice their listening skills.

Talk to Us

As we mentioned earlier, our one-to-one conferences each day help us make decisions about next steps in teaching. More importantly, conferences humanize teaching. We tend to both academic demands and the needs of young people. Although the content of the conference is unpredictable, the language we use to solve problems with students carries our values and beliefs—about students, about our content, and about the work we ask students to do. As we learned from Peter Johnston's important book *Choice Words* (2004), even if we haven't stated our beliefs, our language shows students what we value. For example, Figure 1.2 suggests what students might learn from the common kinds of questions we ask in conferences.

We believe nothing has a more positive effect on our young readers and writers than regularly meeting with them in one-to-one conferences—this is the talk that anchors our classrooms. We model that we don't have all the answers, often because our students know more than we do—we haven't read all their books and we haven't lived their lives. When we talk to them, our

When we say . . .	Students learn . . .
"You haven't been reading much lately, Sarah. What's going on?"	We pay attention to them.
"What kind of challenge do you want to give yourself next quarter?"	We nudge them.
"What are you thinking?"	We value their ideas.
"How might you make this writing better?"	We trust them to make decisions.
"How might I help you?"	We care about them.
"I brought this book from home. Do you think you might be interested in reading it?"	We think about them outside class, and we believe every kid in this class will be a reader.
"Look at how I wrote this. What moves do you notice I made as a writer?"	We will write beside them.
"What craft moves do you notice in the mentor text?"	We pay attention to great writers.
"I understand where you are coming from. I am having a bad writing day, too."	We struggle alongside them.

Figure 1.2 Our Language Carries Value

students gain confidence because they know we value their experiences. When we talk to them, we raise expectations, as students work harder to clarify their thinking. Students have often told us they try harder because they know we will soon sit together and discuss their progress as readers and writers. But the talk we do in conferences does so much more than simply raise expectations; conferences are where we connect with our kids. They are where our students *learn a lot about us.*

Teaching Clip

See multiple reading and writing conferences in the online video

Talk to One Another

As you will see in the chapters that follow, some of the deepest conversations we had about reading all year happened when we gave our students opportunities to talk to one another— during book clubs and when studying a core work together. We saw what Peter Johnston and Gay Ivey found in their research (2015), that personal and interpersonal interactions expanded the students' ability to imagine themselves into others' minds, transforming their understanding of themselves and each other, along with their moral development, their relationships with others at school and at home, their self-regulation, their empathy, the possibilities they imagined for their futures, and their happiness.

Talk to Bigger Audiences

Engagement is often fueled by audience. Students invest in their writing when they know that someone other than the teacher will be reading their work, so we plan opportunities for our students to publish their writing beyond the walls of our classrooms. As we collaborated on this project, we mixed our students together to talk (through writing) in virtual book clubs and writing groups, and we saw how strongly our students were motivated by interacting with peer audiences.

During the year we also extend the talk to even bigger audiences. We plan for students to create digital compositions, record dramatic readings of literary passages, record podcasts, and make public service announcements—all designed to be viewed or heard by broader audiences. Through these experiences, we coach students to

- speak with poise and confidence
- organize and deliver a talk designed to influence others
- moderate their language and disposition to invite listeners into a conversation.

Practice Listening Skills

We teach students about the difference between listening and hearing in conversation, and in podcasts and other media. We teach them to carefully consider what a person said and did not say in a conversation, and to build on each other's thinking when they discuss.

We Believe in the Practice of Approximation and Fearlessness

To grow, writers have to be willing to try things that are new and challenging. They have to learn to accept their own approximations—sometimes even failures—and to try again. Students who write regularly without teacher intervention develop a fearlessness that is necessary for their growth as writers. In the safe space of their writing notebooks, our students are encouraged to experiment. Practice in notebooks is celebrated, but not graded. The notebook is a place to collect ideas, not to perform. We sketch, gather, and notice in order to be more attentive to what we're thinking and understanding. We personalize and demystify writing through daily, ungraded invitations. We take risks with form and ideas. In their notebooks students generate possibilities for longer pieces of writing.

Writing by hand in notebooks helps students see what revision looks like. Those who haven't written regularly often see revision as a move writers make at the end of the writing process. In notebooks, we lead our students to the habit of revising *as their writing unfolds*, a constant rethinking of the ideas they are trying to communicate well. We model this practice by revising our own emerging drafts in front of students on the board or under a document camera as we quick write together each day.

The collection of quick writing and revising that grows over time in a notebook helps students see the gains they are making in volume and in honing the clarity of their thinking by rereading and tinkering with words. Their writing improves with practice, and they can see it.

We Believe in Grading Less and Assessing More

To help you understand this particular belief, let's start by looking at a piece of student writing. Here's an unedited excerpt from Hector, a ninth grader, recalling an incident that occurred in the sixth grade:

> I yelled at my teammate "aye pass me the ball I'll put it away for us." Because we just got done playing soccer. So i dribbled it and juggled it all the way to the rusty old ball cage. With my whole class waiting for me to get into line. While they were waiting for me they were screaming at me with frustration and anger you suck hurry up I ignored them. While I wasn't paying attention a big teacher waited for me there at the ball cage. She was looking at me with madness like if she was about to explode on like a firework on the fourth of July.

This excerpt comes from Hector's "best draft" version, a narrative that had already gone through revision and had been submitted for grading. We don't need to show you the rest of the draft for you to understand that this is a ninth-grade student writing below grade level. And yet, here the paper sat, awaiting the teacher's evaluation.

So what grade would you place on Hector's paper? Before you answer, consider the following: Hector is a reluctant writer, with a long history of receiving poor marks on his writing assignments. He is new to your class, he has shown some beginning-of-the-year willingness to write, and this is his first paper of the year to be submitted for grading. You are only a couple of weeks into the school year, and Hector will be a student of yours for eight more months.

So, now, what grade would you place on Hector's paper?

You might focus on Hector's problems with fragments and his inability to punctuate dialogue properly and conclude that this paper is "below average" for a ninth-grade writer. If grading is simply a task of sorting who gets an A, who gets a B, and so forth, Hector receives a D or an F and we move on to the next paper in the stack.

But, of course, it is not that simple.

Before placing a grade on Hector's paper, we need to be mindful that the central goal for our writers is that everyone will improve. Our students come to us with a wide range of abilities—from students like Hector who are writing below grade level to students who are writing at the honors level—but our goal remains the same for each and every one of them: everyone gets better. To help achieve this, we plan a rigorous writing year in which we'll possibly ask them to write more than they have ever written in a single year.

Which brings us back to Hector. What will happen to him if his first "big" paper of the year is shot down by the teacher? What effect do you think this will have on his motivation to move forward? We already know the answers: for many students like Hector, starting the year with a low grade is all they need to go into shutdown mode. They already believe they are poor writers, and our grading immediately confirms this to be true. The first grade of the year places them back in a cycle of failure and embarrassment, and for self-protective purposes, they revert to shutdown mode. And just like that, early in the school year, we have already lost Hector.

The negative effects of grading don't just apply to struggling writers like Hector; they can stifle our best writers as well. We have all had honors students who stay in their comfort zones so long as we tell them exactly what it is we want them to write. They write the five-paragraph, identify-the-central-theme-in-this-novel essay, they write it well, and we place a good grade on their papers. This approach has produced a lot of students who have become expert in writing lame essays really well. They create voiceless, cookie-cutter, fake-school writing that blandly answers the teacher's question. They are happy with this arrangement because it brings them good grades, and they leave our classes thinking they are good writers.

But this is not good writing. Good writing arises from experimentation, from risk-taking. Good writing happens when creativity is encouraged and nurtured. Recognizing this reminds us of a national writing study done by Judith Langer and Arthur Applebee (1987), who warned that grading has been found to be harmful to the creative process:

> When students assumed that an assignment would be evaluated, they were likely to treat it as a display of what they had already learned: they would present their ideas carefully and fully, but were likely to stay close to the known and the familiar. On the other hand, when they assumed that the writing was part of an ongoing instructional dialogue, they were more likely to use it to explore new ideas—taking more risks and accepting more failures. (71)

We believe exploration, risk, and failure are essential components in a writer's growth. But when students know their papers will be graded, they "stay close to the known and familiar" and, as a result, their growth is stunted. Grading increases the fear of failure, and an increased fear of failure reduces the willingness to take chances. Why take a risk if the result of that risk might lead to a lower grade?

This is why we believe in grading less and assessing more.

Assessment and grading are not the same thing. Grading is a "finish line" evaluative tool. Assessment, on the other hand, is ongoing, something we do every day to inform our instruction. Ongoing, daily assessment drives the kinds of feedback we give our students—feedback that has its roots in coaching, not criticism. Grades tell us where our students ended up, but assessment—the key ingredient in responsive teaching—tells us where we are going.

We Believe Collaboration Is Essential for Professional Growth

Earlier, we described how it took us four hours to plan the first two days of instruction. Our slow pace was not a result of laziness or an inability to focus; it came from the challenge of aligning our practices with our philosophies. We found we were unable to plan a school year without veering into important philosophical conversations. Kelly gave Penny some new thinking on grading practices. Penny gave Kelly some new thinking on features of the writer's notebook. Kelly shared new thinking on creating Thought Logs. Penny shared new thinking on conferring. And so on.

We are mindful that isolation is often listed as one of the reasons so many teachers leave our profession. Even in the busyness of a school day and with hundreds of young people crowding the halls, teaching can be lonely. It isn't the proximity to others that we need; it is the conversations about how we plan for instruction and the risks we are taking in order to engage more students. It is processing the frustrations we all experience in teaching, in grading, in finding a way to inspire the young adults we care so much about. It is sharing the burden of being close to students who have been abandoned or brutalized.

In *Professional Capital* (2012), Andy Hargreaves and Michael Fullan suggest that this inherent isolation in teaching can be countered by bringing "professional capital" to our school sites. This professional capital is made up of three subsets: human capital (accumulating background knowledge in the field and the research to support our beliefs), decision capital (based on what I know, what am I going to do?), and social capital (we are smarter together, and when we try to figure out things together it leads us to practices that move our work forward).

We brought a lot of human capital and decision capital into this project, but it was our social capital—the thinking that occurred via ongoing, focused collaboration—that moved both of us toward new practices and understandings. It would have been a lot easier to remain in our teaching silos, but we recognize there is a significant benefit that arises from interacting with other teachers. Every teacher gets mired in the minutiae of his or her school, which is why sometimes the views of others outside our schools help us see our students and our practices in a new light. These views from outside our respective systems enabled both of us to stay focused on the bigger picture and prevented us from going down unproductive teaching avenues. We had a full year of intellectual conversations: planning lessons together, calibrating our plans in response to student work, and then evaluating the learning occurring in our classrooms.

Charles Darwin said, "In the long history of humankind (and animal kind, too) those who learned to collaborate and improvise most effectively have prevailed" (Darwin Center for Biogeology 2009, 1). We don't know about the word *prevailed*, but we can say with certainty that our collaboration elevated our teaching. Our curricular conversations always returned to these important questions: What do these students understand right now? What do they need next to engage deeply in reading and writing? How do we recover momentum when it lags? The times when we wrestled with something difficult together—like Penny's resistance to moving to a core text at the end of semester one when she still had so many students who were not regular, habitual readers—were important to both of us. Challenging each other helped us plan, teach, and respond to students with confidence and resilience. We met student resistance with creative energy and strength. We cannot count how many times one of our suggestions prompted the other to think, "I hadn't thought about it quite like that." We learned from each other; we learned to trust the thinking of each other. We found more joy in our work. We wish that for every one of you.

✦ Closing Thoughts:
The Budget of Time Is Limited

There is only so much time.

Kelly has a confession. Early in his career he was teaching *To Kill a Mockingbird* to a sophomore class, and as part of the final project he had his students actually build a scale-model version of Maycomb, Alabama. Kids were divided into groups, and each group selected a structure from the novel (e.g., Boo Radley's house, the Finch house, the courthouse) to build. The kids were given two weeks to complete their structures, and they really got into it. One group chose Miss Maudie's house (which burns to the ground in the novel), and they outfitted their structure with a hidden remote-control fan that blew "flames" (strips of red and yellow cellophane) out of Miss Maudie's windows. When the projects were complete, the students invited the rest of the school to tour their "town," plying the visitors with lemonade and Southern treats. Kelly has no doubt that his students had a lot of fun building the town of Maycomb, and he would bet that many of them still remember this project all these years later.

But was it worth the time?

Sure, the project certainly helped build a sense of class community (it is not often that students ask if they can come in on a Saturday morning to voluntarily work on their projects). Additionally, they no doubt learned the value of collaboration when it came to planning and building their structures. But all these years later, Kelly still gets queasy thinking about how much reading and writing time this project took away from his students.

Today, more than thirty years later, the stakes are even higher. We will be working with college-bound students who are in a heated competition to secure college admission. We will also be teaching students whose reading and writing skills are significantly below grade level. We must make sure that our 180 days are spent wisely. The days when we gave up significant chunks of time to build Maycomb, Alabama, are over. All planning now starts with this essential question: *Is this worth the time?*

Establish Daily PRACTICES

When students walk into our classrooms on the first day of school, they come loaded with questions: *What will this English class be like? How high are the teacher's expectations? How much will I be asked to read and write in this class? Will I fit in with my peers? Will this class help me grow? Will my experiences and ideas be honored here? Can I hide in this class? Does the teacher care? Is the teacher qualified? Will the teacher like and respect me? Will the teacher understand me?* These questions remind us why the routines we establish in the first few weeks of school are critical. On the first day students start figuring out the answers to these questions, and this is when they begin deciding whether they will get on board with us or not. How we spend our time at the beginning of the year sets the tone for all the days that follow. We invite students into a world of words, of images and ideas, of composing meaning from the raw materials of their lives.

Conversation Clip

See "A First Day with Seniors"

✈ Day One Sets the Tone

On the first day, we greet our students at the door. When they enter they see our classroom libraries organized into categories that make book shopping easier—libraries wrap around every wall. Our classrooms tell students that reading matters. We have selected piles of books for each table and students are encouraged to speed date books, spending a minute reading a few pages, browsing many titles. We observe them closely, noticing which students browse thoughtfully and which give up with a single glance.

We take photographs of students because learning their names quickly matters. We ask them to talk to each other as they browse and we look for connections between them. We seek to build a compassionate, purposeful community of learners even in this first hour together.

Writing matters too, of course, and we have pictures of former students and their writing or sketches displayed with pride. We take students on a tour of our notebooks, demonstrating how we notice, how we collect, how we write. We tell our students that we play many parts as writers. Sometimes we write to vent rage. Sometimes we write of something that thrills us. Sometimes we write to delve deeper into something we want to think about. Sometimes we write so we can share our thinking with our students. Sometimes we write knowing no one else in the world will ever get to see our words. We play many parts as writers, and we want our students to play these parts as well.

We get them started right away. We hand them writing notebooks and ask them to respond to two questions: *Who are you as a reader? Who are you as a writer?* We write our own answers under the document camera and many students will read a bit of our writing as we write, then return to their own thinking and writing. After several minutes we model how we reread our writing to make it clearer, showing students how we listen to our writing and revise it, something that will become a habit for all of us this year. We invite students to reread their writing and consider ways to make it better. We ask them to talk about their revisions or their writing with a student nearby; we wander among desks and listen.

Next, we ask our ninth graders to write a letter to themselves. This letter will be returned to them on their last day of their senior year. We ask students to share their hopes, their dreams, their goals, and their fears. We encourage them to ponder the questions they have as they enter high school, and we ask them to make predictions as well. We tell them they can put words on the page in any way they'd like—in prose, in poetry, in list form—whatever helps them express their ideas. We encourage sketching. We tell brief stories of former students receiving their letters and photographs in the heat of early summer as they check the fit of their caps and gowns on the brink of all that lies ahead of them.

As our students write their letters, we project a letter we have written, outlining our dreams and aspirations for this school year. We want to establish the idea that we will be writing throughout the year. While they work on letters we sit beside a few students and talk with them, establishing a natural, nonthreatening conferring environment where we listen and learn from our students. We choose one letter excerpt to share at the end of class—to establish the routine of ending class with beautiful words: theirs.

Notice what we did not do on the first day of school: we did not review rules, or the class syllabus, or the procedures, or the letters we send home to parents. We do not want our first class period with our students to produce the same brain-numbing effect we experienced in our back-to-school faculty meetings. Our goal on day one is to actively engage students in thinking and writing, and to set the tone for the rest of the year.

⚡ Practices Support Beliefs: The Template of One Day

In this chapter, we'll explore the *what* and *why* of the daily routines we establish—starting on day one—for the entire year. Teachers are decision makers. We choose the daily practices that ignite curiosity and critical thinking in our students. No matter how much control is placed over us by school districts, department chairs, PLCs, common standards, curriculum pacing guides, or assessment criteria, our values and beliefs guide us to make our own decisions. As we demonstrated in the last chapter, we think deeply about the *why* that grounds good teaching so that our classrooms resonate with the power of our convictions. As much as this book will show you what we teach, it will also show you *how* we support the development of increasingly sophisticated readers and writers.

It all begins with daily practices.

What do we plan for students to do every single day they are with us? Every day our students will follow these practices:

We know we want students to engage in these practices every day, and the most efficient way to accomplish this is to develop routines for each practice. Whether students are preparing for college or are significantly below grade level, we work to make every moment matter. We plan to teach bell-to-bell. Routines save management time because students quickly learn when to have their books out, how they can tackle a quick write, what happens in text study, and how conferences work. To that end, we each follow a daily template for instruction. Figures 2.1 and 2.2 are skeletal views of templates of both our schedules. Though the total amount of time (fifty-three daily minutes versus eighty minutes every other day) differs, in both our classrooms we repeat the same daily practice routines.

Time in Minutes

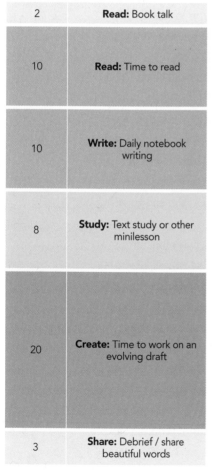

Time in Minutes	
2	**Read:** Book talk
10	**Read:** Time to read
10	**Write:** Daily notebook writing
8	**Study:** Text study or other minilesson
20	**Create:** Time to work on an evolving draft
3	**Share:** Debrief / share beautiful words

Figure 2.1 Kelly's Classroom: 53 Minutes Every Day

We put these practices into place with the goal that we will use our precious, limited time with our students wisely. How we spend time in teaching is about the conditions for learning we create in our classrooms as much as it is about the standards we are reaching for. Students will become more independent, more proficient readers and writers if they confer regularly with teachers and each other, have choice in what is read or written about, and have time to practice re-reading and revision. We seek to establish lifelong literate habits in our students, and we know these repeated practices give us the best chance of achieving this goal.

When setting up an everyday structure for these practices, three key ideas come to mind:

- *This structure is not grade specific.* While this book will focus on our year teaching ninth-grade students, we also both teach seniors, and we adopt the same practices in our twelfth-grade classrooms. If we were middle school teachers, we would use the same model in a sixth-grade class. This is sound instructional practice for readers and writers of all ages.

- *Students control the pace and focus of their work during 75 percent of each class.* As you will see in the descriptions of our daily practices that follow, there is a predictable movement between direct instruction and healthy stretches of time for students to work "off" that teaching on their own.

- *The sequence and timing of moves in a workshop are malleable.* Though we will stay true to this structure on most days, depending on where we are in any unit and the needs of our students, we may spend more or less time in any one of these daily practices.

Let's take a closer look at each of these common elements. First days are important, so we'll share what we've found to be critical in establishing these daily practices at the beginning of the year.

Read: Book Talk

With book talks our goal is to expose our students to as many good books as possible across the year and generate interest in reading. Reading aloud is central to engaging students in books, so we almost

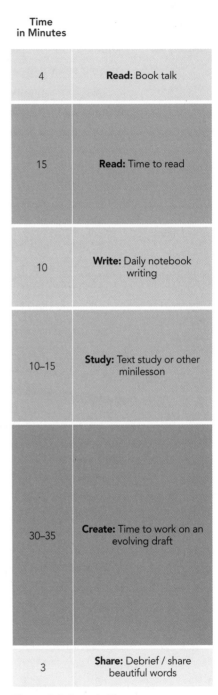

Time in Minutes	
4	**Read:** Book talk
15	**Read:** Time to read
10	**Write:** Daily notebook writing
10–15	**Study:** Text study or other minilesson
30–35	**Create:** Time to work on an evolving draft
3	**Share:** Debrief / share beautiful words

Figure 2.2 Penny's Classroom: 80 Minutes Every Other Day

Teaching Clip

See multiple book talks and speed dating with books in the online video

always read briefly from the books we're sharing. In addition to books, we might also share an interesting poem or article, or a book trailer (found on YouTube or Amazon). Students, parents, administrators, support staff, and older siblings in the school are invited to share book talks with our students as well.

At the beginning of the year, books talks are critical because they generate interest in reading and help students make plans for reading. Here are some guidelines to keep in mind as you plan the first book talks of the year:

- On the first day, have students "speed date" with books spread out on tables around the room.

- Make a case for engaged reading. For the first few days, talk about multiple books, not just one a day.

- Choose high-interest books—the best you can find.

- Confer with students to help you make decisions about which books to share; match books with readers.

- Feature short stacks of books with the same theme, author, or genre.

CONSIDER This...

We are often asked if we use reading levels to match readers with books. We do not. Measures of reading fluency ignore a reader's motivation and prior knowledge. Frank Smith (2006) reminds us, "Children shouldn't all be expected to learn to read at the same time or at the same rate or from the same materials, for the simple reason that children are individuals. . . . The fact that a 9-year-old reads like an average 8-year-old is not in itself cause for dismay. It doesn't mean that the child will never catch up. No one ever talks of a 30-year-old reading like a 29-year-old, and we all read like a beginner when we are having difficulty reading" (151). Our students choose books based on their interests and keep up with the scheduled reading as best as they can, sometimes relying on the support of others in book clubs to help them make sense of the reading.

If they get frustrated with a choice, we let them choose a different book, just like we would with independent reading. We have found that student interest trumps reading level every time. Put a great book in readers' hands and the effort that students will put into sustaining engagement to understand will amaze you. Researchers agree. As Paul Silvia of the University of North Carolina said, "Interest is at once a cognitive state and an affective state, what researchers call a knowledge emotion. The feelings that characterize interest are overwhelmingly positive: a sense of being energized and invigorated, captivated and enthralled. As for its effects on cognition: interest effectively turbocharges our thinking. When we're interested in what we're learning, we pay closer attention; we process the information more efficiently; we employ more effective learning strategies, such as engaging in critical thinking, making connections between old and new knowledge, and attending to deep structure instead of surface features. When we're interested in a task, we work harder and persist longer, bringing more of our self-regulatory skills into play" (quoted in Paul 2013). Skill develops with a will to read. Every year students prove this to us: reading depends more on what they are willing to do than on their skill level when they begin.

Read: Time to Read

Students read daily for ten to fifteen minutes (independent reading selections, book club books, or a core work the entire class is reading). Providing daily class time to read shows students that we value their regular engagement with reading. We establish this habit *in our classrooms*, because we know that if our students are not reading in school, most will not read at home. We have found that this little bit of reading keeps the individual lives of readers at the center of our vision. While it feels like it's not enough time, especially for our least skilled students, just ten minutes of daily reading can have a significant impact, as shown in Figure 2.3.

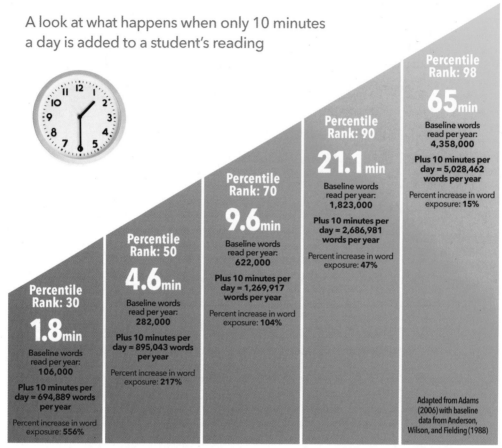

A look at what happens when only 10 minutes a day is added to a student's reading

Percentile Rank: 30

1.8min

Baseline words read per year: **106,000**

Plus 10 minutes per day = 694,889 words per year

Percent increase in word exposure: **556%**

Percentile Rank: 50

4.6min

Baseline words read per year: **282,000**

Plus 10 minutes per day = 895,043 words per year

Percent increase in word exposure: **217%**

Percentile Rank: 70

9.6min

Baseline words read per year: **622,000**

Plus 10 minutes per day = 1,269,917 words per year

Percent increase in word exposure: **104%**

Percentile Rank: 90

21.1min

Baseline words read per year: **1,823,000**

Plus 10 minutes per day = 2,686,981 words per year

Percent increase in word exposure: **47%**

Percentile Rank: 98

65min

Baseline words read per year: **4,358,000**

Plus 10 minutes per day = 5,028,462 words per year

Percent increase in word exposure: **15%**

Adapted from Adams (2006) with baseline data from Anderson, Wilson, and Fielding (1988)

Figure 2.3 The Impact of Time Spent Reading

Source: Beers and Probst (2017, 135)

Here are the guidelines we follow as we plan for the reading block at the beginning of the year:

- Be aware that some students will take longer to find a book they want to read.

- Confer with students. Start right away to get to know students as readers and learn what they need.

- Establish a library checkout routine for reading.

- Communicate with parents about the importance of students' engagement in independent reading (see online resource 2.1). Let them know you are mindful of the appropriateness of the books students check out, but remember that the definition of *appropriateness* varies. Some parents see value in reading a book like *Crank* (about drug addiction), while others might find it objectionable.

- Generate data that helps you know your students as readers through writing prompts such as "Who am I as a reader?" and "How's my reading going?"; reading surveys (see online resource 2.2); reading rate calculations (see online resource 2.3); and so on.

- Show empathy for those who struggle, excitement about the possibilities, and clear expectations that remaining dormant as a reader is not an option. Let students know, *there is no hiding here.*

CONSIDER *This...*

We know that ten minutes is not enough time to establish reading flow. As Penny's student Callum reflected, "I think a habit I have is that I have to be reading for a while until I actually start to picture what is happening in the book. Like the fifteen minutes we have in class is not enough to really capture and remember what happened in the book. So that's what makes me forget where I am in a book, and then I have to go back and read it again."

It is challenging to divide a workshop into parts. We struggled with this all year. We would prefer thirty to forty-five minutes of independent reading, and although that is an unrealistic daily goal, we both had times during the year when we let students read for longer stretches. Once students become engaged in books, they beg for this time, and when they sink into reading, they practice all the skills we've been working on; time to read is never wasted time.

Conversation Clip

See "Daily Time for Independent Reading"

Conferring with Readers: Beginning of the Year

As we explained in the last chapter, every day while students are reading, we confer. In a ten-minute period, we aim to talk one-to-one with three to five different students, and this time helps us understand our students better and design instruction that meets their needs.

In our first round of reading conferences, we focus on getting to know our students' reading habits. We are always pleased when we discover students who like to read, but one of the goals of these initial conferences is to develop an understanding of our students so that we can start to chip away at the reluctance found in our nonreaders. Their answers to our initial queries determine where the conference goes next, as shown in Figure 2.4.

Teaching Clip

See, for example, Kelly's conference with Andrew: "Reading *Arch Enemy*, by Frank Beddor"

If a student indicates that he or she likes to read, we follow up with . . .	If a student indicates that he or she does not like to read, we follow up with . . .
• What do you like to read? • What are your favorite genres? • Who are your favorite authors? • Do you have a favorite series? • What are you currently reading? • How do you find time to read? • Where do you read? • When do you read?	• Why don't you like to read? • Did you like reading when you were younger? If so, when did you stop liking reading? What caused this shift? • When was the last time you selected a book on your own to read? • Have you ever read a book you liked? • Can you name an author you like? • What interests you? What do you do in your free time?

Figure 2.4 Possible Conference Directions

With these questions guiding us, the initial round of reading conferences are fact-finding in nature. The year we did this work together, here are some of the things we learned about our young readers.

Some of our students were downright hostile to the idea of reading. *These students saw reading as a school-mandated assignment that had very little relevance to their lives. They had never been strong readers, and they carried with them long histories of being forced to read books that had always been chosen by the teacher.*

Many of our students had not independently read a book of their own choosing in a long time. It was shocking to hear how many of our high school students readily admitted that they had not chosen a book to read on their own since the fourth or fifth grade. They complained that what they were required to read was often "boring" or too hard for them. Many had lost the desire to select books on their own.

There was a lot of fake reading occurring. *Many students admitted that they often do not really read assigned books. They rely on classroom conversations and SparkNotes to get through the unit. In three years of surveys with Kelly's seniors, over 90 percent of his students admitted they had fake read their way to the twelfth grade. We also found that fake reading was not just a strategy adopted by struggling readers; honors-level students were just as likely to skate by without actually reading books.*

We had serial abandoners in the room. We had a number of students who followed a predictable pattern: they would select books, pretend to read a chapter or two, abandon the books, select different books, pretend to read a chapter or two, abandon the books, and so on. Our theory is that they had adopted this strategy sitting in classrooms where it was easy to hide one's fake reading. We were surprised how many students told us they could not remember the last time they read a book cover to cover. We even had a couple of students admit they had never read an entire book on their own.

Many of our students did not align with any specific author or genre. When we asked, "Who are your favorite authors?" about half of our students could not generate a single name. When we asked, "What is your favorite genre?" we received a bit more response, but we still found a large number of students who said they did not favor any genre. Not one.

Many of our students lived in print-poor homes or apartments. Many of our students lived in poverty and lacked access to reading materials outside school. One reason they did not read books at home is because they did not have books at home.

There was a lot competing with our students' reading time outside school. Many of our students indicated that they did not read more outside school because they often had trouble finding the time. Some of them had band practice until 6:00 P.M. and then went home to face lots of homework. Others had after-school jobs or were required to take care of younger siblings when they got home. Although we feel the "I do not have time to read" excuse is often overused, after our initial conferences, we recognized the claim carried legitimacy with some of our students.

Some of our students were avid readers. Some of our students could easily identify their favorite authors and genres, and they read frequently because they liked books. We are always happy to find these students because having model readers in the room is helpful when it comes to selling reading to their peers.

These findings confirmed what we already suspected: if our kids are to become habitual readers, they need a classroom structure that provides time to read in class every day. They need a classroom environment where they are surrounded by high-interest reading materials. They need to connect with a teacher who knows them and who knows books.

Conferring with Readers: Across the Year

After our initial round of conferences, we continue to check in with students daily to gauge their reading progress, to help with comprehension frustration, to nudge them to set goals, to diversify their reading diet, or just to listen to the thinking they have about a book. In these conferences, we do not have a preset list of questions in mind. Instead, we want our conferences to mirror the natural talk of readers, to be responsive, and to start with questions that hand the direction of the conference to the student. Questions such as "How is it going?" or "Talk to me about your book. Is it a good fit for you?" tell students not that we are measuring their reading, but rather that we believe there is a "good fit" book for every student and we are confident they have interesting things to say about their reading. Our goal is to learn, to think with a student, and to problem-solve. We listen closely, encouraging students to do most of the thinking (and talking).

Eventually, we expect students to begin reading conferences with something *they want to talk about.* To help them progress to this point, modeling is critical, especially early in the year. We model things they may track while reading books: a character's development, a big idea that is emerging, their confusion, interesting rhetorical decisions made by the writer (reading like a writer), and literary elements (e.g., symbolism, setting, conflict). We show students the things we think about in the books we read. Reading is for discovery and growth: a student should leave a conference feeling stronger, empowered to discover more in reading without us.

CONSIDER This...

Beyond our reluctant readers, providing time to read in class also reawakened a love of reading in our honors-level students. Many of our most proficient readers had stopped reading independently because they were burdened by the homework demands of numerous Advanced Placement classes. Reading had become nothing more than a school chore they must do—and do quickly—to prepare for the next round of exams. At the end of the year, many of these students expressed appreciation to us for helping them rediscover the joys of reading.

As students become more comfortable with conferring, we ask them to lead each conference, teaching them the conversation moves that adult readers engage in to clarify their thinking when reading. When a student indicates he is confused, we might model what readers do when confronted by confusion. If the student is enjoying the book, we might suggest other books in the same genre for her to read next. If the student is deep into a book, we might discuss the development of themes or other big ideas. Conferences go in many directions, but they all start with the same kinds of questions: "Talk to me about what you're thinking about in this book; what is worth talking about here?"

Because of daily reading conferences, students can't hide as readers. Our students are never more than two to three weeks away from conferring with us about their reading progress. We both take advantage of the greetings at the door as students arrive to check on how they like their books, to recommend a next book, to check with many students each day. Informal, daily checks help students know we pay attention to their lives as readers, and they feel more responsible for reading because of this.

To help us keep track of our conferences, we collect notes on each student over the year. We record their interests so we can begin matching them with books they might like. Conferences provide us with ongoing formative assessment, enabling us to know what our students know (and what they don't know). They give us time to differentiate instruction, which is vital given the increasingly diverse readers in our classrooms. We focus on one student at a time. Our conferences, which demonstrate not only our care and interest in each student but our thinking about the process of reading, often benefit those close enough to overhear. Teacher talk in a classroom carries values and beliefs. Ours are demonstrated in conferring daily with our students: we are here to encourage, support, and challenge our readers.

Write: Daily Notebook Launch

After reading, we transition our students into notebook writing. In the first few days we ask students to divide the notebook into the parts listed in Figure 2.5.

We are aware that having required sections will alter a student's relationship with his or her notebook. As Ralph Fletcher (2016) said, "If you tell a student how to organize their writing notebook, it is no longer theirs." But we also recognize that students need a place where they collect and study the craft moves writers make. We believe the notebook can be a place where both things occur—where students generate their own thinking and where students practice the skills and techniques employed by writers. It is why we call these notebooks, not journals: they are

Pages 1–70	**Writing:** This is the "meat" of the notebook, the place where students will write daily.
Pages 71–90	**Passage Study:** A section for studying and imitating the craft and convention moves made by other writers. Entries will be written during minilessons crafted by the teacher.
Pages 91–100	**Word Nerd Study:** A section where students collect words they find in their independent reading (and in life) that intrigue them. Entries include where they found the word and what they understand its meaning to be.
Inside front cover	**What I'm Reading List**
Inside back cover	**What I Might Read Next List**

Figure 2.5 Required Notebook Sections

Teaching Clip

See
"Notebook Tour"

working tools in our classrooms. We seek a balance between collecting thinking as writers each day and the frequent practice of study and imitation that increases confidence and skill.

Generate Thinking

Each day we give students something to spur notebook writing depending on the discourse we are studying at the time. For example, throughout the year, but particularly when we study narrative, we write next to poems. Poetry is big thinking in a small space—a few words—and accessible to all. The heart and voice of the writer is at the center of poetry, and student voices rise as they give their own ideas power. We peel off the voice of the poem and wrap it around our own thoughts and ideas. Poets compose in metaphors and images. We write beside these beautiful words, which enables our own phrases and sentences to tumble out.

When we are studying informational texts, we write next to a chart, an infographic, or short, engaging articles. When studying argument, we react to a current event, a spirited review, an editorial, or perhaps a letter to the editor. In every instance, we choose texts most likely to engage our students and invite a response. We want to open up a live circuit between our students and beautiful writing in the genre we are studying.

The balance between practice with features (like dialogue) and freewriting is key. Writing every day in notebooks does not mean teaching a technique every day; it means getting students in the habit of transferring thinking into words and sentences. And this can be tricky. In Penny's school last year the administration launched a focus on four-part objectives and insisted that every class period focus on one skill. This is a mechanistic view of an expansive subject: the teaching of writing. Freewriting is not about practicing a skill; it is about practicing the generative, pleasurable act of writing in order for students to begin to believe in the power of their words to express ideas. Confidence and clarity in writing can't always be completed in one class period, no matter how clear your objective.

During notebook time, everyone in the room—the teacher and each student—writes. When we write, we show our notebooks under a document camera so students can see our first-draft thinking (and often, our struggle). Every day we model the construction of ideas into sentences and make visible the decisions we make as writers.

CONSIDER This...

We write in response—instantly, while our thinking hums inside us— and we write with ease because we're hearing the author's voice as we write. We feel a play with language that drives us to be playful, *if* the conditions for this writing are set up for ease. For ungraded play. For lowering expectations of our writing in order to free ourselves to spill words on the page. Think of a child turning cartwheels on the lawn— one and then another and another. "Mom! Watch!" Joyful practice first, then performance. It's how we've all learned how to do anything. If Mom instead has a clipboard and a rubric and grades every cartwheel, the child will stubbornly refuse to try. Pressure removes joy from learning. Pressure prevents experimentation. Pressure to perform creates barriers that manifest as behaviors. An obsession with grading everything creates dependent writers out of our most willing, most able students ("What do I have to do to get an A?") and cultivates disinterest in writing in those who struggle. Every writer, from child to adult, must experience the satisfaction of finding writing that names something important in order to understand what writing is for and what writing can do. This will lead to *why* writers work so hard to do it well. Everyday freedom to write cultivates this understanding and removes barriers that trap our students in failure.

Practice Revising

After students have written for four to eight minutes, we model two minutes of revision on our lousy first drafts. Some days we think aloud and ask students to pay attention to the way we listen to the words we have written and to observe how we tune them for better language and clarity. Almost every day we give students a couple of minutes to reread and make their notebook writing better, clearer, and stronger. We want students to experience how revision occurs in the drafting stage as we reread and listen to our evolving texts: revision is not simply an end-process move that writers make.

Occasionally, we have students select a sentence that they have significantly revised and then write their first and second drafts of the sentence side by side. We post these revisions to our Google Classroom page or add them to an anchor chart. We often ask students to turn and share their revisions and the thinking that led to their changes. We listen as they talk to assess what they understand about revision. Students come to expect this rhythm of read, write, and talk every day in our classrooms.

Because it's handwritten, daily notebook work helps students develop critical focus in writing. All writers experience the starts and stops of thinking. How do we develop the discipline to keep going? We eliminate distractions that take us away from the writing. When we both write in the early mornings at home, we turn off email and other notifications. If our students were on laptops, they too would find distractions a click away. We've all seen it happen: a student wants to listen to music in order to focus on writing, but ends up on YouTube for ten minutes looking for a song and getting distracted by other videos. We eliminate technology's distractions and have students focus their attention on words and sentences for part of each class period. Writing by hand also creates a different kind of thinking. Stanislas Dehaene, a psychologist at the Collège de France in Paris, notes:

> When we write, a unique neural circuit is automatically activated. There is a core recognition of the gesture in the written word, a sort of recognition by mental simulation in your brain. And it seems that this circuit is contributing in unique ways we didn't realize. Learning is made easier. (quoted in Konnikova 2014)

Zebra Pen (2014) reports on the research of Pam Mueller and Daniel Oppenheimer showing that when students write by hand, (1) they build stronger conceptual understanding of the material; (2) they tax different cognitive processes; (3) they develop better short-term and long-term memory; and (4) they focus better because there are fewer distractions.

We believe a balance between handwriting and typing is worthwhile.

Here's what we've found is important to do to encourage notebook writing at the beginning of the year:

- Supply students with notebooks (or have them get their own) and organize them for the work you will do.

- Find engagements (connected to the first discourse study) that prompt students to write but still give them lots of choice and help them focus on the rich writing ideas in their own lives. Possible prompts include writing or sketching in response to poetry, photos or images, text excerpts, or music.

- Make sure the quality of the writing you share inspires students to write well.

- Write alongside your students and share writing and thinking about revision.

- Be transparent. Share your struggles to write clearly about things that matter to you.

- Value and celebrate the diversity of student thinking and writing.

- Have fun! Pleasure matters. Writing isn't supposed to be hard all the time.

We also planned for talk about reading and writing—in groups and partnerships—with prompts like those in Figure 2.6 to jump-start the talk.

- Turn to your partner and share what you are thinking right now.

- Share with your partner what surprised you in this reading.

- Turn and read your draft to a partner. Read it the way it should be heard.

- Respond to your partner's reading of her draft with one question and one comment.

- Tell your partner what you noticed about his writing.

- Tell your partner what you wonder as you read her writing.

- Share with a partner one revision move you made that really improved your writing.

- Discuss which of your revisions are surface level and which are deeper level.

- Select one of your Thought Log (see Chapter 3) entries and explain to your group why it exhibits your best thinking.

- As a class, let's look at excellent student writing together. What do you notice? Share your thinking in your groups.

Figure 2.6 Prompts to Wrap Talk Around the Daily Practices

Teaching Clip

See "Studying the Craft of *Station Eleven*, by Emily St. John Mandel"

Study: Text Study or Other Minilesson

After reading and writing practice, we teach students to read like writers by studying texts deliberately. Naming and noticing the craft of writing in any genre is an essential understanding for writers. On one day we might study a text that demonstrates the power of word choice. On another, how the author crafts (and punctuates) dialogue. On yet another, how the text moves from one scene to another. We study writing-craft moves such as how to vary sentence lengths, how to open an essay with a vignette, or how to blend genres to argue effectively in an editorial.

In genre study, a flood of mentor texts answers the questions, "What are we writing? What does it look like? How long is it? How is it organized?" The study of models was identified in a meta-analysis of the teaching of writing (Graham and Perin 2007) as one of the eleven strategies that move adolescent writers. We will provide many models in each unit of study so that students continue to learn the essential, transferable skill of reading like writers.

Text study is always about inquiry. If we want students to be independent—to learn a process as writers for learning from texts they read—we must give them time to practice that inquiry and learn from each other. We ask students to read a text or passage and discuss the writing craft they notice with a partner. When they share their thinking, we list what they found on an anchor chart, and we add our observations to the list if we feel students have missed something important.

Even when we're not studying texts together, we know that students are always learning because reading and writing are symbiotic. When we read, we absorb the lines and phrases, noticing the style or tone of the author, but not focusing on how those lines were crafted. As we help students notice what writers are doing and have them imitate those moves to make their own writing better, they will recognize more of these moves in their independent reading. We know that the ongoing lessons about writing craft that arise from regularly reading will carry our students farther than any given minilesson.

We learn from conferences with our students and from their drafts what we must teach next, and we respond with targeted teaching in minilessons. The key here is *the development of curriculum under the influence of the work students produce*. Our engagement with student learning, class by class, student by student, dictates what we teach next.

Text study and minilessons will always be connected to the discourse we are

studying in writing, of course, but here are some guidelines for this daily practice at the beginning of the year:

- First, assess what students do and don't know about the craft of writing by sharing a passage and asking them what they notice.

- Model how to name craft moves in texts.

- Honor what students notice and encourage them to have confidence in their ability to see what writers are doing.

- Watch and learn how students work together by pairing or grouping them for text study in different ways.

- Look at multiple examples that vary in complexity from a single author. This will give students an understanding of how craft is connected to voice and style.

Create: Time to Work on an Evolving Draft

We transition into workshop time with the words "Let's get to work" or, when we connect the work of the minilesson to students' evolving drafts, "Today in your writing, I'd like you to consider how . . ." Sometimes students will all draft the same assignment (e.g., writing a letter to a presidential candidate); other times students will return to their writer's notebooks to select ideas they want to develop alone or in writing groups. And sometimes they will use this time to create new writing from scratch.

Conferring in Writing

Just as we do in the reading block, we confer with our students every day as they are writing. We sit beside as many writers as possible, offering encouragement and suggestions, and keeping notes on our interactions. Much like our reading conferences, most of our best teaching of writing occurs in these one-to-one interactions. We teach ways of working with ideas that lead to joy and satisfaction: planning, organizing, and playing with structure or individual sentences. As the room quiets, many students learn to think about writing in expansive ways by listening to us problem-solve in conferences. Conferring is about seeing the student—the reader, the writer, the composer of ideas—and reading body language, leaning in to listen, notice, pay attention. We determine the focus of the conference by doing this research on the student in that moment in time. We know what we're teaching—not so much kinds of writing as ways to enter a conversation with the world. We are seeking not compliance to a behavior (finish this work) but rather a commitment to the higher purpose of discovering and sharing experiences and ideas. In our first round of conferences, we learned the following about the writers in our care:

Many students lacked writing confidence. *Too many of our students had avoided writing for years—completing assignments with little revision and little success. Some had such a limited understanding of the structure of sentences and paragraphs that they found it difficult to begin. One of Penny's students continually resisted writing anything. He finally told her, "I like you, and I don't want you to see all I don't know." Not only did students feel wobbly about their writing abilities but they did not trust that they had important stories and ideas to write about. Even our strongest writers lacked confidence in imagining the way stories can go—an imagining that requires complex, flexible thinking they hadn't practiced enough in school.*

Writing conferences made many students uncomfortable—at least initially. When we sat beside our young writers for the first time, the room got very quiet. Students were initially reluctant to share their thinking or their writing with us. Part of this reluctance can be attributed to their lack of confidence, but it was also clear that many of them had little or no experience with one-to-one conferences with teachers. We learned that for some students it would take a number of conferences before they would develop a comfort level with this close talk, especially for those students who had never conferred with a teacher while developing an idea.

Some students were flummoxed by choice. *Many students were not used to generating their own thinking and they'd had little experience making decisions about the direction of their writing. They were much more practiced in answering the teacher's prompts and questions. In our initial conferences we encountered students who did not believe they knew how to generate or organize ideas. They did not feel they possessed the capacity to create experiences that engage readers.*

Each writer had idiosyncrasies. Though we learned much about our classes as a whole, the first round of writing conferences also proved invaluable in helping us begin to know each student individually. We learned that Ramon has difficulty staying focused. We learned that Celeste is very fluent but doesn't reread her writing as she works. We learned that Ta writes, deletes, writes, deletes, and ends almost every class period with a blank page. We gathered invaluable intelligence specific to each child.

> **Students who thought they had nothing to say had a lot to say.** *Students were not used to tapping their lives as a source of writing inspiration. Many believed they had nothing to say, but listening to and then encouraging these students in these initial conferences proved otherwise. Many of our students have had extraordinary experiences, and we began to unearth these as we encouraged them to tell the stories only they could tell.*

We seek to align our habits as teachers to the bigger purpose of meeting writers where they are and providing help or nudging them toward greater confidence. This individual time with writers is critical to our success, but it doesn't mean it happens easily or quickly.

At the beginning of the year, when students are first starting this hard work on their evolving drafts, here's what you can try to do:

- Recognize that conferences are critical. Get to know your students as writers and find out what they need.

- Look for signs that notebook work (write, revise, write, revise) and text study are influencing students' work on drafts.

- Communicate empathy and understanding for the hard work you are asking students to do.

Share: Debrief / Share Beautiful Words

As we confer during workshop time, we keep our eyes out for good things our young writers are doing. We quietly encourage students to share their writing with the rest of the class. We save this sharing for the last three minutes of the period. We honor the struggle to write well by sharing the beautiful words our students have created.

Teaching Clip

See "Choose a Line"

Here is what you should keep in mind about this practice at the beginning of the year:

- What you choose to share sends important messages about what you value, so highlight risk-taking, experimentation, and approximation.

- Some students will need more time than others to get comfortable sharing their writing with the class.

CONSIDER *This...*

In the opening days of the school year, we do not grade the work we ask students to do. It would be unfair to grade them on what they have retained from prior experiences in school. Our daily assessment of students' engagement with reading, their ability to write for several minutes and rewrite their first thinking, and their engagement in small-group work is just that: assessment. It helps us to understand students' needs and to plan instruction. We also do not give grades for participation or for returning signed permission forms.

⚡ Closing Thoughts: The Efficiency of Daily Practices

When we both started teaching, planning for how long something would take was hit-or-miss. We quickly learned to have a stack of worksheets to do in case a lesson ran shorter than expected. In this reading/writing workshop model, filling a few extra minutes can be as simple as having students pull out their notebooks and write next to a rich spoken word poem or asking them to dive back into their independent reading books. We no longer need the stack of worksheets to bridge a gap: we have powerful practices that are worthy of repeating.

These daily practices will be evident in the yearlong map of teaching we will plan for reading and writing (Chapters 3 and 4). We need a map to set the pace and to organize our thinking. We need a deep understanding of where we are going and how units connect to intentionally deepen our students' skill sets in reading, writing, listening, speaking, and critical thinking—and to connect each day's teaching to the ones that come before and after. There are so many things to talk and write about that we must plan units with purpose and vision from the start, or we risk a curriculum of parts that won't help students understand the whole of literacy and their own dynamic, changing processes of reading and of writing. There is an intentional, planned arc to a school year, just as there is an arc to a lesson, a unit, a book, and an individual piece of writing. We know we are not moving students through books or units, but rather moving students toward greater independence and control of their decisions and experiences as readers and writers. We love the challenge of this complex work.

Map a Year of READING

We believe in books.

It seems obvious to say this, but we believe in the sustained *engagement* with one book and then another as a primary focus for every English class every year. We love literature. We love nonfiction. We love words. We love the promise of books that lead us to people and places and thinking we wouldn't find otherwise. We believe you want this, too.

Adolescents, however, are rebellious and fiery and move fast. Most fill their time with friends, music, jobs, sports, and technology, and too many no longer see how books are worth their time. In the words of Peter Johnston and Gay Ivey (2015), "While we are busy teaching children to read and write, the students are also trying to make sense of being human. Pressures to focus on the 'basics' and 'academic rigor' often distract us, and we forget that healthy development and well-being require children to experience a sense of autonomy, relatedness, and competence" (51). Our students find autonomy and competence as hunters and lacrosse players, drum majors and workers in a variety of businesses. Why not also in their lives as readers?

English curriculum has long been anchored in required canonical texts. There is evidence that students are unengaged, yet many schools stick to the same texts, the same crawl through one required book and then another. Louise Rosenblatt, an immensely influential reading researcher said, "Especially in the high school years, we should help young people to discover the power of literature to enable us to experiment imaginatively with life, to get the feel and emotional cost of different adult roles, to organize and reflect on a confused and unruly reality, and to give us pleasure through the very language that accomplishes these things. Both our classroom atmosphere and selection of reading materials should therefore be guided by the primary concern for creating a live circuit between readers and books" (1956, 70).

We are determined to create a live circuit between our students and books, and so we map out a year of study we hope will do just that. This chapter is devoted to our belief in a balance of time devoted to three experiences we know are valuable in a reader's life:

- the ongoing development of interest and independence in reading (50 percent)

- the opportunity to engage with a community of readers in book clubs (25 percent)

- the power of a classroom of readers studying the same text at the same time (25 percent).

This 50-25-25 balance of reading experiences is subject to the continued revision we've always done in our work. After this book is published, we will continue to confer with students and consider how our everyday practices are moving each reader in the room. If need be, we will shift these percentages.

Figure 3.1 is the map of reading that represents this 50-25-25 balance.

With this balance of reading experiences, our goal is to move students from dormancy to engagement, and then to a higher volume of regular reading. Once our readers are engaged, we can lead them to choose increasingly complex, literary texts. Every move takes time. Over the course of the year, we will look for evidence that students

- have increased the volume of their reading

- can self-select books to read

- can read with understanding: What does the text say? What does the text mean? How is it said?

- can deepen understanding through writing about books and the ideas within them

- have developed an identity as a reader, aligning with genres and authors

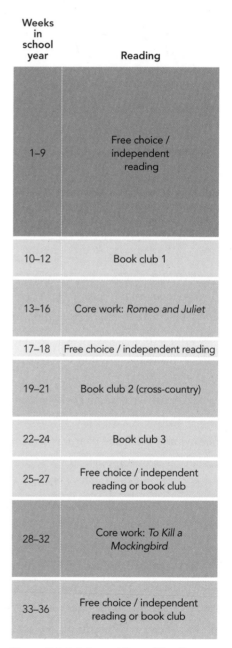

Weeks in school year	Reading
1–9	Free choice / independent reading
10–12	Book club 1
13–16	Core work: *Romeo and Juliet*
17–18	Free choice / independent reading
19–21	Book club 2 (cross-country)
22–24	Book club 3
25–27	Free choice / independent reading or book club
28–32	Core work: *To Kill a Mockingbird*
33–36	Free choice / independent reading or book club

Figure 3.1 A Balanced Year of Reading

- have developed the stamina to read for an hour or more at one sitting and to track their thinking over the course of a long book

- have increased the complexity of their reading

- can deepen understanding through talk in book clubs and in whole-class discussions.

Students grow at different rates, of course, so these goals (and our map) must be personalized, and when needed, revised. If we keep our heads down studying our map, we miss the rich gifts of experimentation, of study, of adaptation, and of looking for trouble in teaching so we can search for answers.

Independent reading is a critical foundation for all that will follow, so we dedicate significant class time for students to read what they have chosen. We focus our attention on motivating, supporting, and nudging all readers in the room to find books that will keep them reading. We seek deep engagement: reading more than they believed was possible, discovering passions and a widening understanding of their own emerging identities as readers. And what can they read? Again we turn to Louise Rosenblatt for advice:

> No particular type of reading is being urged here as the panacea. There is
> no formula: not contemporary literature as against literature of the past, nor
> minor as against major works, nor even syntactically simpler as against more
> demanding works. Rather, we need to be flexible, we need to understand
> where our pupils are in relation to books, and we need a sufficient command
> of books to see their potentialities in this developmental process. Our main
> responsibility is to help the student to find the right book for growth. We must
> scrutinize carefully the way in which teaching methods and approaches will
> either foster or hinder a lasting sense of personal meaningfulness. (1956, 71)

The challenge of personalizing this method for each student is precisely why we dedicate so much of the year to independent reading.

A quarter of our reading year is focused on book clubs where students develop their thinking in community with others—which increases engagement with the act of reading (Johnston and Ivey 2015). Although limited by the books we have or can borrow, or the focus we establish for the book club study, students still choose what they will read in a book club. Our goal is to hand over book clubs to students by the end of the year: at that point they not only choose the books and the pace of their reading, but direct their own discussions and operate like the book clubs we've both participated in as adults. In our reading year map, book clubs represent three rounds of three weeks each, but we also know that throughout the year some students will choose to read the same book with others during independent reading, blurring the lines between these two categories.

Lastly, a quarter of our reading year is devoted to the study of two core texts we choose. We plan for four to five weeks to study each of these two texts, knowing we will have to make decisions about what we teach and what we leave out. We plan to teach core texts near the end of each semester, after students have had time to develop a habit of regular reading and to build the stamina necessary to tackle a complex, literary text. Our goal is for all students to nurture their lives as independent, engaged readers even while also engaged in book clubs and in core text study. Most adults we know read more than one book at a time, and it is, of course, a basic expectation in college.

We have matched these reading experiences to our writing units' map. Students will read and write every day all year. This consistency is essential. There are also points of intersection between the two: students write literary essays during the study of core texts, for example. We integrate the support of both independent reading and the close reading of mentor texts within each writing unit. We plan time for both as we lead students to grow as readers within a writing unit of study.

The rest of this chapter is divided into three parts and will detail how we support readers in developing independence, in participating in book clubs, and in studying core texts.

✈ Independent Reading

Reading is a personal art. We imagine a book as we read; we enter a world, direct the movie of what happens, and imagine the characters as living, breathing human beings. We follow them into homes and cultures we would never otherwise encounter. We fall in love, we experience loss, we grapple with universal human struggles. The world opens and we fall in. We read because books surprise and delight us, teach us, and challenge us to consider our decisions and to live our lives differently. A book can lead us to understand what we never knew we knew. We find parts of ourselves in books. Most importantly, we control the pace of experiencing a book. We can slow down and reread when we are confused, but also when we just want to live in a moment again. We can set aside a book just as it gets to the end so as to prolong the reading of that book. We might skim ahead. We can write in the margins and revisit our thinking years later. We can share our thinking with other people and discover how they read the book differently than we did. We will understand it more deeply as we listen to them.

We raise expectations for all readers by providing time to read and choice, and by conferring regularly with students to listen to their thinking. Every day we send a consistent message: *Everyone reads in this class.* Helping students gain traction as readers is critical in the
first quarter, and then consistent expectations show students how important it remains all
year—and beyond.

As we launch independent reading, we ask our students to consider the following essential
questions (and we revisit them throughout the year):

- How do readers find books of interest?

- How do readers balance "vacation" books, "just right" books, and "challenge" books?

- What can the book I'm reading teach me about writing? What do we learn when
we recognize a writer's craft?

- What strategies help readers manage distractions in order to read for extended
periods of time?

- What clues help readers identify where they got lost in the text? What do we learn
when we recognize a writer's craft?

- Which "fix-it" strategies help readers repair confusion?

- How does sharing thinking help readers understand more?

- How can readers use a conference with the teacher to increase strategies for
approaching difficult texts?

Support for Independent Reading

The daily practice of book talks described in Chapter 2 supports independent reading. Our
readers are as diverse as their clothes, hair colors, and musical preferences. In one class in the
first week of school Penny watched two students, both of whom had not finished a book in the
previous year, choose classics (*In Cold Blood* by Truman Capote and *Of Mice and Men* by John
Steinbeck) while others chose young adult novels, nonfiction, poetry, and graphic novels. Kelly
had a student, Guadalupe, who selected *1984* to read on her own even though she knew the class
would be studying it later in the year. Our book talks are conscious choices each day to connect
students with books that appeal to their needs and interests.

We both read regularly and share that reading with our students in informal ways. We
might cover the door to the classroom with titles we've read that year or simply share our reading plans on the whiteboard, as shown in Figure 3.2.

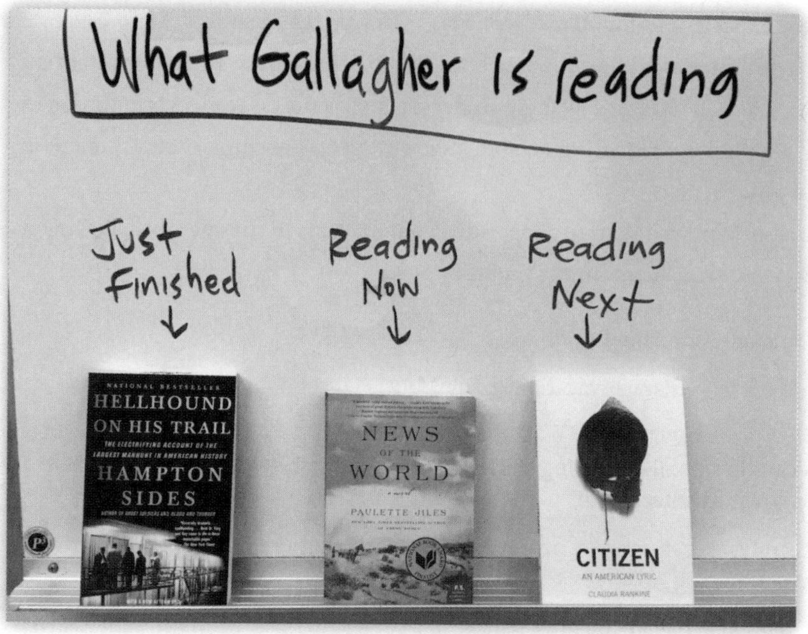

Figure 3.2 Kelly's Whiteboard Showing Reading Choices

Modeling the range of reading we do honors the diversity of texts and the purposes for reading that, of course, vary by reader. (Students enjoy recommending books to us, sometimes stacking them next to our whiteboards. We often read what students suggest to us. Why? It deepens the conversations we have with them and helps us know new titles to recommend to others. Mostly, it shows students we take their thinking seriously and have confidence in their tastes as readers.)

We also have a number of management structures in place that support independent reading. They include

- *Reading list.* Students keep track of their reading on the inside front cover of their writing notebooks (see online resource 3.1) and we reference this while conferring.

- *Next list.* An ongoing list of titles students might want to read next. This list comes primarily from book talks and book shares with other students. This list goes on the inside back cover of their notebooks.

- *Clipboard.* Students record the page they are on each day in class. Each week they total the number of pages they read.

- *Reading ladders.* Each quarter students sort books they have read into a ladder of difficulty and reflect on their individual reading goals, analyzing the balance between easy reading and challenging reading in order to set goals for the next quarter (see online resource 3.2).

- *"What have you read?" posters.* Book covers are posted on the wall and students sign below if they've read the book. This helps us see which books are most popular and forms connections between readers in different classes.

- *Checkout system.* Penny uses Classroom Organizer from Booksource. Kelly takes pictures of students with their books, which he deletes upon return.

- *"What should the teacher buy next?" list.* On a classroom chart, students suggest titles for classroom purchase.

- *Student recommendation shelf.* Just like in a bookstore, students put sticky note reviews on the covers of books and the books are displayed on a shelf.

- *"Dear Reader" letters.* Students recommend books by writing brief reviews on the inside covers of books.

Figure 3.3 What Should Mrs. Kittle Buy Next?

We believe students should have agency in the classroom library. We ask them to help us organize it and students are invited to make suggestions for purchases for our classroom library (see Figure 3.3).

Teaching "into" Independent Reading

We assess what our students need through individual conferences and plan minilessons and demonstrations—like the ones that follow—to meet those needs.

Navigating the Complexities Any Reader Faces in a New Book

We do not prepare ahead for this lesson; we simply show students the questions we ask as we encounter confusion with a book we pick up for the first time. *What is happening here? Who is telling the story? What is the relationship between these characters/people? What do I know about where this story takes place?* We model why reading is hard at the start of any book. Students who frequently abandon books are often stuck in this hard place. They struggle with ambiguity.

They find reading confusing because they never get past the work required to *enter* a book. It helps students understand why a reader must focus attention more closely in the beginning.

Tracking Thinking About Plot, Character, and Ideas Throughout the Book

We begin by encouraging our students to map central plot points in order to hold onto their thinking as they read. We prompt students to pay attention to character development over time. We ask, "What do we know now about this character that we didn't know at the beginning of the book?" Additionally, we teach students how an author uses story to enable big ideas to emerge and to watch for how these ideas are developed throughout the book or series.

Managing Multiple Narrators in a Work of Fiction

An increasingly common structure of YA novels is to have multiple points of view tell a story. Showing students how to track multiple narrators (e.g., in a T-chart) is a point of focus in a mini-lesson and is followed up when needed in conferences.

Reading for Writing Craft

We have students collect sentences of beautifully crafted language to sharpen their focus on writing. We model this with passages from the books we read. We also study one chapter of a book to show the development of thinking both in plot and in theme through the use of asides or commentary from a character.

Understanding an Unfamiliar Time or Place

When a student was reading *Escape from Camp 14*, Penny suggested, "Read with your phone beside you." It is natural to search for images or news articles of North Korea in order to deepen understanding of this memoir. This lesson can be essential for helping students sustain interest in nonfiction, especially when they enter a text without deep prior knowledge of the subject.

Identifying Predictable Moves in Fiction

We understand the moves that are "hidden" in books, and we want our students to develop the ability to recognize them on their own (e.g., the weather may foreshadow a turn in plot; an interruption of the flow of the plot may indicate that the reader should pay closer attention; repeated focus on a time or place may be a hint of an emerging symbol). Classroom time will be allotted for students and teachers to share how they identify the predictable patterns found in fiction.

Studying One Author's Work

We show students how to find other books by an author—by looking for additional titles listed at the beginning or end of a novel as well as consulting online resources like Goodreads. We show students author websites and interviews with authors. We challenge students to read more than one book by a favorite author and to consider how each author has his or her own moves and techniques.

Making the Most of an Audiobook or a Podcast

Research supports the use of audiobooks to engage readers. Many of our students were not read to as children, and this can be the ideal invitation to a world of reading. During book talks, we share excerpts from audiobooks read by authors or actors (*The Hate U Give* by Angie Thomas and *Born a Crime* by Trevor Noah are highly recommended).

Abandoning a Book or Skipping the Boring Parts

There are too many wonderful books in the world to waste time on books we don't love. We give our readers permission to abandon books and show them why we do.

CONSIDER This...

Even though we began the year by giving our students the freedom to choose what they wanted to read, we noticed that many of our most reluctant readers did not begin to gain reading traction until after they were placed in book clubs. Exposing them to good books and giving them time to read them were not enough to awaken them from dormancy. This changed when they participated in book clubs. Having to meet with their peers each week motivated them to get going. Accordingly, as we get a sense of the students in a new school year, we may reposition the first book club so that it occurs earlier in the year.

Conversation Clip

See "Adjusting
the Reading Map
to Start Book
Clubs Earlier"

✦ Book Clubs

Penny's interest in high school book clubs began ten years ago when four senior girls in one class decided to read *Lolita* together. They set a schedule for two months of reading and asked for time to meet in class to discuss their thinking. Two months is a long time, but all four girls continued to read independently as they also slowly studied this common text. As an observer, Penny was enthralled with what she saw happening in their conversations—both inside class and in notes they passed to each other that they shared with her. Prior to this experience, she had noticed pairs and trios of friends reading the same book at the same time. She had encouraged students to read in these informal book clubs, but there were always students who chose to read all year on their own. Watching the girls talk, Penny knew she wanted to replicate the opportunity for rich conversations with all of her students.

Kelly also recalls his first foray into book clubs. Many years ago his students had just finished reading *All Quiet on the Western Front*, and Kelly had secured funding to purchase numerous other books about war—both fiction and nonfiction (ranging from World War II to the then-current Iraq War). Like Penny, Kelly was immediately struck by his students' spike in enthusiasm and motivation, even though the teacher had chosen the big topic (war) to be studied. It was Kelly's first experience with the power of choice and collaboration, which are inherent when students, on their own, get together to discuss books.

There were many realizations in our first experiments with book clubs. One, book clubs decrease social isolation. The classroom community strengthened with an increase in both casual and academic conversations between students who had not spoken prior to book clubs. Two, there was an intensity in student-to-student listening that we had not seen before. Conversations about reading deepened. Three, students supported and encouraged each other without the teacher's intervention. In fact, we saw how little they needed us at all. When we sat and listened to a book club conversation, they ignored us. Students did not need teacher questions to explore big ideas in their books. They took the work of comprehension seriously; they wanted to understand and explore their own questions as they read. There was laughter and a shared spirit of inquiry. It was magic.

Teaching Clip
See a variety
of book club
conversations in
the online video

We planned for three book club experiences across the year in which our students would discuss books face-to-face in our own classrooms and in cross-country Google Doc conversations with students in each other's classrooms. What follows are some of our key decisions when implementing book clubs.

Select Titles

For book clubs, we look for high-interest books that encompass a wide range of reading abilities. For example, here are the five books Kelly chose for his students' first book clubs:

- *The Curious Incident of the Dog in the Night-Time* by Mark Haddon
- *Thirteen Reasons Why* by Jay Asher (chosen before the Netflix series came out)
- *Between Shades of Gray* by Ruta Sepetys

- *Unwind* by Neal Shusterman
- *Escape from Camp 14* by Blaine Harden

Choosing from a list of five books constitutes very limited choice, but we are public school teachers, after all, and budgets are tight. We have been forced to invent creative ways to secure book club selections. All students need their own copy of the book in order to continue reading at home. Penny begged for funds from her principal and department chair. She asked the librarian to collect books from nearby libraries. She swapped books with colleagues. And yes, she also spent too much of her own money.

Kelly's department gets curriculum cycle monies every few years, and teachers thought hard about how to spend that money. Instead of buying five hundred copies of *To Kill a Mockingbird*, his colleagues decided to buy one hundred copies. With the leftover funds, they purchased fifty copies of book A, fifty copies of book B, and so on. The amount of money that was allocated for the curriculum cycle hadn't changed; what did change was how that money was spent. Kelly also tapped Title 1 funds to purchase sets of books, and he secured district-level funds to pilot an ELA classroom that values book club experiences.

When we joined classes for cross-country book clubs, the selection was much broader:

- *Every Day* by David Levithan
- *Under the Feet of Jesus* by Helena María Viramontes
- *League of Denial* by Mark Fainaru-Wada and Steve Fainaru
- *The Nazi Hunters* by Neal Bascomb
- *The Shallows* by Nicholas Carr
- *A Thousand Splendid Suns* by Khaled Hosseini
- *Aristotle and Dante Discover the Secrets of the Universe* by Benjamin Alire Sáenz
- *Side Effects May Vary* by Julie Murphy
- *Outliers* by Malcolm Gladwell
- *Enrique's Journey* by Sonia Nazario
- *Revolution* by Deborah Wiles
- *All American Boys* by Jason Reynolds and Brendan Kiely

The more diverse the book club selections are and the wider the range of text complexity is, the more likely it is that all students will be able to find something they want to read. For our final, student-directed book clubs of the year, students chose their own books to read together in clubs.

Group Students by Choice

With book talks followed by time to peruse titles, students choose books they want to read from the selections we offer and then we form groups based on those choices. When we combined our classes, the most popular choice by far was *Every Day* (twelve students from Kelly's class and nine from Penny's), so we ended up with three different groups reading the same book.

CONSIDER This...

Sometimes students choose books that aren't a good fit. Three of Penny's students selected *Under the Feet of Jesus*. The reason they selected it soon became obvious: it was the shortest book on the list. However, the boys did not connect with it, and they were uninterested from the start. In the spirit of responsive teaching, Penny quickly rustled up three copies of six different books in her classroom so they could make a new choice. The group chose Laurie Halse Anderson's *Twisted* as a replacement.

When students selected their own books in the final book clubs of the year, they also selected their club's members. Just as adults in book clubs do, friends chose to read together.

Create a Reading and Meeting Schedule

After groups are formed, the next step is to create a schedule. For their first book clubs, Kelly allotted one month for students to read their selections. Students were told they would meet once each week to discuss their books, and then each club planned their own schedules for reading.

In our cross-country book clubs, we also gave students a month to read their books, but we created a schedule of weekly due dates for the reading. For example, Figure 3.4 shows what the schedule looked like for four of the titles.

In the final book clubs of the year, students gained control by setting their own schedules for reading and by determining the focus of book club discussions.

Book Club	Week 1	Week 2	Week 3	Week 4
Every Day	p. 83	p. 165	p. 243	Finished
Side Effects May Vary	p. 79	p. 165	p. 249	Finished
Aristotle and Dante	p. 107	p. 155	p. 233	Finished
All American Boys	p. 85	p. 180	p. 265	Finished

Figure 3.4 Sample Reading Schedules for Book Groups

Give Students Tools for Discussion

We developed several tools to help students capture their thinking to bring to book clubs. Discussions happened around tables in our own classrooms, and in Google Docs in our cross-country collaborations.

Thought Logs

We gave each of our students a seventy-five-page college-lined spiral notebook—a Thought Log—and then had each student glue a "Track Your Thinking" chart in the inside front cover (see Figure 3.5).

Using the suggestions on this chart, students tracked their thinking as they read. On book club day, students used their Thought Logs to generate meaningful discussion. We often launched the discussion by asking, "What is worth talking about?" but then the discussions were quickly turned over to students.

Many students were not comfortable with the openness of the Thought Log approach. They were much more familiar with being told what to think and how much to think, but we each explained to them the value of generating their own thinking: "I already know what *I* think; I'm much more interested in what *you* think." Of course, the students immediately asked, "How much should we put in our Thought Logs?" but we resisted directly answering the question. If students write too much in their logs, they will kill the books; too little, and they will not be demonstrating that they are thoughtful readers. This vagueness can be unsettling, but we want students to start making these judgments.

After the students' first group discussion, we collected the Thought Logs. We saw a range of thinking as we collected excellent examples to share in class the next day. "Look at what

TRACK YOUR THINKING

I used to think _____, but now I think _____.
I still think _____, but I'd like to add _____.
Others think _____, but I think _____.

Things to track over time

A character:
- How does the character change?
- What insights does the character gain?

What big ideas are being developed?
- What conflict arises?
- What do these conflicts tell the reader?
- What claims does the author make? What passages support these claims?

What techniques/moves does the writer make?
- What literary devices are used? (e.g., foreshadowing, personification)
- Where does the author use punctuation and sentence structure effectively?
- What are the key passages? Why?
- Notice beautiful sentences/passages. Comment on them.

Track your confusion.
- What is confusing at the beginning of the book? Does the confusion remain or does it clear up?
- What passages/sentences/words do you find confusing? Show evidence that you are wrestling with the confusion.

Thought starters:
- I noticed _____.
- I wonder _____.
- I was reminded of _____.
- I think _____.
- I'm surprised that _____.
- I'd like to know _____.
- I realized _____.
- If I were _____.
- The central issue(s) is (are) _____.
- One consequence of _____ could be _____.
- If _____, then _____.
- I'm not sure _____.
- Although it seems _____.

"That" statements

This passage makes me think that _____.
This makes me feel that _____.
The author is suggesting that _____.

Figure 3.5 Track Your Thinking Chart

Source: Donna Santman and Kelly Gallagher

Andrea did here" and "I like the thinking Ruben exhibited here" proved powerful in motivating students who were slow to get started in their logs. After showing several excellent Thought Log entries, we asked those students who were underprepared to "turn it up" for the next week's discussion. As the four weeks progressed, students' work in their Thought Logs—and the discussions generated by this work—markedly improved.

One Comment, One Question

In our cross-country book clubs, we asked students to bring one comment and one question to the "discussion" in their group's Google Doc. Here's an example from Garrick, who read *Outliers*:

> *Until I read this chapter, I never realized why it can be very hard for American children to learn to count. I wonder if Americans would be better learners if our numbers were like Chinese numbers. First of all, they don't take as long to say. It says, "They have a logical counting system. Eleven is ten-one. Twelve is ten-two. Twenty-four is two-tens-four . . ." What do you guys think of this? Do you think we might benefit from changing the way we count? I feel like we would, except it would take a very long time too accustom to this new system. Maybe if the words for our numbers were easier to say, they might be easier to remember.*

Starting with a comment and a question was an effective way to get the conversations rolling, and the questions helped engage others in the group. That said, we had a number of students who were engaged with the books and thinking about important issues, but their responses did not invite others to respond. Here's an example from Foster, who read *All American Boys*:

> *The book* All American Boys *really makes you think about the problem of racism existing in the U.S. even today. It connects with many of the recent news stories in the U.S., where a white police officer has unjustly beaten, wronged, or even killed a black person. I agree with Kelly, that if Rashad had been white maybe the whole incident wouldn't have happened. This makes me think about how often people today judge other people just based on their appearance. I think that Paul made the assumption that Rashad was stealing just because he was black and sagged his pants. I think that this will cause a lot of racial divide in their city.*

Conversation Moves

We conducted minilessons to teach our students how to participate in ways that invited others into a deeper level of conversation. In these examples from students reading *Every Day*, the bold text represents some of the conversation moves we taught.

> **Emmet: I really agree with the point you brought up, Yaylene, since** A had met Rhiannon, the rules that he created to protect the lives of the people he became have slowly deteriorated into almost nonexistence. For example, when he was the kid about to leave on vacation, A would have never run away if he still held those same values and rules.

> **Ashton:** Convincing Rhiannon that A doesn't have a body is really difficult for A. At first Rhiannon thought it was a prank set by Justin. Well I have two minutes to go. **I would like to hear your thoughts.**

> **Imanol: I agree with your comment, and I'm also wondering** how A will confront Nathan. I think that Nathan may be thought of as someone different from who he really is. A is obviously not hurting anymore, but Nathan thinks he is. Why would Nathan think this? It shows the reader that he is a little more crazy than we thought. I think that Rhiannon will realize that A doesn't have a body when she starts to believe he is not joking. **I'm interested in hearing more of your thinking.**

Notice how the students are being taught to respond to the comments of others as well as to invite an additional response to their ideas. We also taught students to address specific comments in the threads. For example, here is a posting from Jassmyn, who was reading *Side Effects May Vary*:

> ***To Victoria and others who think Alice and Harvey's relationship is toxic***—*I think that Alice is just unsure how to deal with the fact that she loves Harvey, so she tries to push him away. Harvey understands that so he lets her do whatever she wants while he tries to pull her in.* ***Please respond with your thoughts!***

Teaching Clip

See two students discuss online book groups in "A Conversation About *Outliers*, by Malcolm Gladwell"

Interacting with peers in other schools motivated our students to talk more about their reading in our classes. They were driven by a curiosity about how others read and understand both the books and their responses to the texts.

The Shape of Story

We want our students to understand that *where you are* in a book helps to determine *what you might be thinking*. The shape of a story is well known to English teachers: exposition, rising action, turning point, resolution. Why is it important for our students to know the shape of a story? Because where you are in a literary work can drive the kinds of questions you should be considering and the text answers. Our friend Donna Santman, an author and a remarkable teacher in New York City, suggests that readers consider the big-idea questions in Figure 3.6 as they navigate through a book.

We teach students these questions because knowing this shape helps them generate the kinds of thinking we do when we read. It's true that predictability makes reading easier, but knowing what to expect also paves the way for surprise in plot or character development; we expect one thing and the author turns us to another. This is part of the richness of author's craft. When students are in book clubs, writing helps prepare them for the discussions to come—they have a chance to work out their thinking as they are reading and can enter the conversation with confidence.

Self-Directed Book Clubs

For the final book clubs, we told students there would be no traditional requirements—no Thought Logs, no quizzes, no end-of-the-book essays. They were simply to read their books and meet once a week to discuss them. When we announced this to our students, they stared at us, stunned. We found it interesting, but not surprising, when one of our students blurted out, "What's the catch?"

There was no catch. Both of us belong to book clubs, and neither one of us compiles Thought Logs or writes essays to share with our groups (indeed, if those were requirements for our book clubs, we would drop out). We attend our book clubs because we like to read and we like to discuss our reading with others. We want our students to have this same experience—to understand the feel of a "real" book club. Sure, they might mark a passage or two to bring to their discussions, but not because we told them to. We simply asked them to show up prepared to discuss their books. They were charged with deciding what "prepared" meant.

Exposition	Rising Action	Turning Point	Resolution
Who is here?	What trouble is brewing?	What is changing?	What loose ends are tied up?
How are the characters connected?	Where are the obstacles?	What is propelling the change?	How are the characters affected by change?
What are the characters like?	How do the characters deal with them?	Who wins the conflict?	How will life go on (or not)?
What kind of place is this?	How do the characters interact?	How is the conflict resolved?	
What's the trouble?	What's the impact of setting on character, plot, and conflict?		

Figure 3.6 Questions to Navigate a Story

CONSIDER *This...*

So how did the student-directed book clubs turn out? Some read and discussed in pairs, others in small groups of four or five, but almost without exception, each group came prepared and ready to talk. Though the talks were completely student directed, it was fun to see students discuss what English teachers want their kids to notice (e.g., the themes, the conflicts, the author's craft). We understand that some teachers might be concerned that kids will not do the reading if all accountability measures are removed, but we found the opposite to be true. Our students' participation *increased* when they were given the freedom to select their books, to choose their partners, and to decide how they would share their thinking. One of our goals at the beginning of the year was to help our students become authentic, self-motivated readers. For most of them, these self-directed book clubs were evidence that we had achieved this goal.

Conversation Clip

See "Independent
Book Clubs"

✈ Core Texts

In *Books for Living* (2016), Will Schwalbe writes: "Reading is the best way I know to learn how to examine your life. By comparing what you've done to what others have done, and your thoughts and theories and feelings to those of others, you learn about yourself and the world around you. Perhaps that is why reading is one of the few things you do alone that can make you feel less alone; it's a solitary activity that connects you with others" (7).

An interesting concept, isn't it? That reading alone helps us to connect with others. We have already discussed in this chapter how our students made meaningful connections by bringing their thinking into small book clubs, but we also believe it is important to find some space in our curriculum to deepen these connections through occasional shared, whole-class reading of core texts. We want our students to compare their thoughts and theories and feelings to those of others because doing so gives them insight into themselves and into the world. We believe there is a synergy—a level of insight—that occurs when an entire class huddles around a core text that does not always happen in independent reading or in small book clubs.

When reading works that contain big ideas, we want as much diverse thought as possible thrown into the mix. And when it comes to generating this diverse thought, thirty-eight heads are better than one.

As part of a balanced reading diet, we made room on our map for the study of two whole-class works during the school year, one at the end of each semester. This timing was intentional, as we knew the work students would do in independent reading and in book clubs would build the skills necessary to deeply read a challenging literary work. During each whole-class reading experience, we maintained our classroom routines. We still conducted daily book talks focused on books that thematically connected to the whole-class text, we still led students to quick write daily, and we still read in class every day (though now the reading and our conferences largely focused on the core work). Students continued to discuss the whole-class texts in small groups, and they used Thought Logs to track their thinking.

What follows is the planning process we used for teaching a core text.

Select a Text

When it comes to selecting works for whole-class study, we have always liked Carol Jago's guidelines. In *Classics in the Classroom* (2004), Jago suggests choosing books that

- are written in language that is perfectly suited to the author's purpose

- expose readers to complex human dilemmas

- include compelling, disconcerting characters

- explore universal themes that combine different periods and cultures

- challenge readers to examine their beliefs

- tell a good story with places for laughing and places for crying. (47)

Works that meet all these criteria deserve a more measured reading; there is a deeper texture to them than is found in some books students choose for independent reading—and we want our students to experience this richness. These books have something worthwhile to say to all readers. All readers.

Using these criteria, we selected William Shakespeare's *Romeo and Juliet* for our students to read at the end of the first semester. The classic play met all the criteria, we thought our students would connect to it, and we were excited to plan a unit of study around the text together. The plan was for our students to study the novel within our classes and then to write to each other across the country.

CONSIDER This...

We had originally planned to study *Romeo and Juliet* earlier in the year, but we delayed it until the very end of the first semester so students could get an additional four weeks of reading under their belts before tackling the complex play. We were afraid that if we started the play when originally planned, we would lose some of the very tenuous momentum we had begun to see take hold in our most reluctant readers.

For the second semester, we planned to do the same sort of study and collaboration with Harper Lee's *To Kill a Mockingbird*. We both love the book, and given the events happening in our country at the time, we felt it was a relevant and timely read. We couldn't wait to get started.

Then the real world intervened.

When Penny polled her students, she found that many of them had already studied Lee's classic text in middle school. This put her in an uncomfortable spot and raised interesting questions: Should she teach a novel that many of her students had already studied with another teacher? Is there enough value to be found in rereading a text with a new teacher? Or would it be better to select something different for whole-class study? After all, there were a lot of great books her students had not yet read. And unfortunately, the students who had read *Mockingbird* spoke only of how much they hated it, poisoning the atmosphere of a whole-class study of this book.

Kelly, on the other hand, had a different dilemma. Though he had spent the previous three quarters getting students to increase their reading volume, he could not overcome his sense that *To Kill a Mockingbird* was too hard for many of his inexperienced readers. What good would it do to "teach" a book that is too hard for many of his students to read? Kelly was concerned that requiring his students to read *Mockingbird* would lead to more fake reading and drive them away from the hard-earned momentum they had gained via independent reading and book clubs. While some of his students were ready to read the book, others were not.

Because of our respective concerns, we decided to begin exploring other books our classes might read together. In looking at potential titles, we asked ourselves the following:

- Is the book worthy of whole-class study?
- Can the book be used as a springboard to examine big ideas in today's world?
- What have students already read?
- What book would help keep our students' reading momentum?

CONSIDER *This...*

Teaching these novels required both of us to wrestle with some big questions: Is a whole-class reading experience the right move for these students right now? Which books are worthy of whole-class study? How do we teach these books in ways that will engage our students? These were important questions, and answering them required a great deal of thinking. And let's face it—it is hard to find the time and space to do this kind of big thinking, but finding it is critical. Wrestling with these questions increased our confidence in our teaching. In contrast, when we don't give much thought to text selection, it creates problems *while we're teaching*: we can't defend our choice of text or don't anticipate the problems that arise in the unit.

When we don't make the time to think deeply about our decisions, we empower well-meaning curriculum directors and publishers to make the decisions for us. But it is the struggle with these decisions that develops our insights as teachers. The more we think about which texts to choose, the more we think about where our students are as readers and where they are in their emotional development as adolescents. We take the time to consider the challenges we may encounter as we teach the books, and doing so helps us decide how to frame the units.

These questions helped us consider our students more specifically, and for a number of reasons we decided to part ways and to select different novels for our second whole-class text. Penny's students would read Sherman Alexie's *The Absolutely True Diary of a Part-Time Indian*, and Kelly's students would read George Orwell's *Animal Farm*. No single book addresses the needs of every student, of course, but we believed the themes and the author's craft in these two books made them good choices for whole-class study.

Pace the Reading

When planning to teach a whole-class work, we think hard about the pacing. If students read too fast, they will miss some of the deep beauty of the work. If they read too slowly, the text gets chopped up so much that the whole of it becomes unrecognizable. Where is the balance between too fast and too slow? Where is the tipping point?

First Core Text

For *Romeo and Juliet*, we decided to budget four weeks to read and study the play. We know that we could have spent much more time, but we were concerned that drawing it out any longer would risk turning Shakespeare's great play into an extended worksheet. Any shorter and we would have felt we were not doing the play justice. Four weeks seemed about right (and in Penny's schedule, this represents only ten class days). Figure 3.7 shows our pacing for the actual reading of the play.

Second Core Text

For the second study of a core text, we were more than three-quarters of the way into the school year, and we wanted to take advantage of our students' increased fluency and stamina. They were better and more willing readers than they had been seven months earlier, and this influenced our planning. Our students had changed, and so we adapted to their newly gained strength.

We decided students would read the entire book before any discussion would occur. By reading the entire novel first on their own, students generated their own meaning-making before the teacher and other students intervened. This is the whole-novels approach (Sacks 2014) developed by Madeleine Ray at Bank Street College in New York City. Because the novels we selected were short, and because we felt our students were ready to read for longer, uninterrupted chunks at a time, we gave our students two weeks to read, allowing them to determine their own pace. We knew some students would race out and read the books in one or two gulps. We knew others would read at a more measured pace, taking advantage of our daily time to read in class. We trusted each of them to map out their own reading pace, just as we do in our own reading lives.

Conversation Clip

See "Keeping Momentum Going When Studying a Core Text"

Hour	Acts/Scenes Read	Key Plot Points
1	Prologue	Overview of the play
2	1.1	Near fight on the street
	1.2	Romeo loves Rosaline
		Romeo and his friends are invited to the Capulet party
3	1.3	Paris courts Juliet
	1.4	Romeo ignores his gut and decides to attend the party
4	1.5	The kiss
5	2.1	The balcony scene
	2.2	
6	2.3	The Friar agrees to marry Romeo and Juliet
	2.4	Comic scene with the Nurse
7	2.5	The Nurse tells Juliet the good news
	2.6	The Friar marries Romeo and Juliet
8	3.1	Mercutio is killed by Tybalt
	3.2	
9	3.3	Romeo learns of banishment
	3.4	Old Man Capulet moves up Paris-Juliet wedding
	3.5	Old Man Capulet has his meltdown
10	4.1	The Friar devises fake death plan
	4.2	Wedding preparations are underway
	4.3	Juliet drinks the potion
	4.4	
11	4.5	Juliet is found "dead"
	5.1	Romeo buys poison
	5.2	The message does not get to Romeo
12	5.3	Romeo finds Juliet
		Romeo kills Paris
		Romeo commits suicide
		Juliet commits suicide

Figure 3.7 Pacing Chart for *Romeo and Juliet*

Pose Essential Questions

With limited time to teach a core text, we have found that anchoring the study in an essential question helps us keep our focus and make good planning decisions.

First Core Text

For *Romeo and Juliet*, we created two essential questions:

1. What is true love, and how do you know it when you have found it?
2. How do decisions shape our destiny?

The first question was critical in getting our students invested in the play. What fourteen-year-old is not interested in love at first sight?

We had students write next to Taylor Swift's "Love Story" and we wove in some clips from the excellent PBS program "*Romeo and Juliet* with Joseph Fiennes." We asked students if they believed in love at first sight, and from there we had students share whether they had ever seen "true love" in their lives. This generated lively writing and discussion (see Figure 3.8 for student thinking about this question).

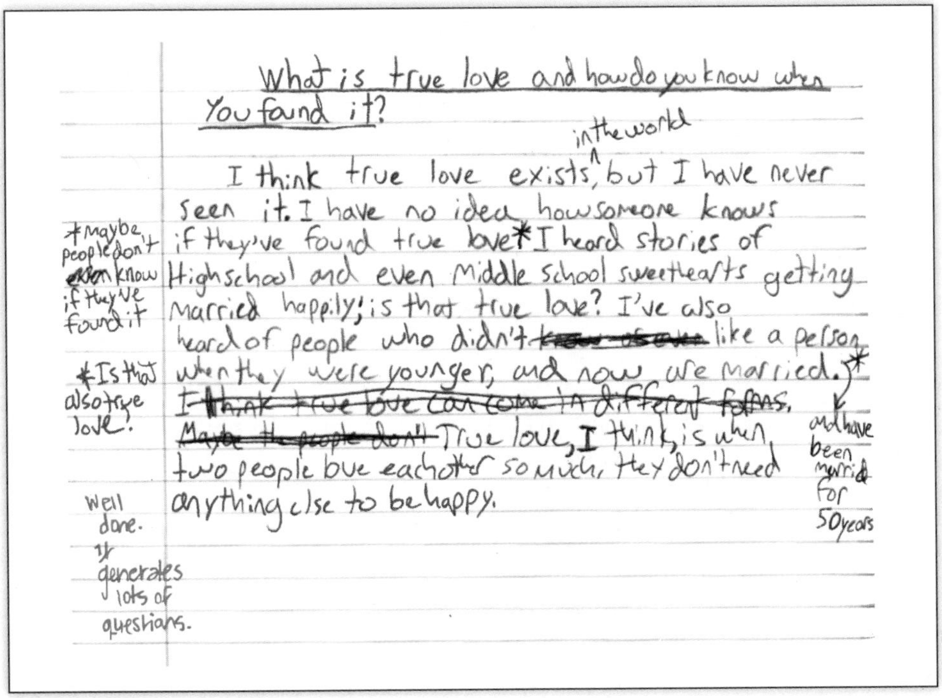
What is true love and how do you know when You found it?

I think true love exists in the world, but I have never seen it. I have no idea how someone knows if they've found true love* I heard stories of Highschool and even Middle School sweethearts getting Married happily; is that true love? I've also heard of people who didn't like a person when they were younger, and now are married.* ~~I think true love can come in different forms.~~ ~~Maybe the people don't~~ True love, I think, is when two people love eachother so much, they don't need anything else to be happy.

*maybe people don't even know if they've found it

*Is that also true love?

and have been married for 50 years

Well done. It generates lots of questions.

Figure 3.8 What Is True Love?

The second question—How do decisions shape our destiny?—is one we returned to repeatedly over the course of the play. To get students thinking in this direction, we had them quickly write in notebooks to the following prompt:

> All humans make choices or decisions daily. Some are important; some are
> not so important. We choose what clothes to wear. We decide whether or
> not to do our homework. We choose certain people for friends. Sometimes
> the decisions we make change our lives.
>
> Discuss an important decision you have made in your life. Explain the
> decision and how it affected you. Tell whether you would make the same
> decision again.

This writing also spurred interesting discussions, and it provided our students with a lens through which to read the play. We had students create two-page positive/negative charts in their Thought Logs to track the decisions made in the play. After each act we stopped and had students examine key decisions made by the characters.

Second Core Text

Because *Animal Farm* is an allegory, the essential question that framed Kelly's study was "What is Orwell *really* saying?" At the time of the study, the country was involved in a highly contentious election season. There is probably a nicer way of saying this, but never in our lives had we seen and heard so much crap being peddled. The general public was force-fed a steady diet of half-truths and downright lies, and worse, these lies were seemingly spewed with the cynical confidence that they would go unchallenged. And, sadly, this is exactly how it played out: some lies were repeated so often that people started to accept them as facts. What Orwell is *really* saying in *Animal Farm* was, of course, perfectly suited to the times.

The Absolutely True Diary of a Part-Time Indian was equally suited to exploring the essential question Penny's students had pursued all year: "How do others see the world differently than I do?" The book is about friendship and families in the midst of violence and alcoholism and what it means to come of age in such turmoil. She considered Alexie's rationale for writing his books: "I write books for teenagers because I vividly remember what it felt like to be a teen facing everyday and epic dangers. I don't write to protect them. It's far too late for that. I write to give them weapons—in the form of words and ideas—that will help them fight their monsters. I write in blood because I remember what it felt like to bleed" (2011). The book honors the experience of Native Americans, and since we believe strongly in diverse books to enlarge the experiences of our students, the question made perfect sense as an anchor for the study of Alexie's book.

Decide Which Skills to Highlight

The next step in planning how you'll teach a whole-class text is to settle on the specific skills you want to address in the study. Different novels, of course, invite different possibilities.

First Core Text

After lengthy discussion, for *Romeo and Juliet* we selected the following skills to highlight in the study:

- Understand the structure of a sonnet.
- Recognize how characters were defined by the decisions they made.
- Appreciate Shakespeare's use of metaphorical language.
- Analyze theme and foreshadowing.
- Read at different levels: What does it say? What does it mean? How is the text crafted?
- What do you learn as you read like a writer?

With these skills in mind, we were ready to decide on the quick writes and mentor texts we would use, the minilessons we would craft, and the book talks we would conduct. Figure 3.9 shows a compilation of teaching resources from both our classes (for a complete list of books that compliment *Romeo and Juliet*, see online resource 3.3).

In addition to our whole-class teaching, we also had students explore their thinking about the play in email exchanges between our classes. Students developed their skills as they worked to clearly articulate their thoughts to an outside audience, as you can see in this exchange between Tania and Taylor.

Tania wrote:

> In the play *Romeo and Juliet* I only know it is surrounded by the idea of love. And I for one know little of that topic. There is a quote by Romeo that says "A madness most discreet, A choking gall, and a preserving sweet" that is how he describes love. He explains love as everything and nothing, as a medicine, something crazy, and something deathly. I wonder how love feels like and wonder if it something as great as he describes.

And Taylor responded:

> I feel like love can be all of those things, however it is what you make it. If you allow it to be deathly it will be, If you let it get crazy it will be crazy. that's just how it works. I have a really hard time connecting to anything in *Romeo and Juliet* because it is all so over-exaggerated, and unrealistic.

Quick Writes and Mentor Texts Used	Minilessons We Conducted	Book Talk Titles
Songs • "Love Story" by Taylor Swift **Poems** • "First Kiss" by Joseph Stroud • Sonnet 43 ("How do I love thee? . . .") by Robert Browning • "Not Anyone Who Says" by Mary Oliver • "The Type" by Sarah Kay **Films** • *Romeo and Juliet* (2013 version) • *Romeo + Juliet* (1996 version) • *Romeo and Juliet* (1968 version) • "*Romeo and Juliet* with Joseph Fiennes" (PBS) **Books** • *No Fear Shakespeare* • *Romeo and Juliet* graphic novel by Gareth Hinds • "Love's Vocabulary" by Diane Ackerman (excerpts) • *Because a Little Bug Went Ka-Choo!* by Dr. Seuss	What are the elements of a sonnet? What is iambic pentameter? Writing a sonnet Analyzing metaphor: "A rose by any other name . . ." Close reading to analyze foreshadowing Close reading to analyze theme Close reading on three levels: What does it say? What does it mean? How is it said? Sharing strong Thought Log entries with the entire class Strategies for memorizing lines (we modeled our struggles) Analyzing filmmakers' decisions in different versions of the same scene	*Romiette and Julio* by Sharon M. Draper *Keeping You a Secret* by Julie Anne Peters *Aristotle and Dante Discover the Secrets of the Universe* by Benjamin Alire Sáenz *13 Little Blue Envelopes* by Maureen Johnson *Juliet Immortal* by Stacey Jay *Love Walked In* by Marisa de los Santos *The Spectacular Now* by Tim Tharp *The Sun Is Also a Star* by Nicola Yoon

Figure 3.9 Resources for Teaching

Second Core Text

Because we designed the study of our second core text around the idea that "students must first read and experience a work of literature wholly and authentically" (Sacks 2014, 3), we removed the annoying stop signs that teachers often place after each chapter. We still conferred with students about the development of big ideas, but the bulk of our teaching occurred before and after our students read the novels. Figures 3.10 and 3.11 show the different teaching supports we offered our students.

Teacher Support *Before* Reading the Text	Teacher Support *While* Reading the Text	Teacher Support *After* Reading the Text
Briefly explained that this book was chosen because of its relevance to the modern reader. Introduced allegory and had students explore the concept. Teased students into the book by stating, "This is a book about talking animals on a farm, but it is not really a book about talking animals on a farm. It is an allegory. As you read it, try to figure out what Orwell is *really* saying." (Kelly does not discuss the Russian Revolution until *after* the book has been read). Read Old Major's speech in Chapter 1 out loud to the class to help students get into the book. Placed students in small book club groups for discussion, even though every student in the room was reading the same book. Reviewed the kinds of thinking students should be striving for in their Thought Logs as they read the novel.	Provided class time for students to do some of the reading. Continued one-to-one conferring. Provided audiobooks for lower-level readers. Gave book talks with thematic connections, for example, *V for Vendetta* (overcoming oppression).	Revisited allegory and outlined the key players in the Russian Revolution. Facilitated a discussion in which students made the connections. Choose close reading passages for students to study. Facilitated a Socratic seminar discussion of the novel. Shared exemplary thinking found in the students' Thought Logs. Posted related articles in Google Classroom to help students understand the thematic connections between the novel and current events.

Figure 3.10 Kelly's Teaching Support for *Animal Farm*

Craft an Assessment

We return to where we started the unit: What do we want our students to take from this reading experience? Different novels suggest different assessments. We plan ahead for assessment, so that we align our teaching with our intended outcomes throughout the unit.

First Core Text

For *Romeo and Juliet*, we decided on a four-part final assessment:

1. **Write a sonnet.** Students were asked to write a sonnet using the Shakespearean rhyme pattern (ABAB CDCD EFEF GG) on any topic. Some of our more advanced students dabbled in iambic pentameter, though that element was not required. To model this process we first created our own sonnets in front of the students. Students recorded the reading of their sonnets into online voice recorders.

Teacher Support *Before* Reading the Text	Teacher Support *While* Reading the Text	Teacher Support *After* Reading the Text
Explained that this book was chosen because of its relevance to discussions about race and class in our country. Connected the book to our ongoing essential question. Reminded students of the significance of the National Book Award for literature. Introduced students to the author in an interview in which he responds to the challenges to and banning of this book in some schools. Reminded students of our fall study of Chapter 2, "Why Chicken Means So Much to Me," and had students revisit their notebook responses on the chapter. Created night writing expectations to coincide with the reading. This included a range of free responses (I noticed _____, I wondered _____), research on Native American tribes, and sketching.	Gave book talks on all of Alexie's books, his collections of poetry, and a collection of books from First Nations authors in Canada. Gave book talks with thematic connections, for example, *Black Like Me* (racial and ethnic identity). Continued conferring with readers one-to-one. Read aloud sections of the text to a student who was struggling, as well as providing the student with the audiobook. Encouraged all students to consider the audiobook as a companion after sharing an excerpt in class (there is a free sample narrated by Alexie on Audible.com). Assigned daily quick writing using poetry and photographs of Native American people. Selected passages from the book for quick writing responses. Had students choose a sketch from the text to imitate and/or transform. Celebrated night writing by sharing student sketches and writing under the document camera. Had students share research on Native American tribes in their writing groups.	Had students discuss the book in small groups and then in two whole-class Socratic seminars. Posted related articles in Google Classroom to help students understand the thematic connections between the novel and current events. Facilitated quick writing followed by small-group discussions that examined the book's relevance to the modern reader. Used a student's notes on a big idea as a mentor for developing thinking across the novel and transferring that thinking into a literary essay. Conferred with students one-to-one to develop literary essays and assess their understanding of the development of theme in the novel.

Figure 3.11 Penny's Teaching Support for *The Absolutely True Diary of a Part-Time Indian*

2. **Complete a quote ID exam.** Students were given key passages from the play and asked two questions for each passage: (1) What was happening in the play? and (2) What was the significance of this passage to the development of the play? We selected passages that encouraged our students to demonstrate they had a grasp on the skills we taught: recognizing a major theme, understanding foreshadowing, appreciation of the author's use of metaphor.

3. **Create a digital element.** We asked each student to create a digital *Romeo and Juliet* miniproject. For voice recordings, many students used the Google Voice app found on our class laptops. Digital projects were then emailed to us. Here are some projects brainstormed by our students:

- Perform a scene from the play and film it. Students could use Shakespearian language or they could translate the scene into modern slang.

- Create a two-minute play. This is a speed summary project. Students were asked to orally summarize the entire play in under two minutes. This was inspired by the "Ten Classics in Ten Minutes" series, which can be found on YouTube: www.youtube.com/watch?v=GBA0NbPfDHU.

- Interview a character for a podcast.

- Memorize twenty lines from the play and record yourself reciting them (Penny's students were given an additional two weeks to complete this).

- Create a "Thug Notes" summary of the play. This was inspired by the "Thug Notes Summary and Analysis" series: www.youtube.com/watch?v=K-qgVms V3hMShakespeare.

- Create a digital collage of ideas and images that encapsulate the play.

4. **Write a literary analysis essay.** For the literary analysis essay, we took two different approaches. Kelly's approach was more traditional. His prompt asked students to revisit one of the essential questions:

> *While reading "Romeo and Juliet," we have been looking at the decisions made by the characters. Of all the decisions made in the play, which decision was the most critical?*
>
> *Identify the play's most critical decision. Explain who made it and why, and analyze why this particular decision is crucial to the development of the play.*

Kelly knew that many of his students did not know how to organize their thoughts into a "literary essay," but he planned to take them step-by-step through the process. However, reality interceded and he found himself crunched for time with only two days for students to write their essays before winter break. Kelly decided to give his students a model essay he'd written analyzing a key decision made in *Hamlet*, a play they had not read. Because the focus was on the structure and craft of the writing, it didn't matter that students didn't know the play.

CONSIDER This...

Kelly's model essay had some interesting effects on his students' writing. For example, José was one of those students who consistently wrote underdeveloped pieces, but with Kelly's model as a guide, he was able to stretch his writing (and his thinking). This isn't really surprising. In order to write a literary analysis essay, a student has to know what a literary analysis essay looks like.

While Kelly liked how the model essay elevated his students' writing, he noticed that it came at a cost: a lot of his students' essays had a sameness to them. Even though they generated their own analysis, their essays *looked* the same. Certainly, there are many ways to write a literary analysis essay, but showing them one way to do it created a lot of papers that hewed very closely to the original. This raised an interesting question: Is it worth living with shades of formula if the formula itself helps students write more competently in the discourse? Generally, our answer is no, it is not worth it. But the literary analysis essay is a bit of a different animal. Analysis has value in helping students think about literature—but the literary essay has an element of fake school writing to it. And because it is a unique "school" kind of writing, the shades of structural formula in the students' essays did not disturb Kelly as much. We don't like it, but in this specific genre the trade-off was worth it to get kids to write competently in this discourse (in a two-day window of time).

In order to sharpen analytical thinking without the support of online essays on the text, Penny used a comparison of film adaptations of the play to lead her students to analyze. Why? Because analyzing the craft of digital texts is a critical skill for students to develop. Here is the literary essay assignment she gave her students:

> As we continue to read Romeo and Juliet, *we are adding a layer of analysis by studying short film segments from directors Zeffirelli, Luhrmann, and Carlei. We will identify **decisions** each director makes that **influence and**

enhance *our viewing experience. This practice will help you understand*
this play more deeply, yes, but you will also learn to apply a level of
analysis to examine art, music, film, or other plays more deeply.

After students watched the different film segments, they wrote to analyze

- how the setting reflects the major themes and motifs of the scene

- how the language of the play communicates symbolic meaning and tone

- how the sound effects and lighting selected for a scene communicate mood as they
  direct attention to an object, gesture, or facial expression to show what is important

- how the costumes reveal information about a character, including his or her other
  motivations.

Teaching students how to analyze scenes from film adaptations had three parts. First, as a
whole class, students studied two film adaptations of the balcony scene, recording on a T-chart
differences in the director's decision-making when it came to setting, language, music, and
costumes. Second, students analyzed a different scene with partners. Third, on exam day, each
student demonstrated his or her ability to critically analyze the components that make up a complex scene. Through this gradual release of responsibility, students discussed the scenes in class
with increased confidence and skill, demonstrated in the following two excerpts from final essays.

From Sam's essay:

In the very beginning of the scene, eight or so drunken, unhinged and slightly
deranged Montague men stride through the cobblestone street, hooting, holler-
ing, yelling, whistling, and calling Romeo like a dog. Romeo scurried up the tree
and sits in the canopy, watching his friends cause a rowdy ruckus in his wake.
They carry torches through the now noisy, dark street while aimlessly peek-
ing all over. After a slow pursuit of Romeo, the Montagues stroll on, forgetting
about him and remembering of their alcohol. Romeo quietly whispers "He jests
at scars that never felt a wound" and continues to Juliet. This shows how loud
and boisterous the Montagues are, and how Romeo and Juliet will be secretive
and quiet in their relationship until they ultimately are discovered.

As Romeo walks towards Juliet's balcony, the landscape is dark and
extremely quiet while he pushes through the forest of vines around him.
The balcony itself is made of stone and is a pale color. I think this displays
the journey Romeo takes to get to Juliet, and how there is always Unknown
around the corner.

From Danielle's essay:

When Juliet tells Romeo his intent is marriage she is holding up her palm, which makes me believe that Zeffirelli is trying to refer back to earlier in the play when Juliet says at the party that it's holy palmers hand they use in prayer. After they agree to be married the music becomes quick fast. When the Nurse calls for Juliet the music slowly decreases and turns into a very slow song. When Juliet says goodnight and heads off into the house the music is soft and calm again, very similar to when Romeo first sees Juliet at the house. To finish off the scene Zeffirelli pans the camera over to a tree with lots of leaves and branches and has the sky change to change the scene. I think Zeffirelli decides to end the scene like that because at the beginning of the scene Romeo was making his way through all of the trees and bushes to get to Juliet.

Second Core Text

Even though we were teaching different novels, we agreed on three common assessments for the second core text:

1. Students wrote literary analysis essays. They were given this prompt to consider: *Choose one big idea the reader can take away from the novel and analyze how the author develops this idea.* In our minilessons, we supported students by modeling how to track a big idea across a text.

2. Each student wrote a scene from the novel that did not exist. This enabled them to revisit the narrative writing skills they had learned earlier in the year.

3. Each student selected a two-page spread from the novel and recorded a dramatic reading.

✦ Closing Thoughts: The Case for Engaged Readers

In "Engagement with Young Adult Literature: Outcomes and Processes," Gay Ivey and Peter Johnston (2013) ask why "calls to make engaged reading an essential component of adolescent literacy curricula go unheeded," especially when engaged reading has been proven to increase reading achievement and to reduce achievement gaps. Johnston and Ivey continue, "Perhaps the failure of prior research to provide these insights is due to the absence of personally relevant texts in secondary English classrooms where required canonical texts from American and British literature, rather than engagement, anchor the curriculum" (1). We know that the use of self-selected young adult literature establishes student autonomy and relevance, which are recognized conditions of engagement. We are hopeful that the traditional English curriculum that engages too few of our students each year will shift to the power and possibility of student agency and joy as all teachers work to achieve a better balance in the middle and high school reading diet.

We don't want to build compliant readers; we want to build engaged readers—and we believe this engagement springs from providing our students with choices. Let's give them numerous high-interest books and provide opportunities for them to read independently. Let's mix in book club experiences. Let's stretch their thinking with whole-class novel study. Let's create a balanced reading diet that builds healthy readers. And when we think of the term "healthy readers," we return to Will Schwalbe, who says in *Books for Living* (2016), "I'm on a search—and have been, I now realize, all my life—to find books to help me make sense of the world, to help me become a better person, to help me get my head around the big questions that I have and answer some of the small ones while I'm at it" (10). We, too, are on this lifelong reading search, and we want to do everything we can to invite our students along as well.

Map a Year of WRITING

In the introduction to *The Best American Essays* (2005), Susan Orlean says:

> All indications to the contrary, our voices matter to each other, that we do wonder what goes on inside each other's head; that we want to know each other, and we want to be known. Nothing is more meaningful—more human, really—than our efforts to tell each other the story of ourselves, of what it's like to be who we are, to think the things we think, to live the lives we live. (xviii)

Our students need this connection more than ever, and it is through writing that they will come to know each other, and to be known.

We plan our year with writing and writers in mind. Most of the daily practices you read about in Chapter 2 support students' growth as writers. And while it may be clear how daily notebook writing and text study support this growth, time spent reading does important work as well. The research is clear. Students who read write with greater fluency, clarity, and organization. Frank Smith, author of *Reading Without Nonsense* (2006), says:

> All the nuts and bolts of writing—including spelling, punctuation, and grammar, but more importantly the subtle style and structure of written discourse, the appropriate organization of sentences and paragraphs, and the appropriate selection of words and tones of voice—are learned through *reading*. The point deserves emphasis. *You learn to read by reading and you learn to write by reading.* (118)

We plan our writing year with balance in mind too, and before we share the specific units we mapped out for the year, let's first consider this important planning concept.

✎ Finding a Balance Between Tasks, Assignments, and Freewriting

Our writing year map (and this book) is a call for teachers to find a better balance between writing for tasks and assignments and writing that frees and inspires students. Why must we have both? For student investment in the writing process. Just as we plan for students to choose companion books while studying *Romeo and Juliet* and will maintain time and support for independent reading while students are studying a core text, we will seek opportunities for individual choices and passions in each of our writing units. For example, in informational writing students first will play with the forms and possibilities in writing reviews in their notebooks. They might choose a time span and place (such as thirty-six hours in Honolulu) and detail the stops travelers should make in that place. They might review local restaurants or places to track deer. This approach helps students own their writing in that unit of study.

Generating ideas for writing is a college-bound skill. As James S. Murphy (2016) noted, "In a recent survey of K–12 and college teachers, ACT found that college teachers considered the ability to generate ideas the most important skill for their students to possess, *twice as important* as the ability to analyze texts" (italics ours). Twice as important. This raises a critical issue: What should the balance be between analyzing texts and generating ideas in high school English? Freewriting in notebooks—as a regular practice—generates ideas and confidence. We vary the prompts to inspire students and we resist turning notebook practice into a task. For students who initially don't invest in notebook writing, we persist. We continue to work, to write, and to invite our students into writing because it provides such important riches for those who try— who make the notebook a catchall for joy and struggle and essential experiments that light fires in their imaginations.

We have been involved in this thinking about balance for a long time. Because balancing choice and teacher-chosen texts and writing assignments is a reimagining of the way English should be taught, what we are proposing here may not be easily and immediately accepted by your colleagues. We know you may not be able to immediately implement all of this thinking into your curriculum. However, we are certain change is necessary.

Teachers as Writers: Practicing What We Preach

We have learned that what we understand and practice ourselves in writing profoundly influences what our students learn. We can only teach well what we know well. We have studied writing to determine what is essential to teach, and we invite you to think this through with us—and then to continue to study writing on your own. We all have a lot to learn.

Why must we study how writers work? Because it will help us to resist with confidence the "good ideas" of others, particularly in a time of professional learning communities that privilege standardization over agency in teaching. Teaching students to write in formulaic ways, for example, is a bad idea because of all the hidden practices it teaches at the same time. Students become adept at following a pattern, not at thinking of the best ways to develop and communicate their ideas. Students become lazy in their thinking because so little thinking is required in order to write five paragraphs of similar construction from class to class, year after year. Formulaic writing not only leaves students unprepared for writing in college and the world, but dulls interest in writing and handcuffs divergent thinking. Those are enormous costs. Additionally, students who write primarily in formulaic ways do not see the deep connection between reading and writing. How will they learn to read like writers when they only write what they never read?

When we listen to what writers say, we make different decisions about our teaching, our assignments, and our grading practices. For example, what do you reconsider about teaching if you listen to Leslie Jamison, American novelist and essayist, talk about what she learns as she writes? Jamison (Jamison and Prose 2015) says, "Writing hasn't felt like getting progressively better at a single task; it's felt more like stumbling toward the bewildering call of each new project" (BR39). If you have felt the impossible struggle of determining what you want to say in an article, poem, or memoir, you understand why she says the call of that particular writing project is bewildering. All of the writing we both have done for this book has circled, advanced, and retreated from one idea to the next. We recognize that as the writing process. We organized and reorganized our writing as each day of work revealed more of what we hadn't realized we meant to say. A chapter that seemed focused when we started to write it too soon was lost in a maze of ideas that were revealed as we wrote.

Planning ahead for writing will only get us so far; it is the writing itself that leads us to develop our ideas. This is why, just like with reading, we must give students time to write in class, so that we can offer feedback and adjust instruction in conferences with students as they

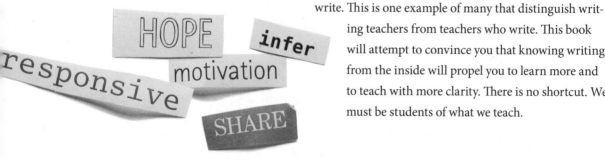

write. This is one example of many that distinguish writing teachers from teachers who write. This book will attempt to convince you that knowing writing from the inside will propel you to learn more and to teach with more clarity. There is no shortcut. We must be students of what we teach.

◂ Units of Study in Writing

We mapped out our writing year to reflect our understandings of writing and to build not just rhetorical and textual knowledge, but also persistence and flexibility in our young writers. We planned a study of genres that mirrors our understanding of student interest: a study of story first, in fiction and in memoir, before writing about literature; (writing to explain and inform both in print and media to expand student flexibility with composition; and then writing to inform and argue a position both in print and media for wider audiences.)Lastly, we planned to end the year with multigenre, a place where students have control of both the form and the focus of their content. This arc of the writing year leads students to use the writing process to create increasingly sophisticated texts, but more importantly, students grow to see themselves as empowered writers who choose form purposefully to deliver their content most effectively. Figure 4.1 shows the map of the writing year we taught together.

Our map for a year of writing follows a predictable pattern. Alfred North Whitehead, a scientist and philosopher, believed that all learning moves from romance to precision to generalization. He suggested that this process is how we learn anything: a romance or interest in the subject leads us to the specifics of the subject, which leads us to generalize that understanding and to connect it to other learnings.

In designing our writing units, we charm students into a romance with writing—daily quick writing that is ungraded, and thus safe, leads students to a romantic attachment to the act of writing (they develop an interest in finding

Weeks in school year	Writing
1–2	**Writing unit 1:** Open choice
3–4	**Writing unit 2:** Short memoirs and narrative scene writing
5–7	**Writing unit 3:** Narrative multiscene writing
8–10	**Writing unit 4:** Multinarrator writing or digital storytelling
11–14	**Writing unit 5:** Inform-and-explain writing
15–17	**Writing unit 6:** Literary essay
18–19	Revising literary essays, midyear exams (Penny's school), and writing about reading in book clubs
20–22	**Writing unit 7:** "Where I'm From" digital writing
23–27	**Writing unit 8:** Argument and public service announcements (digital)
28–29	**Writing unit 9:** Literary essay
30–34	**Writing unit 10:** Multigenre project
35–36	End-of-year portfolio

Figure 4.1 Map of the Writing Year

CONSIDER This...

Looking back on the year, we find that our greatest regret is that we did not build a unit into our map dedicated solely to the reading and writing of poetry. We believe poetry deserves a place at the table right next to narrative, argument, and informational texts. Our students did read a lot of poetry—we often used poems as "seeds" to spur notebook writing—and some wrote poems for multigenre projects. We know this was not enough. Poetry deserves its own dedicated unit of study.

The following year, poetry was elevated in each of our classrooms. We created a poetry "smackdown" based on a March Madness basketball bracket. We selected sixteen poems (eight written poems on the left side of the bracket, eight spoken poems on the right side of the bracket). Students then studied two poems at a time, choosing a "winner" to advance to the next round of the poetry tournament. In selecting which poems would advance, students were asked to use the "glossary of poetic terms" from Nancie Atwell and Anne Atwell Merkel (2016, 186–187) as they debated both the technical skills and the emotional appeal of each poem.

The poetry smackdown study coincided with students' writing original poems. They performed them and submitted them digitally at the end of the unit. Some recorded dramatic readings of their poems; others created films. To see examples of some of these digital poems, see the online resources.

By the time you read this, we will have already implemented a full poetry unit into the year's curriculum, a practice we intend to repeat for the rest of our careers.

words and watching them knit together and feel good about the risks and rewards of writing). Then we move to learning and practicing the precise moves of a genre. We lead students to generalize the conventions of a genre to all forms of writing. We connect the thinking in one writing unit to the next—showing how in each unit writers repeat the same moves, no matter what they are composing.

As you can see in the writing map in Figure 4.1, most of our writing units are chunked into three- and four-week units. This does not mean that each student will compose only one text during each of those units; instead, they will often write many smaller, ungraded experiments before choosing pieces to take through the writing process. In Section II of this book, we detail the teaching of writing in the different discourses you see on this map. In this chapter, we'll consider more general factors that influence mapping a year of teaching these different discourses.

❧ Start with the Finish Line in Mind

Just as in reading, our curriculum map for writing has a destination. At the end of the school year, we want our students to be independent and empowered writers who show evidence that they

- have developed confidence in generating words to express their ideas
- have learned to reread their writing as readers, listening to how their words work together to communicate effectively
- have learned how to make their writing better through revision
- have maintained a writer's notebook that is as individual as they are
- can write in the following discourses: narrative, inform/explain, argument, and poetry, and can synthesize their learning in multigenre projects
- have developed an understanding of how genres blend—how narrative can argue and how great nonfiction often informs through a strong narrative line
- have used writing to deepen their understanding of reading in both fiction and nonfiction
- have improved their syntax and deepened their understanding of the intention of conventions
- have learned to compose with digital tools—crafting ideas through images, text slides, voice-overs or narration—and can choose music or other background effects to create an engaging experience for viewers.

The challenging thing about keeping the finish line in mind is that once we meet our students, the line can seem very far away, at least for some of them.

Move Students from Victimhood to Agency

You know this kid. His notebook has little writing in it. The computer screen before him is a block of white—no words, just haunting blank space. He checks his phone every thirty seconds or so—anything to avoid writing. (If you write, you know this place—you have lived there many times yourself: *I have nothing to say.*) When you sit beside him he has no ideas, rejects every thread you suggest, tells you repeatedly, "I'm not a good writer. I can't write. I hate writing." You invite him to stay after school. He doesn't. You insist. (Even call his mom.) He shows up, and he talks to you—even tells you a story or two—it's nice spending time with this boy. You listen; you encourage him to tell his story into a voice-to-text software program, but he won't. You walk across the hall to give him space for ten minutes or so. He stares at a blank page. After forty-five minutes that you could have spent planning, reading student work, or answering email, you've still got nothing. He leaves and you rest your forehead on your desk.

This student remains locked in place.

You despair of ever moving forward, much less reaching the finish line.

One of the issues with planning a year filled with writing is that you don't know how each student (and especially those like the boy in the preceding anecdote) will negotiate the balance between agency and victimhood, as defined by Maria Popova (2017): "The stories we tell ourselves about our public past *shape how we interpret and respond to and show up for the present.* The stories we tell ourselves about our private pasts shape how we come to see our personhood and *who we ultimately become.* The thin line between agency and victimhood is drawn in how we tell those stories" (italics ours).

Popova is speaking of literally telling stories here, but people tell stories of themselves as writers, and we often see a thin line between agency and victimhood in the fragile confidence of young writers. (In the fragile confidence of *any* writer—including teachers of writers.) As we plan for a year of writing, over time we want to help students shift the language they use when describing themselves as writers. Figure 4.2 captures the shifts we want our students to make.

To have any hope of reaching the finish line, to move from victimhood to agency, students first have to *show up* for writing—every day. We explain the importance of this to students with words like these:

> We show up for writing by separating from distractions and then rereading
> a draft, changing one word and then another, and adding thinking, even

shallow, unformed thinking. It is active work: reading, listing, waiting, hearing our words and "speaking" to an imagined reader. We face the limitations of time and refuse to waste it. We practice the discipline of writing by not giving into distractions. It is too easy to say, "I can't." It is too easy to say of a first draft, "It's fine." Trust us, it will get better if you work at it. Writing is never finished—only abandoned. We must face how hard it is to write well just like we face an opponent on the football field: refuse to yield. Discipline alone separates the best writers from those who improve very little. We give you time and space and tools to write—and we work to guide you with our thinking next to yours—in order to move all of you as writers. But the hard work is yours.

As you learn to listen to your writing and shape it, you will be amazed at what you can create. You will learn your own process for shaping writing and improving it. You will learn the power of using words to express what you think, to argue for what matters to you, and to help you think more clearly. Writing well will set you apart from any candidate for a job. It will provide you with unforeseen opportunities; it begins with your willingness to work.

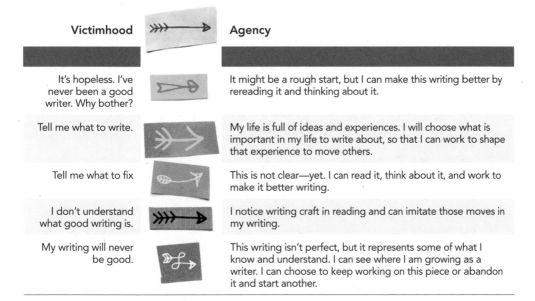

Victimhood		Agency
It's hopeless. I've never been a good writer. Why bother?		It might be a rough start, but I can make this writing better by rereading it and thinking about it.
Tell me what to write.		My life is full of ideas and experiences. I will choose what is important in my life to write about, so that I can work to shape that experience to move others.
Tell me what to fix.		This is not clear—yet. I can read it, think about it, and work to make it better writing.
I don't understand what good writing is.		I notice writing craft in reading and can imitate those moves in my writing.
My writing will never be good.		This writing isn't perfect, but it represents some of what I know and understand. I can see where I am growing as a writer. I can choose to keep working on this piece or abandon it and start another.

Figure 4.2 From Victimhood to Agency

CONSIDER This...

What happened to that unwilling writer mentioned earlier in the chapter? Penny would argue that her attention (and pressure) was getting in the way of his writing—not only that afternoon, but in class. But she also knows this: he'd been allowed to pass the year before without writing much of anything. He failed three of the four quarters last year, but passed for the year. He believes he will pass high school just as he did middle school, moving from one year to the next with little to no evidence of learning. He also believes that reading and writing have little to do with his life—he hasn't read in years and he has found no joy or satisfaction in writing.

In class the next day Penny decides not to confer with him. She focuses on supporting other students. She glances up and sees him staring at his blank screen. His friend—and easy distraction—is absent this day. His table is filled with kids who are writing.

Sometime later, Penny glances his way and sees a cute girl seated beside him, laptop to laptop. He is reading her story and she is encouraging him to write. Conditions that move writers: right there. Boom.

Penny goes by his desk on her way to another writer and sees there are words on his screen. She wants to stop, but she resists. It's too soon—he's found something, and he needs time to write. Ten minutes later, when class ends, he says, "Look, Mrs. Kittle, I wrote today!" She gives him a high five and says, "I can't wait to read it."

This is what she finds: a fire last year was a total loss for his family, and they are still homeless. It is no small thing for him to be willing to live it again in writing.

Time. Patience. Response. These are conditions that move writers.

Planning with the finish line in mind takes faith. And it requires a long view of our work. Students who have trouble getting started might have nothing to show for days. They feel the failure of it. But we have to give them time because the progress of a writer is not linear, not measurable each day, and writers are fragile.

Plan the Teaching That Threads Through Every Unit

When we map out a year, it's critical to remember that so much of the writing curriculum—both process and craft—is *not* tied to any specific form or genre of writing. The "bones" of our writing units—leading students to generate ideas, teaching them to organize and revise them, and then to fine-tune writing—do not change as texts or forms change. There is a distinct difference between teaching genre awareness and teaching students to understand what makes any piece of writing effective, memorable, and powerful. Greater insight does not originate from labeling writing; it emanates from the close study of writing. We want our students to learn that the moves and techniques employed by strong writers are not always genre specific. For example, a strong writer may make effective use of dialogue in a narrative, or in an informational piece, or in an argument. We want our students to recognize this flexibility *across writing types*.

Students will be asked to compose texts in the future that we haven't seen yet, but we teach them to study how a text (print or digital) works and then how to imitate it. When Penny's student, Jake, was selected to give a graduation speech, he did not search in a specific genre toolbox for thoughts on how to pull a speech together. He was encouraged to study graduation speeches to figure out what makes one good. He listened for applause and then looked back at where in the speech it happened. The moves made in graduation speeches cannot be pigeonholed to a specific writing genre. By the end of the school year, we expect all students to move to generalizations in their thinking about writing and apply them to their own ideas, composing in several genres to communicate the complexity of a topic.

In Section 2 you'll read about the genre-specific moves and techniques we taught in different units across the year and will no doubt see that much of it overlaps. But it's the teaching we thread through our units over and over again—by modeling writing ourselves—that teaches students the powerfully transferable curriculum of process. Our demonstrations are holistic (all writers think about _____, all writing moves like _____) as well as genre specific (in writing a *story* I think about _____).

Teaching Clip

See Penny confer with Jake about his graduation speech

Across the year, we demonstrate

- the full process of writing. Writers learn a process in one genre that is largely transferable to other genres, but we also model meeting the challenges in each genre.

- the way we move an idea to a draft.

- how we plan writing that shows an idea from start to finish.

- how we solve problems in a draft.

- how we reread sentences aloud to hear the rhythm: where they work together well and where our sentence structure has complicated the meaning.

- how we use lessons from a mentor text to improve a draft.

- how we develop an ending that completes the journey of a piece.

- how we develop the voice of the text in relation to our audience: the difference between *I am your confidant* and *I am a distant observer.*

- how we seek feedback. We analyze our writing to determine where we need help and then honor students' analysis of our writing to build confidence in their ability to give feedback to each other.

- the struggle of writing well. We show students the frequent setbacks we experience when our writing falls short of our vision. These demonstrations not only develop our empathy for their struggle, but also show students that writers need persistence.

Distilling the breadth of writing curriculum down to these ten essentials helps focus our daily work with young writers and prompts us to be more intentional in our teaching. Connections are key. We are careful to use the same language across units. If we talked about an "ending that completes the journey of a piece" in our narrative unit, we use the metaphor of a journey to talk about endings again in our argument unit, and again in informational writing. In terms of process, we remind students that they've been down similar paths before as writers—solving problems, deciding what feedback they need, listening for rhythm in their writing. In terms of craft, we remind them, there's a value in studying mentor texts.

Understanding the curriculum of writing in this way focuses our work, but it also expands possibilities. We know there isn't a privileged form or genre in writing outside school—communicating well is what's privileged. In public schools, however, specific text types are overvalued. In English class, literary analysis has been the genre of choice as long as we've both been teaching. But when we focus on the writing process and teach students to use it in increasingly sophisticated ways, we position students to continually improve as writers. Based on students' needs and interests, we strive to open our classrooms to all types and genres when we consistently teach and practice the elements that make *all* writing—text or digital—effective.

✈ Plan to Change Your Plans

While it may seem counterintuitive, when mapping out a year of writing, it's important to plan to change your plans. You can (and should) think ahead about the important lessons your students will need to write well in each study. You should think about how you can order those lessons so they lead students through the writing journey they need to take. But you also need to remain responsive to the needs of your students.

Conversation Clip

See "Today's Work
Leads Tomorrow's
Teaching"

We know that when we closely interact with our students, tomorrow's lesson might be revised based on what occurred in today's class. When Penny taught an argument unit with her freshmen, her students became quite animated about gun control issues. To capitalize on their engagement, Penny arranged for the school's police officer to visit the class the next day (a visit that was not originally part of the unit plan). During his visit, the officer brought a different point of view into the classroom, thus challenging the students' thinking, and this interchange of ideas added depth to students' understanding of creating balanced arguments.

Yes, we start the year (or the unit, or the week) with a big picture of how things will unfold, but we also know there is a fluidity that is an integral part of our classrooms. This fluidity is foundational to meeting the needs of our students and to our own growth as teachers. We work hard to revise our teaching because our teaching is responsive, active work.

Sometimes "the right lesson" doesn't come from our lesson plan book (and almost never from a pacing guide someone else has written). The "right lesson" spins out of a close reading of our students and of their needs *that day*. For example, at one point during the year, Kelly's students had an established due date to turn in a draft of letters they were writing to presidential candidates. In reading the drafts, Kelly realized that most of the students needed more guidance in writing effective openings. He decided to add an extra day so his students had time to study the effective introductions found in mentor texts. This, in turn, meant pushing back the due date so his students would have additional time to revise their introductions.

Students' needs often evolve organically and can be unpredictable, and that's exactly why we need to be open to changing our plans. Decisions about changes, however, must always be made with the rest of the year in mind. There is only so much time. What is essential? What is important? And what will we have to let go of as we run out of time? The year we planned

Conversation Clip

See "The
Challenge of Time"

together, we found ourselves facing the challenge of time as the second semester of school started. We discussed our plans and considered the cuts we might make that would best meet the needs of our students.

Plan to Reteach

Planning for whole-class teaching in writing can give us a false sense of effectiveness. We think we can teach the same thing to every writer in the room at the same time. This thinking, which is often institutionalized in pacing guides, misses the mark. Consider a whole-class minilesson Kelly taught on how to write an introduction to a literary analysis essay. He shared a variety of student examples with the class, each modeling a different approach. Students were asked to name the moves made in these sample essays, in hopes that studying them might inspire them. After the minilesson, Kelly conferred with Anthony. The conversation went as follows:

> **Kelly:** How is your introduction coming?
>
> **Anthony:** Well . . . (*Long pause*).
>
> **Kelly:** Think about the introductions we examined today. Did you find any of them helpful?
>
> **Anthony:** Well . . . (*Another long pause*).

So far, not Kelly's best conference. Why was Anthony so reluctant to discuss his introduction? Because, as Kelly soon learned, he was still in the collecting-information stage of prewriting and was not in a position to begin thinking about his introduction. He simply wasn't there yet.

The writers in our classrooms are often in different places, which means that any given minilesson will not connect to all students and will possibly distract them from the important work they need to do as writers that day. Will Anthony remember the minilesson on introductions when he's ready for it? Possibly, but it's unlikely. That's why we schedule individual conferences—to fill those gaps that are inevitably missed when we teach to the entire class.

Matt Glover has often said that conferences are the least efficient but most effective form of teaching because they meet writers exactly where they are. In contrast, minilessons are the most efficient but least effective because the focus will not align perfectly with every writer's needs every day. This is not an argument to abandon whole-class lessons; we see value in both. But if we have to choose one or the other, we know personalizing learning in conferences is most important.

✒ Plan to Study Your Teaching

When it comes to a yearlong map for writing, our in-the-moment decision-making is resting—always—on a foundation of clear outcomes and clear ideas about where we want to lead all of our writers. We are mindful of the impact of today's work on tomorrow and how students will or won't see connections between our lessons. We watch students to see if connections are happening, and we make adjustments to our map when needed. Conferring, of course, is where we help students stay with us.

CONSIDER This...

When we study our teaching, we remember Tom Newkirk's (2009) idea that teachers should be constantly on the lookout for "trouble" in student work. Finding this trouble shapes our focus in the classroom, and it is the first step in helping our students to improve. But if we are honest with ourselves, we must also recognize that we sometimes have trouble with the trouble. We may identify a problem in a student's writing, but there are times when we are at a loss on how to approach it. We want our response to propel the student forward, but it is not always clear what that response should be. We have all sat in front of a highly problematic student paper and thought, "Where do I start?" If we give the student too much feedback, we run the risk of overwhelming a fragile writer. We are also concerned with the delicate balance between suggesting what the student might do next and encouraging her to try to determine her own next steps. How much feedback is too much? How much is not enough? What should the teacher's focus be in a limited conference? When these answers prove unclear, we are grateful we can ask one another, "How would you approach this student?"

It may seem odd to consider conferring so closely in a chapter about planning for a year of whole-class teaching. After all, because conferences are responsive to each student's immediate needs, you can't really plan ahead for what will happen in them. But it's the thinking we do *across* our conferences that so powerfully informs our whole-class teaching. Conferring makes learning visible. We look for patterns. If we have several writers struggling with planning, we can meet with them in a small group the next day or plan a minilesson featuring a student who is making good progress on planning a draft. The conference is an opportunity to see if what we are teaching is having an impact on student writing. We look for evidence that students are applying the features of the genre we are studying (for example, the use of sensory details, dialogue, or transitions between scenes while studying narrative), and we adjust our teaching in response to what we learn.

Hone the Skill of Conferring

Because conferring is so important to both individual writers and our whole-class teaching, every year we work to get better at it. We confer with four goals in mind:

1. Students will **develop confidence** in generating ideas for writing.

2. Students will **use the writing process** to help develop their ideas.

3. Students will **develop independence** by making decisions about what to do next with their writing.

4. Students will **see texts as mentors** of writing craft.

What follows are some big ideas we keep in mind that help us keep our conferences productive.

Give students our full attention.

We begin by choosing which goal to focus on in a conference based on what we learn as we lean in and listen to a student. We show students we are listening with our body language. We turn toward them; their writing and their thinking is important to us. We are not sitting down to correct errors; we are sitting down to learn and to problem-solve. Our students' learning begins with our listening (Graves 1985).

Conversation Clip

See "The Balance of Talk in Conferring"

Begin with listening and then share what we heard.

We help writers understand what a reader will experience as the piece is read. Don Graves believed that to confer effectively, the teacher must provide an active audience for the writer by confirming what is understood in the text and then asking clarifying questions. The language we use is:

"This is what I heard . . ."

"This is what I wondered . . ."

"This is where I was most engaged . . ."

"As a reader, as a member of your audience, I'm thinking this as I read . . ."

"This is where I was confused . . ."

Include a plan for next steps.

The feedback that students receive from their teachers is vital, and it should include suggestions about what a writer might do next. Educational researcher John Hattie (2013) says, "And while teachers see feedback as corrections, criticism, comments, and clarifications, for students unless it includes 'where to next' information they tend to not use it. Students want feedback just for them, just in time, and just helping nudge forward. So worry more about how students are receiving your feedback than increasing how much you give."

Allow writers to make their own decisions.

We believe the ultimate choice of what to do next must rest with the writer. Most often we *suggest* next steps; we do not tell students how to work. The teacher helps the writer understand the writing's effectiveness, but the writer is always in control. We will direct a student toward correct punctuation, of course, but few other decisions about writing can be seen as correct or incorrect. If we tell students what to do, we take away their control of their writing. It is tempting to say, "Do this," but we resist so that the student is doing more of the thinking work than the teacher.

Connect students to each other in small-group writing conferences.

Writing is often lonely work. We both write in the dark before school. When we talk we share the joys and frustrations involved in trying to write well. We read drafts to each other and talk through our thinking. Talk moves our writing and our thinking and is an essential part of the writing process. We gather our students in small-group conferences and have them meet in writing groups to build a community of connection and support. A small-group writing conference might be focused on a feature of the genre we are studying (e.g., creating an effective introduction in a letter) or it might be focused on the process of revising a draft, but in either case it allows students to teach and support one another.

Conversation Clip

See "The Question
of Directness in
Conferring"

Teaching Clip

See Penny's
conference with
Alex about a
multigenre project

CONSIDER This...

Keeping writing conference notes for each student proved to be problematic. For one thing, because of class size (Kelly) and fewer instructional minutes (Penny), it often took three weeks or longer to confer with every writer. Because students rarely, if ever, spent three weeks on a given paper, they would be working on something different each time we conferred with them. A student might be writing a narrative when we first conferred, but by the time the second conference rolled around she might have moved on to writing an argument. We were rarely afforded the luxury of meeting with students more than once on a piece of writing, and this led to conferences that felt a bit "shotgun" in nature. Our notes didn't always inform our instruction because by the time we had compiled them on all students, they had moved on to writing something different. Our notes lagged behind their practice.

The best way to fix this problem is to reduce our class sizes and give us more time to teach, but we know that will happen after hell freezes over. Truthfully, there is no ready solution to this problem. We know we had kids who needed us, and there were times when we were simply unable to get to them. This was terribly frustrating, but we also know that conferring with some of the kids some of the time is way better than meeting none of the kids none of the time.

Figure out what supports students as writers.

When a very reluctant writer came in one morning with a burst of writing he'd done the day before in an after-school administrative detention, Penny asked him how he did it (when he'd done so little writing in her class). The student said he used pictures from his phone to inspire him. He then added, "And I texted the entire time I was writing that day! I told you I can do both at once." Penny asked him to share his experience with the class and had a brief discussion with students about how technology engages as well as distracts. Several students mentioned writing poems and other short texts in the notes app on their phones. They insisted that they are more comfortable writing on phones than on the computer. We recognize that writers should choose their own tools to compose, so sometimes we allow students to write on their phones. It is a complicated management decision, as so many moves in writing workshop are, but because we confer, we are able to adapt our methods to align with our students' needs as writers.

Take notes on writing conferences.
We minimize the notes we take as we talk so that we can stay fully attentive during the conference, but we record what we learned before we move on to the next student. Sometimes we sketch out thinking—in our notebook or in a student's—to plan a story or solve a writing problem. We record what we learn, and we record next steps for this writer, so our next conference can build on this one. We also make notes about anything that might affect our whole-class plans for teaching.

Teach into What You See

Over time, students become more comfortable sharing their writing with us. We are often invited to read writing in their notebooks while we confer, and these conferences are invaluable as they give us insight into what adjustments we need to make in our instruction. To help you understand how what we learn in conferring affects our planning for whole-class teaching, we'll share four realizations that came to light after examining our students' work in writing conferences and how we made plans to address each one.

Lost Momentum in Writer's Notebooks

Halfway through the school year we noticed that too many students had stopped writing a few minutes in, barely uncovering their thinking before giving up. We could not let this disengagement with writing practice continue. We reignited energy for quick writing with controversial poems like Prince Ea's "I Am NOT Black, You Are NOT White." As with all quick writing, we plan ahead to connect what we choose to write about with the big ideas of our unit of study. But it is also important to read the energy around notebook writing and choose poems and videos that demand the engagement of students. Quick writing is designed to tap into our students' passions all year long. When their passion lags, we have to redouble our efforts to find texts that will reignite their passion to write.

When their writing momentum stalled, students sometimes asked, "Why are we doing this?" That's a question we always stop and answer because just as joy and energy are contagious in a classroom, so are disengagement and lethargy. This was the time to gather student notebooks and to look for excellent examples to share with the class. We sought diversity in thinking and responses. We looked for evidence of engagement with big ideas, and then we placed these good examples front and center in the classroom:

"Look what Olivia created in response to reading Sherman Alexie."

"Look at the notes Samantha took on wage inequality after we investigated issues in this election."

"Look at the revision Jamie did after we wrote next to the 'Gun Murders' infographic. This little bit of writing is so much better."

These words are powerful. Celebrations of writing not only reinforce our expectations but show students the brilliance and risk-taking of their classmates. Paying attention to notebooks reminds students that we value their efforts. We are reading their work, and we respect their thinking.

The day Penny invited the school resource officer to her class, it was actually in response to a burst of momentum her students found after she chose a series of quick writes on gun violence. In her northern New Hampshire community, gun ownership, a family tradition of hunting, and a state motto of "Live Free or Die" all contribute to a cultural allegiance to firearms. Using a series of four texts (an infographic, a short newspaper article, and excerpts from two campaign speeches) led to deeply engaged writing about gun ownership and whether teachers should be armed. The short bursts of writing after each text were followed by a longer bit of time to combine thinking between quick writes. After this extended writing, students shared with one another. This notebook work took twenty-two minutes, and her classroom was suddenly alive again with thinking, writing, revising, and talk.

In Figure 4.3 you can see the first four quick writes Penny revised, followed by revisions in different colors as she worked through the thinking with two classes that day. Modeling authentic engagement with ideas is of central importance in leading students to quick write with passion and purpose. Figure 4.4 shows quick writes by one of Penny's students on this same topic.

10:13 In the U.S. we have 3.7 ~~every~~ year.
1. Gun murders per 100,000 residents says that the infographic
    we have more gun violence than 15 ~~European~~
    countries - like Canada and Australia civilized
    and Japan and England
    These are countries we admire. What are they doing
                                    so that people can own
                                    guns but there is less
2: Gun violence can be explained in lots of ways. Violence?
    Suicides, mental illness, criminals ... but
    can't we also have some rules? We don't   Can we
    seem to realize all the possible bad outcomes learn
    of no regulation. Why let criminals   from
    carry ~~assault~~ rifles on the streets?   them?
    other countries think we are stupid & foolish.

    should teachers be armed in classrooms?
    Donald   it would have stopped the violence in a recent
3. Trump says ~~arming teachers is a good idea~~ mass
    ~~I say HE'S CRAZY.~~ In 31 years of teaching grades shooting.
    1L-college in 7 states I've seen more than a few   Well,
    nutty teachers - people who should not only not   at
    be teaching but should not have guns.   Sandy
        Also, ~~what~~ if a kid took the gun? Even having Hook
    one in a teachers jacket could cause an incident   Elem.
    ~~at a school because many kids are stronger~~   the
    ~~than adults.~~   or desk or in the   armed
    And many kids get   classroom   security
    furious w/other kids   guard
                                                      was the
4. 10:31 - 10:35   first one
    Hillary says hold gun manufacturers to blame   shot.
    for violence - that we have a culture of violence
    in our country that must be ~~stopped.~~ We do.
    We are a paranoid, violent country. why is that? why are
    The U.S. has   we so
    We have more murders than ~~16~~ other countries - violent?
    many countries that 1   15
        respect - like Canada, Italy, Spain, Australia, the U.K., I
    France & Norway - it seems like we must be doing think
    something wrong if we have so many murders ~ 3 x those
    as many! - than so many other civilized countries. who
    Have we always had so many? Have Americans   sell
    gotten more violent?   guns
                                                      could
                                                      be
                                                      held
                                                      accountable

Figure 4.3 Penny's Quick Writes on Gun Murders

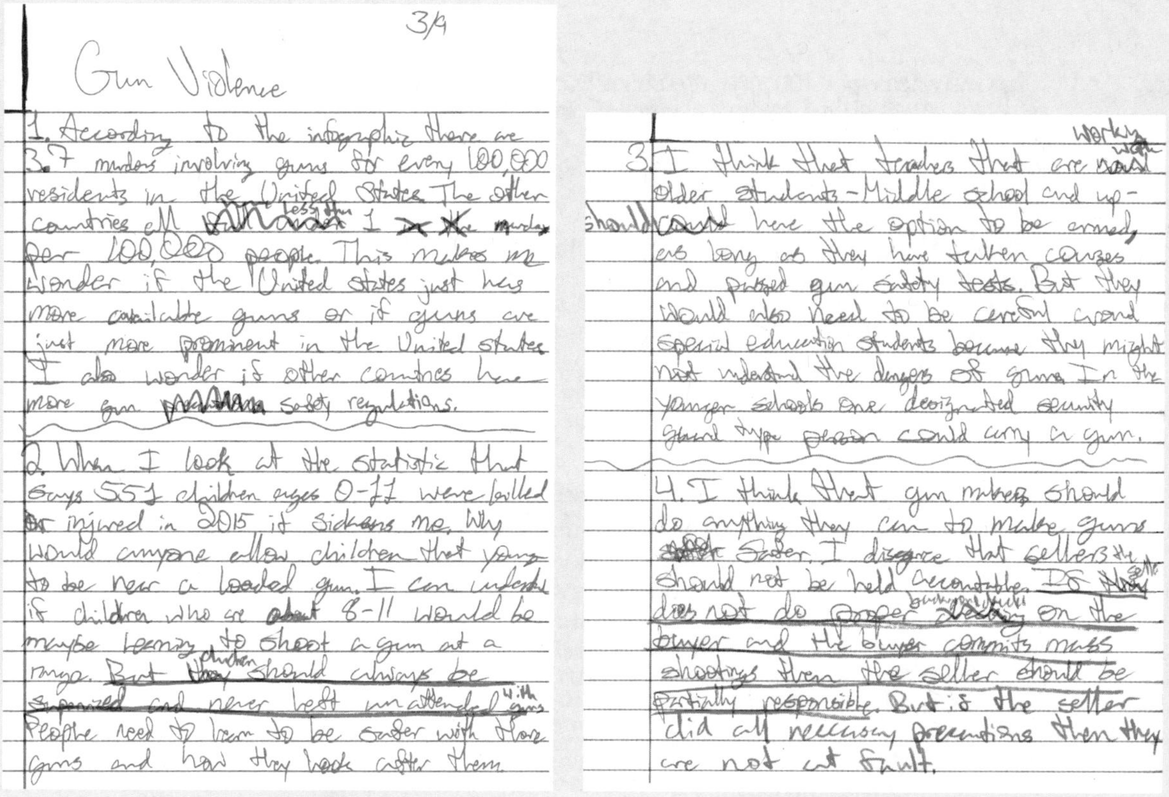
3/9

Gun Violence

1. According to the infographic there are 3.7 murders involving guns for every 100,000 residents in the United States. The other countries all less than 1 murder per 100,000 people. This makes me wonder if the United States just has more available guns or if guns are just more prominent in the United States. I also wonder if other countries have more gun safety regulations.

2. When I look at the statistic that says 551 children ages 0-11 were killed or injured in 2015 it sickens me. Why would anyone allow children that young to be near a loaded gun. I can understand if children who are 8-11 would be maybe learning to shoot a gun at a range. But children should always be supervised and never left unattended with guns. People need to learn to be safer with their guns and how they look after them.

3. I think that teachers that are working with older students - Middle school and up - should have the option to be armed, as long as they have taken courses and passed gun safety tests. But they would also need to be careful around special education students because they might not understand the dangers of guns. In the younger schools one designated security guard type person could carry a gun.

4. I think that gun makers should do anything they can to make guns safer. I disagree that sellers should not be held accountable. If seller does not do proper background checks on the buyer and the buyer commits mass shootings then the seller should be partially responsible. But if the seller did all necessary precautions then they are not at fault.

Figure 4.4 A Ninth Grader's Quick Writes on Gun Murders

When writing engagement begins to lag, we resort to a number of ways to get our students interested in writing again, as evidenced in Figure 4.5.

Underdeveloped Drafts

While most of our students were writing regularly throughout the first semester (some with more enthusiasm than others), we still had a number of writers who were not stretching themselves during the writing time we gave them to work on their own. They remained stuck in the "write one paragraph and stop" mode. With some students this was due to a lack of fluency; with others it was because of laziness or disengagement.

How did we address this issue? First, we planned to focus our next round of conferences on those students who were having problems developing their pieces. We hoped that one-to-one

Ways to Encourage Engagement in Notebook Writing

Use poetry/song lyrics, short videos, photographs, and other engaging prompts from current events. Encourage students to find interesting texts that the whole class writes next to, increasing their agency in this practice.

Sketch next to art postcards. Once a sketch is created, have students write next to or inside the sketch, capturing the mood or the setting or the sensory details inspired by the art card.

Encourage private writing (e.g., a letter to someone who annoys you).

Write alongside the students, engaging seriously with the content. Show them you have good writing days and bad writing days. Struggle. Show them that this daily practice matters—that you find energy in practice.

Have every student tag one favorite entry and then read it aloud to writing groups. Share these with the whole class with student permission.

Have students generate and explore their own writing territories. Have days when students generate their own notebook seeds and write freely. A writer's notebook should bear the stamp of the individual writer.

Figure 4.5 Ways to Encourage Engagement in Notebook Writing

time with the teacher would help spur them to write more. Sometimes in these conference, we became a bit more directive if students appeared to be hopelessly stuck and approaching dangerous frustration levels. We might say to them:

"Can I sketch your idea in your notebook?"

"Have you thought about trying _____?"

"Let's look back at the mentor text."

"Look at how I (or another student) approached this."

"What do you think the reader needs here?"

"As a reader, I might want to know more about _____."

The second adjustment we made was to tinker with our daily schedule to allow for more writing time. On selected days we shortened (or eliminated) the reading block to give students the entire period to write. This enabled us to confer with more writers, and it gave students more time to develop their pieces.

And, of course, we shared models of student writing in which kids were stretching themselves as writers.

Shifting Needs in Conferences

As we headed into the second semester, students had quite a bit of writing under their belts; therefore, it was time for a shift in the kinds of questions we asked in conferences. Early in the year we were more focused on encouraging students to write, but at the midyear point we began asking students to make connections between what we had been teaching and what they were working on in their drafts. Our expectations were higher, and this necessitated a new line of questioning. Previously, we may have asked questions like "How is your draft going?" or "What do you want to talk about?" but as we shifted into the third quarter, our questions became more specific. Here are some examples of the types of questions we began asking:

"What does this text look like that you're making?" (This expects more of students: that they have a clear vision of what they are writing and how it should be written).

"What craft move are you working on right now?"

"What are you doing in this piece to try to make it your best?"

"How are you bringing what you've learned about narrative into this argument piece?"

"What ideas did you take from our previous conference?"

"How is this piece similar to something you've written before? How is it different?"

"What have you learned about writing craft from your independent reading that you could use in your own writing?"

We conducted a minilesson on how conferences would change in the second half of the school year in order to help students show us what they have learned. We front-loaded these questions so they could think about them *before* conferring with us. Our goal was to create a shift. We wanted to move away from being the ones who gave the ideas so our students would develop trust in their own thinking. We wanted them to do more of the work. To make this happen, we consciously took longer on the "research" part of our conferences. We let students talk more at the start to see if they could articulate their thoughts about their drafts. We often responded with "What else?" or "Say more about that" instead of jumping in with our thinking as soon as a student finished talking.

We told some students we expected more from them. ("I expected you to be farther in your draft." Or "You know the qualities found in this kind of writing—I expect to see these qualities in your draft. Do you know what is missing here?") As the year progressed and we started to get to know our students well, we had to watch ourselves in the conferences. It can be quite tempting to waste precious conference time chatting with students about their issues and interests. We tried to save the "Oh, that happened to me" chats for passing time between classes. Instead, we reminded ourselves to stay focused on how to empower the students before us to practice transferable writing skills.

We also began to expand our conferences to include others. Sometimes we brought other students to the discussion—naturally, those seated nearby. When focused on one student's writing, we might ask the group, "What might help this writer?" In these settings, we encouraged the students to speak directly to one another. Sometimes we brought small groups together and said, "Let's practice this one skill together," so that we could explicitly reteach something that still needed to be addressed. We began gathering small groups to increase the range of revision strategies they were using.

Reasons to Celebrate

As we entered the second semester, we planned to stop more often and recognize the good things students were doing. At the end of class, we often shared student writing. We read their work back to them like it was gold—like literature. We made their language feel important—slowing it down when we came to the end. Celebrating it with attention. Sometimes we'd say, "I think this is the best piece you've written all year. Here's why," pointing out a writer's growth and showing we valued it. We started a bank of good student writing by opening a "Beautiful Words" Google document, and every time we came across a good move made by a student writer, we dropped it in this document so that it could be shared later with our students.

Conversation Clip

See "The Importance of Writer's Owning Their Choices"

We encouraged students to try something that is on the edge of their thinking and move beyond simply reinforcing what already comes easily to them. From time to time, we'd choose a student of the day to compose on the board while the rest of the class wrote in their notebooks. At the end of the writing block, the student would share her thinking about her draft just as we had done many times before.

Closing Thoughts: The Case for Engaged Writers

When you begin a journey, there's comfort in having a map in front of you. It doesn't necessarily mean you will follow that map exactly, but it's there to prevent you from getting lost. In this chapter we mapped our vision for a year of writing—not so you will transplant our thinking into your classroom, but so you will consider the complex decisions teachers must make in order for students to discover the power found in words.

We know what moves writers: a volume of practice, choice, the study of models, and feedback. When students are engaged in writing problems, they analyze what they know and focus on addressing their weaknesses with their next composition; they work like writers, not simply students. Engaged writers experience composition as personally meaningful, and they become expert at developing their own thinking and processes. Writing becomes a habit of thinking, and students swim in words and ideas. As Angela Duckworth says in *Grit: The Power of Passion and Perseverance* (2016), "As a teacher, wasn't it my responsibility to figure out how to sustain effort—both the students' and my own—just a bit longer?" (17). We feel hope and possibility at the start of a school year because we know that being a reader and writer is electrifying. The challenge is designing a year that helps our students discover this as well.

BALANCE Feedback and Evaluation

This week, as we're writing this, we read Angie's poem about her mother's drinking, and we are struck by the bravery of the piece. We read Robin's essay where she experimented with using intentional repetition, and we are taken with how the repetition lends power to her writing. We read Dakota's story of her brother's death, where she is trying to weave in flashbacks to strengthen the narrative. We read Antonio's letter to his mother, where he is searching to find his voice as he pledges to her that he will try to leave his life in gangs. All of these drafts are a long way from being finished, but because they are not being evaluated, our students are willing to continue experimenting with them. We are not scoring these drafts on a rubric; we are appreciating students' moves as writers, looking for opportunities to nudge them along. We can see that the conferences we have had with these students have helped. Their writing is better, true, but our few minutes together with these students also inform us of their struggles. Knowing our students as people makes us better teachers.

✒ Grading Doesn't Teach

As we stated in Chapter 1, we both believe in grading less and assessing more. Students like Angie and Robin, Dakota and Antonio, are hungry for response that encourages, that nudges, that lets them know their writing is heard and appreciated. Placing a grade on a student's paper doesn't teach him to write with more clarity and vision; a grade does not teach. The work of a writing teacher is response and encouragement.

But the world, of course, is hungry for grades. In many schools, administrators and parents *demand more grades*, and they insist that these grades be posted digitally for 24/7 access. Some administrators require teachers to post a minimum number of grades weekly, and the message seems to be that the more grades that are posted, the harder the teacher must be working. The more grades that are posted, the more kids must be progressing.

Let's be clear: More grading does not mean better teaching is happening or that learning is occurring. Grades sort winners (As and Bs) from losers (Ds and Fs), but they don't make our students better readers and writers (and in some cases they impede their progress). Today's students are tested (and graded) more than ever, yet one in four who make it to college will be enrolled in remedial courses. Nearly half of these students hail from middle- and upper-income families, dispelling the widely held belief that only low-income or community college students are saddled with remedial courses (Education Reform Now 2016). Today's students—perhaps more than any other students—have been graded and graded and graded, yet their reading and writing skills are not strong enough for college success. Voluminous grading of crappy writing (often essays about fake reading) does not change the fact that the writing is still crappy.

Given the political worlds in which we teach, we must assign grades, but thoughtful planning about how, what, and why we'll grade is essential if we want our students to become better readers and writers. To plan well, we must keep in mind that grading and assessment have different goals. Carnegie Mellon University's (2017) definition helps us understand this important distinction:

Conversation Clip

See "The Problem with Grades"

> Generally, the goal of grading is to evaluate individual students' learning and performance. Although grades are sometimes treated as a proxy for student learning, they are not always a reliable measure. Moreover, they may incorporate criteria—such as attendance, participation, and effort—that are not direct measures of learning.
>
> The goal of assessment is to improve student learning. Although grading can play a role in assessment, assessment also involves many ungraded measures of student learning. . . . Moreover, assessment goes beyond grading by systematically examining patterns of student learning across courses and programs and using this information to improve educational practices.

What does it really mean to grade less and assess more? What does this look like in practical terms? The year we planned together, we had numerous spirited conversations, wrestling with our thinking as we worked to revise and improve our grading philosophies and practices. In this chapter we'll share the guiding principles we decided on for grading, and we'll also describe the culminating portfolio assessment students submitted for a final grade at the end of the year. Then, in the discourse chapters that follow in Section 2, we'll share some of the criteria we used to grade specific assignments during the year.

⚐ Guiding Principles for the Grading of Writing

Principle: Students Need a Volume of Ungraded Practice

In *Holding On to Good Ideas in a Time of Bad Ones* (2009), Tom Newkirk says, "It may seem heretical to make this claim, but I am convinced that we overvalue feedback and undervalue practice—and in doing so have created a purgatory for diligent writing teachers. Volume, to be sure, does not equate with quality, but young writers can't get to quality without volume" (82).

Our students need lots of time to practice the skills that improve writing and to find words to name what they are thinking—to shape their experiences and ideas. Our students need *volume*, but being graded before they've had enough time for this volume of practice scorches motivation. Knowing this, we planned each unit across the year with lots of ungraded practice at the center of our teaching. You've read about the routines for this practice in earlier chapters, but here they are just as a reminder:

Conversation Clip

See "Low Pressure
Writing and
Revision"

- *Notebooks.* This is the place where words are generated and shaped, day after day. The place where ungraded, low-stakes writing and revision occurs.

- *Teacher demonstration.* We write and revise in front of our students so they can learn how writers shape writing from an initial idea to a polished draft.

- *Time to share writing with peers.* Since many of them have poor editing skills, we do not ask students to peer edit. We do, however, encourage and plan for peer response to help writers hear what others see in their writing. We know that students often do not know enough about writing to effectively coach each other in its complexities, but we can teach students to respond to one another's papers in ways that lead them to recognize what they do well and where improvements are needed.

- *The study of model texts.* We spend a lot of time as a whole class with our students identifying the moves of skilled writers. We also encourage students to study the craft of writing in their independent reading.

- *Ongoing work on drafts.* We may have more than one deadline for a paper, and students have days to work on drafts and get feedback before anything is graded.

While all this day-to-day work is ungraded, we do periodically collect student notebooks and give them a grade for their engagement with quick writing and revision. Before turning their notebooks in, students complete a checklist to help us quickly see which assignments they have completed (see Figure 5.1). Each student also selects one entry he or she permits us to read carefully and places a sticky note on it. We ask our students to mark an entry that demonstrates excellent writing. Why? First, we believe writing notebooks should be a place for experimenting, and when writers experiment, sometimes they fail. If we grade the quality of each individual quick write, we compromise that belief. We know we would be paralyzed as writers if we had to share pages and pages of crappy writing with a teacher. Grading is counterproductive to our goal of increasing writing volume and colored-pen corrections will constipate young writers. Second, we respect student privacy. Students may write differently if they know the teacher will not read it. We intentionally give our students breathing room. We afford them privacy, and this, in turn, encourages them to take risks when drafting.

To come up with a notebook grade, we look for evidence of rereading and revising in quick writes because we model this and give students time for it in class. We match points with how many entries show this practice. If a student has written every assignment, she earns 50 out of 50 points; if she's completed seven of the eight assignments, she earns 45 points, and so on. When students are absent, we encourage them to write in their notebooks to earn full credit.

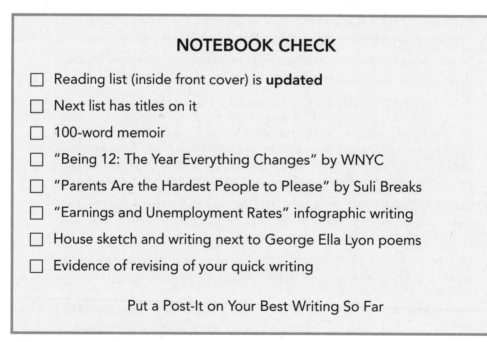

NOTEBOOK CHECK

☐ Reading list (inside front cover) is **updated**

☐ Next list has titles on it

☐ 100-word memoir

☐ "Being 12: The Year Everything Changes" by WNYC

☐ "Parents Are the Hardest People to Please" by Suli Breaks

☐ "Earnings and Unemployment Rates" infographic writing

☐ House sketch and writing next to George Ella Lyon poems

☐ Evidence of revising of your quick writing

Put a Post-It on Your Best Writing So Far

Figure 5.1 Example of a Notebook Checklist

CONSIDER *This...*

In states that have moved to competency-based grading, students cannot receive credit for practice. This doesn't make it any less valuable. Practice leads to competency. We have found that writing together in class next to poetry and other provocative material taps into students' passions. Students participate in notebook writing to express their thinking, not for grades. There were weeks when both of us did not collect student notebooks and the energy for this writing did not decrease. Students value time to reflect and to write what they believe. They do not need constant evaluation in order to practice.

Principle: Students Need Practice in Reading Like Writers

As regular practice we have students read with a colored pencil in hand as we read aloud, then turn and talk at their tables about details they noticed, such as how the author crafted the dialogue. We collect these annotations at the end of class and review them to assess which students are able to do this well. We assess the understanding in order to determine where we need to repeat practice. All of this work is ungraded.

On one day we ended up with a group of students who were not showing us evidence that they understood how sensory details developed scenes. The following day we had those students meet us at one table while others continued work on developing their scenes. We explain how we assess their understanding by collecting annotations so we know how and where to support them. The rest of the students (working on their drafts while we meet with a small group) can ignore us or listen in. Students learn that we read and evaluate their work even when we don't grade it.

After reading several texts together as a class and/or in pairs, we have all students record what they notice on a mentor text without help to demonstrate what they've learned. This one we collect and mark for a grade. Although it is a small part of their overall grade, after many attempts to practice the skill, this grade feels fair (not necessary, just fair).

Principle: Students Need Feedback

We are both comfortable with the idea that our students will do lots of writing that we never read. That's the only way they will get the necessary volume of practice when we teach dozens and dozens of students. We know our writers grow more when we give them feedback in the midst of drafting, so every day we meet with students in conferences, assess their needs as writers, and teach in response to those needs.

We also periodically collect drafts and provide feedback, not grades. To build confidence, we acknowledge strong craft. We also point to difficulties with skills or transitions or focus. We identify areas where revision might occur. Rather than waiting for drafts to be finished, we do this essential work midprocess. We do this so students can revisit their writing with these suggestions in mind. Offering feedback while the writing is in development and evaluating a piece when it is finished are two different things. Evaluation changes the way teachers read student writing, and it also changes the way students work. When we read through a grading lens, we often glue ourselves to criteria we've set, checking off four or five elements as we read. When we do this, we can miss the small gifts embedded in student writing.

CONSIDER *This...*

Sometimes the sheer numbers of students we teach is not the only thing that gets in the way of giving feedback as often as we'd like. Kelly, for example, is teaching a senior class this year that has trouble remaining on task during writing time. He would like to confer more, but he often has to "walk the class" between conferences to make sure his students remain focused. It took his class two months to get to the point where they would stay on task without his having to hover. Kelly is halfway through the year, and his class still has days when their focus is not sharp. It's getting better, but the class' immaturity has cut down on his time to confer.

Sounds good, right? Simply confer with your students, provide them with some coaching tips, give a little written feedback every now and then, and then watch them improve. How great our teaching lives would be if it were that simple. But let's get real for a moment. Though we agree that feedback is what helps our students grow, we are also aware that there is never enough time to give all the students in one class as much feedback as they need. We remain steadfast, however, in getting to as many writers as we can. Our students need to know that we hear and understand what they are writing *as they are developing their thinking in writing*. We do our students no favors when we see a piece of writing once—just to grade it. We know how it feels to have our entire year of teaching "graded" on a single observation by an administrator. Our students feel this same sense of injustice when the first time they receive detailed feedback on their work is when it is graded. It's too late—their confidence is torpedoed.

It is relentlessly difficult to manage a classroom in order to create time for conferring with individuals, to give writers lots of written feedback, and to continue to build confidence in students who believe they will never be good writers. All of it is difficult. It is also necessary. We must do the best we can, given our trying circumstances. We must stay focused on the students in front of us, students like purple-haired Emily, who just yesterday said to Penny as they conferred, "No one has asked me what I think—like *ever*, Mrs. Kittle. It's just weird to have you sitting next to me, talking just to me, and asking what *I* think about this book. It's weird." Penny walked away from her a few minutes later, grateful for the conversation, because what Emily really said was, "Thank you for listening—for noticing *me* in this crowded classroom." Penny thumbs through her conferring notebook and sees eight kids she still needs to get to, and immediately a sense of failure strikes her. But at least she knows she is doing things that *do* move readers and writers. It may not be enough—and she may not give feedback when a student most needs it—but her efforts are making most of her students better readers and writers, one conference at a time.

Principle: Not All Work Is Weighted Equally

Most of our students' writing is not graded, but when we do grade, we ease into it. As you'll see in the chapters in Section 2, each of our writing units is planned so that students produce increasingly complex work as we layer in new skills (not just one big paper that earns one big grade). As students gain footing in the discourse, the value for each assignment increases. For example, Figure 5.2 shows the increasing point values for the four graded products in the study of narrative.

Conversation Clip

See "Increasing
Complexity Across
a Unit"

Assignment	Point Value
Write a 100-word memoir	20
Craft one scene	50
Craft several scenes to tell a story	100
Write a multinarrator story	200
Create a digital story	200

Figure 5.2 Point Values for the Narrative Study

Principle: Grades Should Tell the Truth About Progress

On due dates, we require students to turn in their papers regardless of what shape the papers are in. Penny has her students print their drafts in class and she requires them to physically hand them to her as they walk out the door. Kelly does not have a printer in his room for student use, so he makes sure that his students share their drafts via Google Docs before they exit the classroom. Why do we check to see that every student turns in a draft before leaving? Because we do not want to spend the next week trying to corral students who have not submitted anything. (We also know that students who exit the room without turning anything in are less likely to ever turn it in.) All students have been working on their drafts in class, so every one of them has *something* to turn in. The papers we receive fall somewhere on a wide spectrum of development—from fully developed pieces that have gone through multiple revisions to crappy single-paragraph (or less) first drafts.

Because the deadline has passed, these papers are graded. It does not mean, however, that students are finished writing them. If a student does not like the score he receives on a paper, he may revise for a higher grade. As long as a student wants to continue working, his draft remains in play. This is why we have replaced the term *final draft* with *best draft* in our classrooms. All drafts—even graded ones—remain alive and eligible for revision. There is no final.

Students who turn in badly developed pieces are moved to the front of the conferring line. We continue to work with them (often long after the deadline), exploring ways to get them invested in improving and/or finishing their writing. Over time, students come to understand that turning in underdeveloped drafts doesn't get them off the hook. On the contrary, they learn that turning in substandard drafts earns them one-to-one time with the teacher. We tell our students that they might as well try to do it well the first time, as the papers they are writing will not get any easier next week when we will ask them to revisit them. Once these expectations are in place, almost all of our students soon start to internalize that there are no shortcuts or easy outs, and as a result, their work ethic increases.

Ultimately, we believe that a grade should tell the truth and should accurately reflect a student's *abilities* at that moment in time. This is why we encourage all students to revise until they get to their best drafts, and it's also why we don't factor deadlines into grading. A zero or a grade deduction for being late has nothing to do with a student's literacy skills and it oddly mixes writing skills with behavioral issues. This results in a grade that is a lie. Students who get a zero on an assignment see their grades plummet, even though that grade does not accurately reflect their abilities.

Principle: Rubrics Are Problematic

We have abandoned rubrics as a means of figuring out numerical scores for writing. We have all been in this situation: you are grading a student's argument, and one of the qualities to be assessed on the rubric is the writer's use of evidence to support the argument. This section of the rubric might look like the one in Figure 5.3.

You have read the paper, and then you try to parse words: Is the evidence *limited*, or is it *adequate*? *Strong* or *comprehensive*? You go to the next item to be assessed and this parsing process is repeated. Is the writer's word choice *advanced* or *superior*? You repeat this process for all five elements found on the rubric, and then you add up the five scores and divide by five to arrive at the final grade: $3 + 4 + 4 + 5 + 2 \div 5 = 3.6$. It seems so straightforward and easy.

The problem is, no five-item rubric can capture all the elements of "good writing," and even if it could, evaluation of writing cannot be reduced to a simple math formula. Rubrics parcel out the qualities of writing as if everything should be treated equally in importance, when often there is an element that clearly outshines all others. Writing is more than the sum of its parts, and as such, we believe it should be judged holistically. When we get too granular in grading writing, we lose sight of the work as a whole. We lose sight of its art.

	Superior 5 Points	Advanced 4 Points	Proficient 3 Points	Limited 2 Points	Below Basic 0–1 Points
Evidence to support your argument	Evidence is comprehensive.	Evidence is strong.	Evidence is adequate.	Evidence is limited.	Evidence is missing.

Figure 5.3 A Rubric for Evaluating Evidence

Though we don't like how rubrics are used to divvy up points, we do see the value of giving students descriptors of what we will be looking for in the writing (especially because these are developed with students through the study of mentor texts *before* the unit begins). For example, one of the descriptors for argument writing has to do with developing a claim. It reads, "The claim is supported well with credible reasons and evidence. Explanations clarify the relationship among claims, counterclaims, reasons, and evidence." We do not score these descriptors separately. We write a brief note next to them, often pointing out the strengths of the paper and leaving the student with a suggestion or two. After writing these notes, we step back, take a broad view of the project, and then assign a grade. In the discourse chapters in Section II, we'll share the descriptors we gave students for graded assignments in different genre studies.

Principle: Best Drafts Receive Limited Feedback

Before they hand us their work, students reflect on their understanding of the qualities that make writing effective and how well their writing meets the standards. Our students assign their work a grade before we assess it. Because we have already conferred with them and offered midprocess feedback before their writing is submitted for grading, we do not spend much time writing comments on best drafts. Our students know that any best draft remains eligible for additional revision, so we try to limit our comments to one or two suggestions that might help the student make the writing better. The goal of our commentary is to motivate the student to want to go back and improve the writing.

We are also exploring other ways to provide commentary on graded drafts. Our students, for example, sometimes submit drafts to be graded through turnitin.com, which has a feature that enables us to attach oral commentary to each student's paper. Once a paper is up on the screen, we click a link and leave a recorded message for the writer. What is nice about this feature is that it limits commentary to three minutes, which forces us to be succinct.

⚑ Assessing the Growth of a Reader

Let's briefly recall that we aim for a balanced reading diet in our classrooms, where students are reading independently, participating in small book clubs, and reading whole-class works. These are different reading experiences, and each of them comes with opportunities to know our readers better. Each of these experiences also comes with specific grading considerations.

Independent Reading

We do not quiz or test our students on their independent reading. Ever. We do, however, give students points every two weeks for maintaining their pace in order to reach their goals. That said, we do not believe in establishing a one-size-fits-all reading pace for every student. Telling all of our readers they must read twenty pages a night is daunting for the remedial reader and insulting to the voracious reader. Instead, we have each student determine an individual reading rate (Kittle 2013).

CONSIDER This...

We started the year with a plan to check on reading goals every two weeks. That didn't happen. Somewhere in the middle of the year, this practice fell by the wayside in our classrooms. Why? We would like to give a precise, brilliant explanation here, but the simple answer is that we lost track of it in the frenzy of the school year. It ran away without our noticing. One day we looked up and realized that although students had recorded their progress every day on the clipboard in our classroom, we had not entered a grade for meeting reading goals for more than a month. Though we were pleased with the amount of reading our students did, we also recognize that there was real value in having them set their own reading goals. It wasn't the grading that mattered—it was the goal setting and the students' assessment of progress. Losing track of this practice was not good. We became determined to reinstate student-generated reading goals and are redoubling our efforts to maintain the practice throughout this school year.

To determine a baseline rate at the beginning of the year, students read in their independent reading books for ten minutes. They record the page number they are on before they begin reading, and then at the end of ten minutes they record the page where they stopped. If a student reads, say, six pages, she multiplies that by six in order to understand how many pages she can comfortably read in one hour. We also discuss how reading rates often fluctuate depending on what is being read, and we encourage students to recalculate their rates when entering new books that might make different demands on them as readers (Kittle 2013, 27–28). Students track completion of books on a reading list taped inside the front cover of their notebooks.

Although we give students daily class time to read, we assign reading at home (two hours per week) and we ask them to set goals for finishing their books. Intermittently, students revisit their goals to see if they have met them. We assign points based on how close they came to meeting their goals. This is less than 10 percent of the overall course grade and is tied to regular reading reflections in notebooks as well as the goals students set for sustained engagement with reading both inside and outside of school.

Book Clubs

In Chapter 3 we described the Thought Logs our students keep as they participate in book clubs. These Thought Logs, which contain student-generated thinking, take the place of quizzes and are collected and scored twice during book clubs. We read through the logs and look for good examples to place under the document camera as models for all students to see. In Figures 5.4, 5.5, and 5.6, you will see three examples of students' different approaches to Thought Logs.

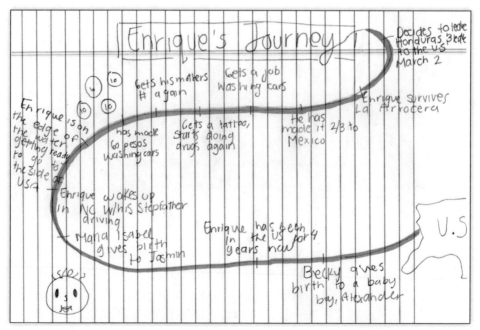

Figure 5.4 Thought Log for *Enrique's Journey*

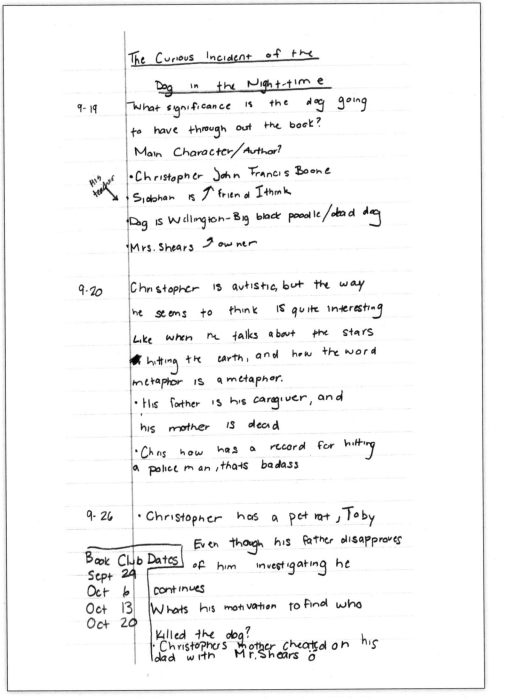

The Curious Incident of the
Dog in the Night-time

9-19 What significance is the dog going
to have through out the book?
Main Character/Author?
• Christopher John Francis Boone
His teacher → • Siobhan is ↑ friend I think
• Dog is Wellington-Big black poodle/dead dog
• Mrs. Shears ⌐ owner

9-20 Christopher is autistic, but the way
he seems to think is quite interesting
Like when he talks about the stars
hitting the earth, and how the word
metaphor is a metaphor.
• His father is his caregiver, and
his mother is dead
• Chris how has a record for hitting
a police man, thats badass

9-26 • Christopher has a pet rat, Toby
Even though his father disapproves
Book Club Dates | of him investigating he
Sept 29
Oct 6 | continues
Oct 13 | Whats his motivation to find who
Oct 20 | Killed the dog?
• Christophers mother cheated on his
dad with Mr.Shears ö

Figure 5.5 Thought Log for *The Curious Incident of the Dog in the Night-Time*   *continues*

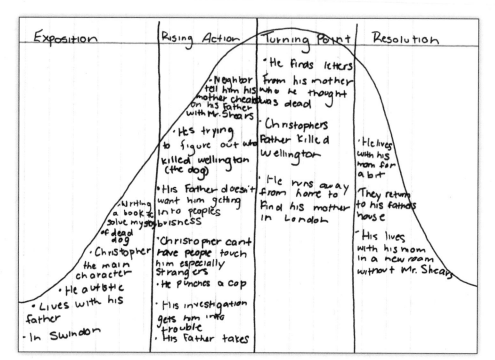

The following handwritten text appears across the plot diagram:

Exposition | **Rising Action** | **Turning Point** | **Resolution**

Turning Point / top of arc:
- He finds letters from his mother who he thought was dead
- Christophers Father killed wellington
- He runs away from home to find his mother in London

Rising Action:
- Neighbor tell him his mother cheated on his Father with Mr. Shears
- He's trying to figure out who killed wellington (the dog)
- His Father doesn't want him getting into peoples buisness
- Christopher cant have people touch him especially strangers
- He punches a cop
- His investigation gets him into trouble
- His Father takes

Exposition:
- Writing a book to solve mystery of dead dog
- Christopher the main character
- He autistic
- Lives with his father
- In Swindon

Resolution:
- He lives with his mom for a bit
- They return to his fathers house
- His lives with his mom in a new room without Mr. Shears

Figure 5.5 *Continued*

(We do not use rubrics to score the Thought Logs; we show students excellent examples and develop criteria together.) A good Thought Log:

- moves beyond a summary of plot points

- demonstrates a student's ability to track thinking about character development or other features in the book over time

- shows analytical thinking and the ability to recognize big ideas hidden in the book

- extends thinking about the book through student-generated research or sketching, poetry, and other artistic expression

- thoughtfully identifies and addresses confusion

- exhibits thinking not found in other students' Thought Logs.

Literary Analysis

Students write essays at the end of each of our two whole-class novel studies. We like to give students a choice of two or even several different open-ended prompts. We tell students to

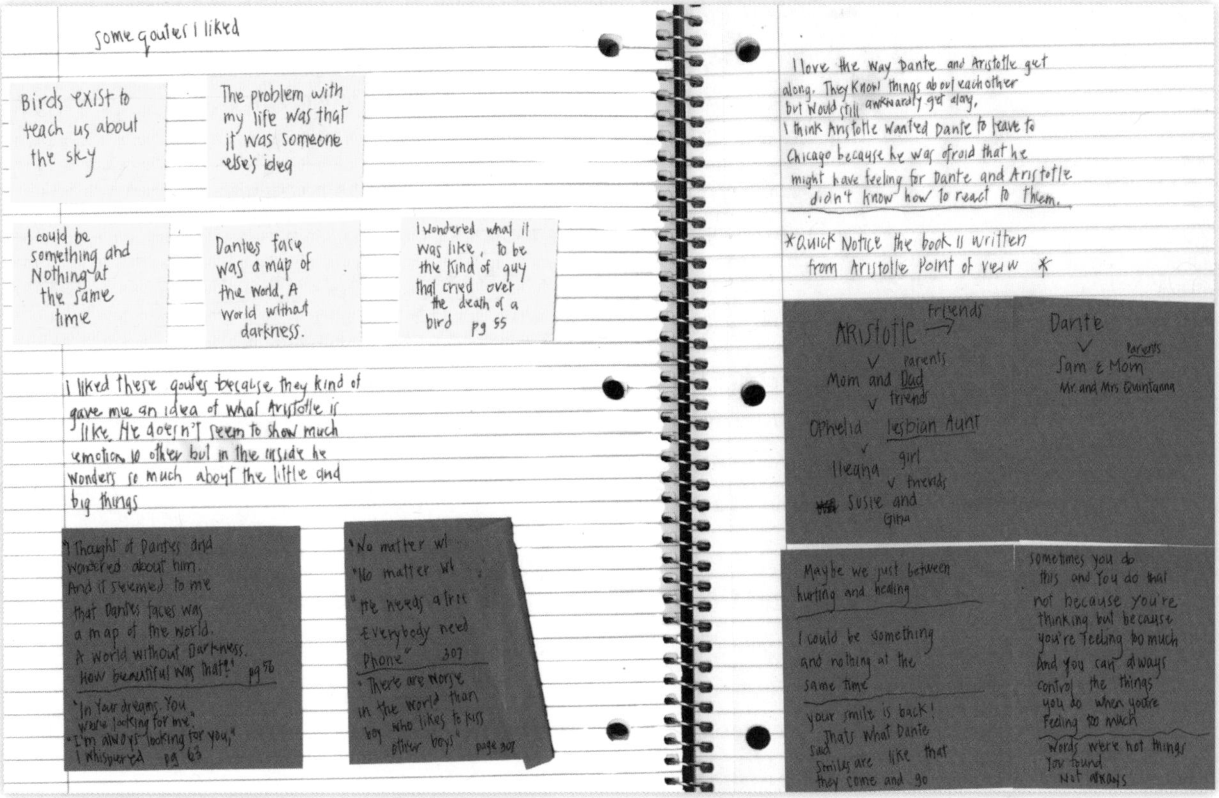

Figure 5.6 Thought Log for *Aristotle and Dante Discover the Secrets of the Universe*

be specific and always cite passages from the book to support their responses. Here are some sample prompts:

- *Discuss one big idea that can be found in your book. What is the author trying to say? How does the author's craft enable this idea to emerge?*

- *Choose any literary device and explain how the author uses this device to explore a central idea. (This prompt is accompanied by a list of literary devices.)*

- *Discuss a change that occurs in your book, and explain why this change leads the reader to consider a big idea.*

- *Choose an item in your Thought Log to discuss. Explain its importance and how creating it helped you achieve a deeper understanding of the book.*

- *The characters in a novel make decisions based on their values. These decisions have consequences. Choose a character and discuss a decision he or she made. What value does this decision highlight in the character? Discuss what the reader learns from studying this character's decision.*

- (For a classic) *One reason this book has remained important is that it gives the reader significant issues to think about. Discuss one significant issue found in this book, and explain how the issue is still important to the modern reader.*

(We give these prompts to our students *before* they start reading so they can consider them as they read.)Before they write their essays, we provide them with the descriptors of excellence for the literary analysis essay (see Figure 5.7). We write (or digitally record) brief comments and then we score the papers holistically.

Whole-Class Reading (to Grade or Not to Grade)

While we both use the literary essay as a graded assignment for whole-class novels, Kelly also occasionally administers reading checks and exams; Penny does not. Let's take a moment to explain this difference in our practices as well as what we do agree on.

Category	Excellence in Literary Analysis
Scope	Demonstrates a comprehensive grasp of a complex idea (or ideas).
Sequence	Exhibits a coherent thesis and strong organization, using appropriate transitions. The introduction entices; the closing inspires.
Development	Contains evidence in support of thesis and related claims. Develops topic with well-chosen, relevant, and sufficient details and/or passages from the literary work.
Craft	Contains strong fluency with explanatory prose, mature vocabulary, precise language, strong voice. Skillfully integrates source and support material with commentary, using citations when appropriate.
Editing	Exhibits attention to and control of conventions throughout the essay.

Source: Adapted from the Puente Project, University of California

Figure 5.7 Descriptors of Excellence in Literary Analysis

Penny does not believe in grading reading checks or having any written "final exam" beyond the essay. She feels the quizzes are unnecessary, as she discusses the book with students in individual and small-group conferences and has students write regularly about their thinking as they read. To Penny, quizzes feel like punishment, especially to students who are struggling to understand the novel, and anything that feels like punishment serves as an impediment to building a love of reading. She does not believe students are motivated to read any more by knowing there will be a reading check on Friday. She knows many other students have become adept at the "passing the quiz even though I have not read the book" game, so she has decided to opt out of this game entirely.

Kelly does occasionally conduct reading checks with his students. With thirty-eight kids in the room, he doesn't feel he has enough time to conduct individual conferences with every student while the class is in the middle of the novel. The reading checks are simple: he writes a single key word on the board (selected from the passage that students were supposed to have read) and students write a brief explanation about the significance of that word. A variation of this assignment is to have each student select the most important word from the reading and explain why that given word was chosen. (Penny uses both of these prompts for notebook writing, but does not grade them separately from other Thought Log work.) Kelly has many students who will do the reading of their own volition, but he also has a small number of students who will pick up their reading pace knowing that a reading check awaits at the end of the week.

We both occasionally add other assessments during the study of a whole-class novel. For example, we sometimes ask students to do passage analysis. We provide students with key passages from the work and ask them two questions for each passage:

1. What is happening in this part of the novel/play?

2. Why is this passage significant to the development of the novel/play?

We select six to eight passages and give them to students to consider before the test date, but on the actual day of the test we randomly select two of them for student response. Our students are asked to pick two passages they believe are significant as well, so the test consists of four responses.

CONSIDER This...

We understand the criticism a passage analysis exam evokes. *Who is the teacher to decide which passages should be designated as "important"?* We believe these concerns are outweighed by both the design and the value of the exercise. For one thing, students select two passages to write about and we select the others. We do not select "gotcha" passages—all of them are key and should be recognized by anyone who read the book. We believe teachers make these decisions all the time—either consciously or unconsciously—and that any time a teacher has taught a novel or play, he or she has had a hand in what was and wasn't discussed. Even with an open-ended question like "What's worth talking about?" the teacher's reaction to what students say plays a major role in what they will think. Because we do not have time to have our students deeply read and analyze everything in a book, we make hard decisions about what will and won't be considered.

As teachers (and as people who have read the core work numerous times), we *know* that certain passages in the book are important. We want to make sure our students demonstrate deep thinking about these critical passages as well. Our students are not drowning in this kind of testing. As part of a balanced reading diet, they only read two whole-class works so they encounter an exam like this only twice a year.

⚡ Setting Up the Grade Book

Once we start generating grades, we set up our grade books into three categories (see Figure 5.8).

Category	Percent of Quarter Grade	This category includes . . .
In-class practice of skills and understandings	10 percent	All notebook work: quick writes, annotation of mentor texts, passage study work, Word Nerd work, evidence of group work thinking, Thought Log work done in class, and some work that directly addresses skills.
Homework	10 percent	Reading done outside class, Thought Log work done at home, articles of the week, and additional invitations to work in the writer's notebook.
Summative assessments	80 percent	"Best" drafts that make it to the teacher for grading, portfolios (including the reading ladder each quarter), and passage study analysis in reading to demonstrate understanding or in writing to analyze the author's craft.

In Penny's school, exams play a role in the final value grade.

Category	Percent of Quarter Grade	This category includes . . .
Exams (Penny's school only)	20 percent of final value grade	Each student receives a grade calculated as above each quarter, but the final value of that grade for the school transcript reflects the addition of one or more exams. Students in a yearlong course take a midterm exam worth 10 percent of the final value grade and then a final exam worth another 10 percent of the final value grade. Students in semester courses take one final exam worth 20 percent of the final value grade.

Figure 5.8 Grade Book Categories

⚡ Grading the Finish Line: The End-of-Year Portfolio Summative Assessment

The last and most important assignment we grade is the end-of-year portfolio. Before the year starts, we envision the skills we want our students to acquire over the course of the year. In portfolios, students collect their best work and show their growth in the skills and understandings we practice. They are required to have four sections: an introduction (title page, dedication, and table of contents), a writing section, a reading section, and a digital section. We share these expectations with students early in the school year so that they hold a clear understanding of the finish line as they work.

We believe portfolios are valuable for both students and teachers. For students, the act of putting a portfolio together requires them to work through three stages: collection, selection, and reflection. In the collection stage, they gather all the writing they have done over the course of the year. This is the easy part, as nothing is thrown out. But the last two stages—selection and reflection—require them to dive deeper into metacognition.

Selection

During the selection process, students wade through all their work, asking themselves these questions: "Why is this narrative better than that narrative? Why is this my best evidence of revision? Which of my article-of-the-week responses shows my deepest thinking?" Deciding which pieces will make the cut and which pieces won't moves students to closely reexamine the evidence of their development as writers. Figure 5.9 shows the writing, reading, and digital composition products we require students to have in their portfolios.

Writing	Reading	Digital Composition
1. Baseline Essay: Students write essays (no revision, editing, or grades) the first week of school. These papers are snapshots of their writing abilities at the beginning of the year. They compare later writing to this baseline as they reflect on progress they have made. **2. The Story of My Writing Year** (explained below) **3. Best Narrative Draft** **4. Best Inform/Explain Draft** **5. Best Argument Draft**	**1. Reading Ladder:** A list of all the books read over the course of the year organized in order from most difficult to easiest. **2. The Story of My Reading Year** (explained below) **3. Best Article-of-the-Week Reflection** **4. Best Close-Reading Passage:** An annotated passage highlighting the writer's moves and intentions.	**Best Digital Composition (either voice recording or movie):** Students are asked to discuss what they learned, the challenges they faced, or any other reflections about one of the following digital projects: • memorized and recorded lines from *Romeo and Juliet* • "Where I'm From" digital movie • recording of a literary passage from their independent reading

Figure 5.9 Portfolio Products

Writing	Reading	Digital Composition
6. Best Literary Analysis Essay **7. The Multigenre Project** **8. Best Writing from Another Class:** A piece that showcases both writing skill and deeper-level thinking in another content area. **9. Best Evidence of Revision:** Passages (or photographs of passages) from notebooks that demonstrate the ability to move a draft into deeper-level revision. **10. Wild Card** (*optional*): Any other writing (poem, email, notebook entry, and so on) that showcases development as a writer.		• public service announcement • multigenre (if applicable—some students did book trailers).

Figure 5.9 *Continued*

Reflection

After the selection process, students move to the most critical element: reflection. We ask them to write two pieces specifically for the portfolio: "The Story of My Writing Year" and "The Story of My Reading Year." As they reflect, they consider where they started the year as readers and writers, where they are at the end of the year, and where they might, as readers and writers, go next. Figure 5.10 shows the questions we give students to help them tell their stories. Students select which questions to answer.

As you can see, the requirements of our portfolio were extensive, and therefore the portfolio was weighed much more than any other assignment. Earlier in this chapter we suggested that grading should be tiered as students take laps through a given discourse (the laps through narrative writing, for example, were scored at 20, 50, 100, and 200 points, respectively). Because the portfolio is the penultimate assessment of our students' skills, it received a much heavier weight. We were mindful of Nancie Atwell's (2015) suggestion that grading should focus less on the journey and more on the finish line. The portfolio is the finish line, and as such, received finish-line weight.

Writing

Explain *some* of the following in a clear and effective story about your life as a writer:

- [ ] Think about yourself as a writer at the beginning of the year and compare that with where you are now as a writer. Have you changed? If so, what caused that change?

- [ ] Discuss how you have succeeded (or not) in developing fluency in writing practice.

- [ ] Discuss how you have improved as a writer (citing specific examples from your work).

- [ ] Share your understanding of what makes good writing and *how* you have learned to define it.

- [ ] Analyze your strengths and weaknesses as a writer. Use your writing projects, both digital and written, as well as your writer's notebook, and cite specific examples from your work across the year.

- [ ] What is the most important piece you've written? Explain.

- [ ] Which piece would you like to burn? Explain.

- [ ] Which piece was most difficult to write? How did you work through the difficulty?

- [ ] Which piece was most enjoyable to write?

- [ ] Discuss specific writing strategies you've used with references to specific texts you've written.

- [ ] Discuss how you have improved some of your previous texts for this portfolio.

- [ ] In what ways do you still need to improve your writing? How will you improve?

- [ ] What are your immediate and long-range goals as a writer? What are your goals for this summer? For next year?

Reading

Explain *some* of the following in a clear and effective story about your life as a reader:

- [ ] Think about yourself as a reader at the beginning of the year and compare that with where you are now as a reader. Look at your beginning-of-year survey and compare it to how you would answer those questions today. Have you changed? If so, what caused that change?

- [ ] Discuss how you have succeeded (or not) in developing a regular reading habit.

- [ ] Discuss favorite books you read this year as well as a clunker or two.

- [ ] Have you discovered any new authors and/or genres that you like? Discuss the skills you used as a reader to determine if a book was a good fit for you; how you made sense of it when you struggled; and when a book kept you reading past the assigned time each night.

- [ ] Discuss what you learned about writing from reading other writers.

- [ ] Discuss how book clubs influenced you as a reader this year.

- [ ] Are you satisfied with the amount of reading you did this year? Yes? No? Explain.

- [ ] Discuss your balance of reading nonfiction versus fiction. What did you learn about their similarities and differences?

- [ ] Discuss reading strategies that you use. Be specific.

- [ ] In what ways do you still need improvement in your reading? How will you improve?

- [ ] What are your immediate and long-range goals as a reader? What are your goals for this summer? For next year?

Figure 5.10 Reflecting on a Year of Writing and Reading

CONSIDER *This...*

> Knowing what we expect our students to demonstrate in their end-of-year portfolios helped us remain focused throughout the year on the essential skills in different discourses that we know students must practice and gain facility with. It reminded us to utilize every one of our 180 days. Establishing the portfolio kept us focused all year on how we spent time. The portfolio created a constant low-level pressure on us, but this was a good kind of pressure. It kept us on track.

Which leads us to the last question on your mind: How did we grade the portfolios? The answer? Very quickly. As students worked on them in class we conferred with them to celebrate and to consider their work with them. We collected final portfolios during the last week of school, leaving us only a couple of days to read through them. We did not mark up the pieces of writing they selected because we were already familiar with them—after all, we had conferred with our students about their writing throughout the year, so we were not seeing these pieces for the first time. Instead, we focused our attention on the reflective letters. We read each of them carefully, stepping back to get the widest view of each student's progress and skill level. We wrote brief comments, and then we placed a grade on the portfolio.

◀ Closing Thoughts: The Heart of the Work

While we were working on this chapter, Penny tweeted the following: "Spent the morning reading and responding to (not grading) student writing—and keeping a list of all I learned." Soon after posting this tweet, she received this response from a high school teacher in Massachusetts: "I love this idea but I have too many kids and not enough time to read work and not put a grade on it." Penny resisted the urge to post a shallow response via Twitter, but here is what we want to say to this teacher:

> Your heart is in this work—we are sure of it—and you want your writers to improve. Grading, however, is not the answer. In fact, it gets in the way. A writer needs to take risks and experiment in order to improve, but student writers suffer when their efforts are treated like bread dough, to be smacked down just as it begins to rise. Surprising moves delight and engage readers, yet students are likely to stumble as they attempt them. If students take risks and we grade every stumble, they will stop moving. When we grade student work, we stop the thinking: revision feels like "more work," and more work to all of us feels like something to avoid. There is enough time in the year to allow for long thinking about writing, but grading practices can prevent this from happening. Overgrading gets in the way of the very thing we seek—extended, deep thinking about writing. The work of a writing teacher is to read and respond, to nudge and to celebrate. That work is best done in a conference. Students should write more and we should grade less.

Our mantra in a profession dedicated to the love of reading and writing should be to embrace experimentation and practice—lots of both—and to minimize, shrink, reduce, and if we had our way, *eliminate* grading. The increase in testing in the last decade has been considerable—anyone who has been in teaching that long has seen it happen—but the 2012 National Assessment of Educational Progress (NAEP) results show that even with all of that grading, there has been no significant increase in proficiency. These results remind us of a farmer's wisdom: you don't fatten a pig by weighing it. Grading is not worth all the energy it steals from us.

Evaluation and testing eat up time that is better spent reading, writing, and talking. We steal time from our daily essential practices with students to measure their progress. We steal time from our own reading and writing in order to mark those tests and submit those grades. Worry about performance inhibits creative thinking and leads writers to choose the easiest path to finish. In contrast, expansive thinking develops over time. Constant evaluation teaches students to be dependent on a teacher's judgment, instead of their own.

We worked hard to try to find the proper balance between the evaluation required of us by our schools and the authentic practices we believe are essential in building literate students. And whenever we felt that balance getting a bit out of whack, we stopped and asked ourselves, "Is this grading practice getting in the way of our students' improvement?"

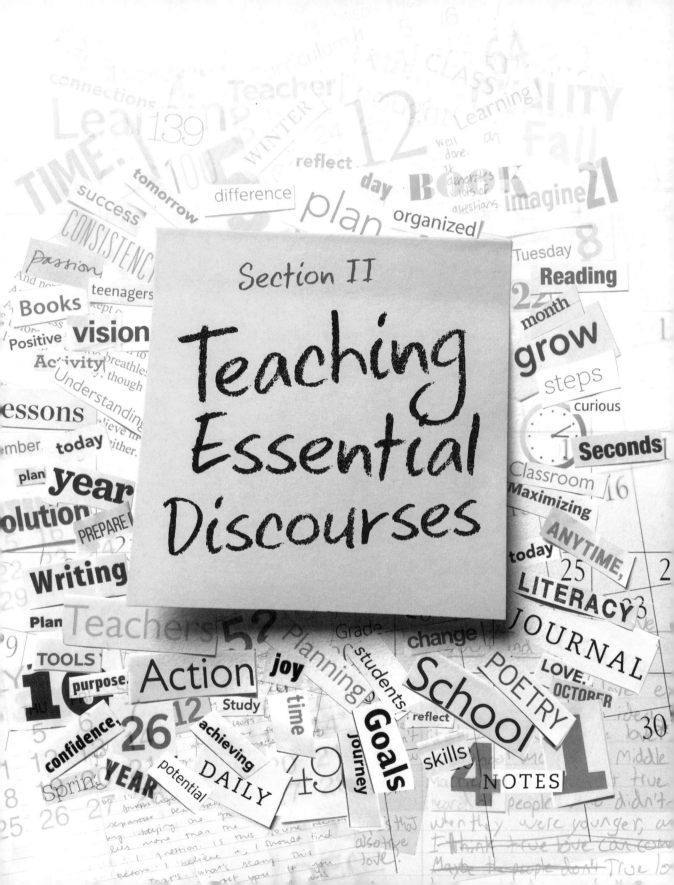

Section II

Teaching Essential Discourses

A... ...pt on the fridge.

Anu... ...ys you had crushes on.

And ...at got worn to a dance at which you danced by yourself, befo - you got too breathless to dance.

Along with, probably, though this isn't worthy of huge thinking, a soul or something.

Anyway, adults don't believe in Santa Claus. They try hard not to believe in Santa Claus in Reverse either.

The chapters in this section detail the planning and teaching we did in four essential writing studies: narrative, informational, argument, and multigenre. Planning a unit that remains cohesive across a number of weeks is always challenging, but there are predictable decisions we know we'll have to make in any study.

✦ Time

As you saw in Chapter 4, before the school year begins, we map out a year of studies in writing and project how much time we will spend in each one. As each unit approaches, we decide how we will use the time we've allotted to move these current students through the work of this study. This decision is tied to the expectations we have for what students will produce in each unit.

✦ Expectations

Instead of spending weeks writing one essay and then moving on—common in the 4 × 4 approach (students read four big books and write four big papers across the school year)—over the course of a study, we plan for students to create a series of texts using a progression of skills. We think of this as "taking laps around the track," and each time we circle back around, we increase the complexity of skills we're teaching in that discourse. Completing multiple laps in any given discourse ensures that our students' writing volume will significantly increase, thus leading to deeper understandings.

In our planning, we decide the kinds of texts students might write in each lap, and we also project how much time they'll need to complete the lap. At the beginning of each unit, we give students a "road map" plan for the laps they will take in the study. Each plan connects the critical habits of *all* writing (see Chapter 4, page 85) with the skills of the specific genre we are studying. The skills detailed in the unit plan are a lot to take in at once, but we believe students are empowered when they know where a unit is going.

⋆ Teaching

Once we know the laps students will take in the study, we plan notebook work to help them generate rich thinking in the genre. We select mentor texts to show the features and conventions we want students to learn, and we decide which demonstrations we will need to do to help students plan, draft, and revise their writing in the different laps.

Once the study is underway, we are constantly assessing student work—in notebooks, drafts, and conferences—and revising our plans based on what students understand. This assessment is critical because when we're planning ahead for the big ideas we want to address in a unit, we don't know what our students do and don't know. For example, in our narrative unit, we expected ninth graders to have experience writing dialogue, but when we assessed their notebook writing, we saw how superficial their understandings were. In response, we revised our plans and slowed down the work on crafting dialogue.

⋆ Essential Questions

Essential questions serve an important purpose in the teaching of writing. We don't want to teach writing as a task; we want our students to study writing and the moves of writers in order to develop flexibility in thinking and in skills. To help them do so, we have developed essential questions in order to move students into a broader, more lasting understanding of writing in every unit:

- What processes do writers use for generating ideas?
- How do writers determine the expectations and the conventions of a genre?
- What can the book I'm reading now teach me about writing?
- What strategies do writers use to communicate in an organized and clear way?
- How do writers choose words and use voice to communicate with fire and precision?
- How do writers determine needed revisions in a text?
- How do writers anticipate questions and objections to a text? How do writers address or refute differing opinions?
- What is the value in sharing writing with others—even crummy first drafts?
- What is the value of listening and responding to feedback on writing?

We believe the teaching of reading and writing is a process of continually circling back to the same big ideas. The act of circling back is at the heart of retention. Students retain what they revisit, which is why we will revisit these essential writing questions throughout the year.

✒ The Rhythm of a Study

In the chapters that follow, we highlight important decisions we made for each of these aspects of planning (time, expectations, teaching, essential questions). While the number of laps may vary, each study follows a predictable, shifting rhythm as it unfolds through time. This rhythm is intentional as we plan for three phases of study regardless of genre:

> launching a unit
>
> heart of a unit
>
> end of a unit.

In a writing study, we retain all our daily practices—books talks, independent reading, notebook writing, text study and minilessons, time to work on drafts, and sharing and debriefing—but they are planned to meet the needs of students. Time devoted to different practices shifts during the unit of study. For example, we extend text study time if students do not yet understand the features of the genre, or we might extend work time to confer with more students as the lap is coming to an end. In those cases, we might skip notebook work that day. The rhythm of our classroom shifts as we assess the needs of our students.

Launching a Unit

There are several goals for the work we plan in the opening days of a unit. First, we want students to find engaging ideas for writing which will fuel the rest of the unit. We typically plan for numerous quick writes so students are collecting a volume of writing practice in the genre. We often follow this notebook practice with time for students to consider ideas and think about choosing one to develop into a longer piece. We confer during this time, and students who've discovered an idea they want to pursue may begin drafting.

We study texts in these early days as we work to name, notice, and understand the conventions of the genre in mentor texts. We give students time to do some of this work in pairs or small groups to discover new thinking and to talk about ideas for writing. We sometimes have students write a short draft in their notebooks to demonstrate conventions of the genre (e.g., one scene in narrative, a short review in argument). These short, first lap drafts give us valuable assessment information about what students do and do not understand about the genre.

Heart of a Unit

We spend most of our time in the heart of the unit. With lots of low-stakes (often ungraded) practice, notebook writing shifts to refining skills and practicing elements of the genre, and students complete a second lap of writing that shows their growing understandings of the genre's conventions.

Choosing texts for study is critical in this phase because a short mentor text can potentially do three kinds of work: evoke ideas for student writing, show excellent craft through passage study, and demonstrate the specific conventions of the genre (e.g., voice, details, and dialogue in narrative; or transitions and organization of ideas in informational writing). We also plan to use evolving teacher and student drafts to reinforce conventions of the genre.

In the heart of a study, there is more time to write and confer with students as they develop a longer, well-developed piece that demonstrates more conventions of the genre. Sometimes we stop the class to address ongoing issues we see in drafts or to deal with widespread confusion. At the end of each period, we debrief the class about what is working and what students learned that day, or we reinforce expectations by celebrating beautiful words or sharing observations we made while students were working.

End of a Unit

At the end of a unit, notebook work focuses on passages students imitate to refine the craft of their writing. Passage study is followed by extended time for students to work at polishing and refining their best drafts. We continue to confer and teach lessons as needed, and students meet in writing groups to share drafts and offer feedback before best drafts are submitted for grading.

◀ Reflecting on a Unit

At the conclusion of each study, we carve out time to reflect on the unit's effectiveness before moving on. We consider the following:

- We look for engagement and growth in students' habits as readers and writers. We expect to see growth in the length of writing, the use of features, a command of revision, and the ability to edit the writing for clarity. We look for participation and collaboration in writing groups and the ability to give and receive feedback.

- We examine the selected mentor texts. Should we revise our selections to better align texts with student interests? Have we found new texts that bring a new energy to our teaching?

- We look for weaknesses in student writing. Did the best drafts show weaknesses that can be best addressed by the selection of a mentor text, a minilesson, or a teacher demonstration? This is particularly important if you are spreading out these laps in narrative over the course of a school year. We use what we learned in this unit to drive how we plan our next one.

- We examine the pace of the unit. Where did the unit have energy? Where did it falter? What was a waste of time? Where did students struggle and need additional support?

When we design a unit, we see the decisions we make as moves, like pieces in a puzzle that fit together in unlimited ways. Unit design is art: it is gratifying, sustaining, and engaging because we create the units anew each year. We believe teachers should create their own units, based on what they learn as they study the work their students are doing. As Sir Ken Robinson (2013) said, "Teaching is a creative profession. . . . Teaching, properly conceived, is not a delivery system." We strive to be more than "assigners." We strive to be responsive teachers.

A. ... pt on the fridge.
And ... ys you had crushes on.
And ... at got worn to a dance at which you danced by
yourself, befo - you got too breathless to dance.
soul or ... Along with, probably, though this isn't worthy of huge thinking, a
something.
Anyway, adults don't believe in Santa Claus. They try hard not to
believe in Santa Claus in Reverse either ...

plan Create

Choice

NARRATIVE

> The storyteller is deep inside every one of us. The story-maker is always with us. Let us suppose our world is attacked by war, by the horrors that we all of us easily imagine. Let us suppose floods wash through our cities, the seas rise . . . but the storyteller will be there, for it is our imaginations which shape us, keep us, create us—for good and for ill. It is our stories, the storyteller, that will recreate us, when we are torn, hurt, even destroyed. It is the storyteller, the dream-maker, the myth-maker, that is our phoenix, what we are at our best, when we are our most creative.
>
> —**Doris Lessing,** *winner of the Nobel Prize*

Lessing's words call like the wind whipping around the house on a winter morning: *The story-teller is deep inside every one of us.* We tell our students, "You have stories that no one can tell but you. You have experiences and ideas that can teach all of us." At its heart, the narrative unit is about finding the storytellers inside each of our students.

Crafting stories always brings a contagious energy to our teaching of writing, and the placement of this study at the beginning of the year is critical for several reasons. Students get to know us as we reimagine and craft our own memories of growing up next to older siblings, of competing in sports, of riding bikes through our old neighborhoods, of battles we had with parents, teachers, and other adults. We—their teachers—have stories only *we* can tell, and we model the creation of our stories in front of our students. When we do, they begin to see us as more than just "teachers," and when our students begin sharing their stories, we begin to see them as more than just simply "students." We get to know them and what they care about outside school. We honor their experiences, and in doing so, we begin forming relationships with them—relationships that are central to building a foundation for our teaching all year long.

We know that in many schools expository and informational writing are more privileged discourses, but we concur with Tom Newkirk, who argues in *Minds Made for Stories* (2014) that all writing is grounded in story, and that teaching students the moves of narrative provides them with an essential foundation for writing in other genres. A well-crafted scene can anchor a feature article based on research, illuminate a key point in an argument, or frame the perfect ending for a college admissions essay. Narrative is central to all writing discourses, so this is another reason we begin here. We will refer to writing a scene throughout the school year to ensure students retain an understanding of its essential features and to help them write well in every genre.

We also believe that teaching the habits of engaged writers (e.g., finding ideas, studying craft, organizing complex information, polishing writing for an audience) is critical in the beginning of the school year. While we study these habits in any genre, we have found that students engage readily in writing stories, especially when invited to write either memoir or fiction. We want our students to see English class as a place to imagine and create, not just to argue or relay information. The narrative unit develops habits of mind about writing that are both intellectual and practical and will support student success in any field or discipline.

Finally, narrative is a good choice for the beginning of the year because it's the genre most of our students are reading independently. They are immersed in stories, so it's easier to make connections between their reading and writing. For example, we started one class with a book talk on Andrew Smith's *Stick*, pausing to read the opening few pages where a character introduces himself. We encouraged our students to notice how Smith draws readers near with a character's compelling, intelligent voice. Regular book talks like this help our students find books, but they also provide an opportunity to demonstrate the writing qualities we seek in this unit.

We might also encourage students to notice the qualities of an effective scene as they read independently—the narrator's voice, for example, or how the plot moves through time. We say *might* because our ongoing assessment of what our writers need drives this decision. Our most important work is to help all students live inside stories through regular time to read. We know that if we make reading a hunting and gathering mission to serve writing, we risk ruining the act of pleasurable reading. What's critical—especially at the beginning of the year as readers

are gaining traction—is that we let students simply read *most* of the time and trust what research clearly shows: students who read regularly, write with greater fluency, clarity, and organization. As Frank Smith (2006) reported, students who were "reading rich, complex, meaningful material produced stories that were creative and interesting" (121).

⋆ Planning a Study in Narrative

As we worked to ignite their imaginations, students studied and applied the conventions of narrative to write either memoir or fiction (we let them choose) during the study. Why fiction? The skills of narrative writing are the same in either genre and many of our students love the opportunity to imagine and create. Writing fiction is neglected in middle and high school. Each year we see students deeply engage in writing when given the opportunity to imagine a setting, its characters and a conflict.

We give our students a list of the essential elements of stories that we will teach, and they paste them into their notebooks. Many students are familiar with these elements, but it is useful to have them in one place to reference as they work and as we confer. Here is our list:

- Story is built on scenes, which contain sensory details of setting, characters, and action. All of this detail is essential to help the reader experience the moment.

- The first scene, or lead, usually jumps into the action. Readers don't want a long introduction; they want something to happen.

- Scenes contain dialogue. If your characters don't talk, then your readers feel like they are watching a silent movie. Make some noise!

- Scenes are often written in the present tense so the reader feels as if he or she is in the moment as it is happening. This is tricky: don't let yourself move back and forth between present and past tense in the same scene or your reader may become confused.

- Story is narrated. The voice of the narrator carries the reader along, be it playfully, sternly, sarcastically, or any other -*ly* you can think of. The voice has to be authentic and it must fit the tone of the piece. You want to use a voice that invites a reader to live in the moment with you.

- Scenes use show-and-tell to bring the action to life. To show what's happening, don't say, "I looked over the edge of a cliff"; say, "My knees trembled and my stomach lurched as I peered over the rim of the cliff."

- And lastly, stories have a "So what?" ending (Atwell 2002). The reader should know why you wrote this moment, why it matters to you.

⋆ Time and Expectations

In our schools teachers are trusted to plan instruction to meet the needs of their students, and we are encouraged to take the time we need to teach well. Because we have so many important reasons to teach narrative, we dedicated the first quarter of the school year to the study of scenes and stories, knowing that the Common Core State Standards suggest a significant amount of time in every grade be dedicated to narrative writing. For example, the CCSS recommend narrative be studied 30 percent of the school year in grades six through eight and 20 percent in grades nine through twelve.

Our plan is shown in Figure 6.1.

We believe that repeated practice with story writing—multiple laps around the narrative track, as we say to students—will build confidence and independence with story construction. However, a teacher could plan to study narrative both early and later in the school year, saving an extended thinking lap for spring.

Weeks	Mapping the Writing Year: Narrative Study
1–2	Swimming in short memoirs
3–4	Craft one scene
5–6	Write several scenes to craft a story
7–10	Extended thinking: craft a story with multiple narrators

Figure 6.1 The Map of the Narrative Study

CONSIDER This...

Having taught this unit, we realized that a fourth option in teaching narrative—digital storytelling—would have wide appeal. The composition skills students learned early in the unit invited them to imagine these same moves in the digital world of storytelling. In the year following our collaboration, Penny's students participated in an Unsung Heroes project with Georgetown University to tell the stories of people in their community through photographs, video, music, and voice-over narration. In the fourth lap, students were given a choice to pursue either a multiple-narrator story or a digital composition.

In the narrative unit, we want students to master the construction of a scene, to elevate their writing beyond just recounting what happened. We teach them to slow down time to unveil setting details and the conversation between characters—to write scenes like those they read in books. We show them how a plot is built on moments in time to show the action and develop the characters. We invite them to experiment with how time moves in a story—with flashbacks and flash-forwards—so they begin to understand the slow reveal of a big idea or the subtlety of an extended metaphor in the crafting of a powerful story. This is all too much to learn at once, so we planned our unit as a progression of building skills as we start simply and then begin to write increasingly complicated scenes and stories.

We took our students through the same first three laps of narrative study and then—based on the needs of our students—went in different directions for the fourth lap. Figure 6.2 shows the progression of craft moves that lead students to increasingly skillful narrative writing. This is a road map for teaching the unit.

Lap One: Swimming in Short Memoirs	**Lap Two:** Crafting One Scene	**Lap Three:** Crafting Several Scenes to Tell a Story	**Lap Four:** Using Multiple Narrators to Craft a Story
Make reading a daily habit.	Read like a writer. Increase the volume of your reading—you'll see elements of effective story writing in everything you read.	Read like a writer. Notice and imitate effective writing craft.	Read like a writer. Analyze how authors craft different points of view.
You have a story to tell that no one can tell but you. Craft your narrator's voice.	Show a moment in time (scene) through the use of sensory details (see, taste, hear, feel, smell) to help readers imagine and live inside the experiences of those in this setting.	Craft several effective scenes to develop a story around an idea, a place, or a quality (like courage).	Develop a voice for each of the narrators who contribute to your story through word choice, sentence structure, and tone.
Generate a lot of story possibilities in notebooks.		Organize scenes to create momentum and to best develop the purpose for readers. Use flashbacks and flash-forwards effectively.	Recognize your power as a writer to change thinking. Tune your voice to persuade, to explain, and to tell with passion from different points of view.
Explode a moment by zooming in on details. Slow down time.	Balance show and tell to establish the pace of the scene and to show readers what matters.	Create effective transitions to link scenes and bring cohesion to the story.	Choose the genre (letter, email, poem, Snapchat, scene narration, etc.) that would best represent this character's point of view and voice at this place in the narrative.
Use all your senses to describe people, places, and events.	Use dialogue to reveal characters both in what is said and what is not said and through the words of other characters.	Engage readers with a dynamic lead.	Experiment with metaphor, symbolism, and other literary devices to develop your ideas, your setting, and your characters.
		Create an effective ending to reflect on why the story is told or why it matters.	Use different points of view to deepen thinking about the ideas in your story.
	Use word choice to create a believable, consistent voice for the narrator of the scene.	Craft word choice to create the tone of the piece and to develop the narrator's voice.	Organize scenes to create momentum in the plot, smoothly transitioning between narrators and events.
	Polish your writing for an audience by proofreading line by line.	Use major and minor characters to interpret or elaborate on the big idea(s) or theme of your story.	Conclude with a new understanding of the big idea.
		Proofread, edit, and polish as you write.	Read your writing aloud. Hear how it works and fine-tune it. Recognize errors in sentence structure and eliminate them.

Figure 6.2 The Laps We Planned for Narrative Study

⟡ Lap One: Swimming in Short Memoirs

Early in the school year we are confronted by many students who have lost confidence in their ability to write well. They don't like to write. They don't believe their stories matter. They search for details and find they can't recall them. Most do not know how to build a story from an idea— or how writing itself helps them recall details. They do not know—or they have forgotten—how to generate rich ideas for stories. So in this first important lap around the narrative track, we planned lots of notebook writing to help students recall meaningful moments that will generate investment in their writing. We know that investment in an idea leads to greater attention to revision and craft throughout the unit, so we spent time demonstrating how *we* find ideas for stories we want to tell well.

We all learned to swim by first wading into the water. We use poetry to get our students to splash around in the narrative writing pool. A poem invites an emotional response and leads us to our life stories. We share a poem with students and we all write. We ask them to write quickly without stopping. Our goal is to generate a lot of words on the page. They choose the form for their writing: a list of ideas; sentences about an experience; or one idea written quickly with line breaks like a poem. If we see that students rarely choose to sketch an idea, we may model this. We demonstrate different responses in different classes and leave them under the document camera the next day in order for students to see the possible range of writing next to poems (see Figure 6.3).

We may ask students, "Did anyone do anything interesting in their notebooks?" The key is, we want students to discover new thinking *as they write* and learn to trust that the act of writing will lead them to great stories.

Teaching Clip

See "Writing Next to Ralph Fletcher's Poem 'The Last Time I Saw Don Murray'"

Writing Connected to Place

On one day, we selected poems from George Ella Lyon's collection *Many-Storied House* (thanks to Linda Rief for this idea.) We started with "Kitchen Table," in which the narrator recounts significant events that have occurred at the table. We read the poem aloud, picked a favorite line, and then wrote to capture our first thinking for a few minutes. We repeated this same process with other poems such as "Upstairs," "Interior Design," and "That Chair." We chose this particular collection because we know we all have memories that originate in our homes—often emotional ones. We hoped students would connect to Lyon's ideas and experiences in order to write their own.

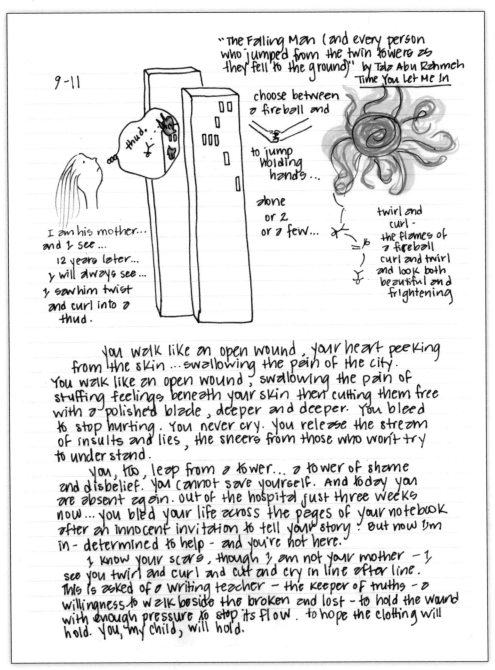

Figure 6.3 Responses to Poems from Penny's Notebook

After a few rounds of writing from these poems, we had students list the addresses of places they have lived, then select one place and sketch its floor plan. We had both already done this in our own notebooks, and we showed students how to label key events on their sketches. Together we spent a few minutes jotting memories, and then students shared them with one another. We know that talk is a foundation for generating thinking, so we encouraged students to add memories that came from this sharing. Students created many rich narratives connected to place.

Writing Connected to Objects

On another day, we had students write next to Sarah Kay's spoken word poem "Hands." We played the YouTube video of Kay performing her poem, spent a few moments sharing lines we loved, then had students open their notebooks to a clean two-page spread. On one side we had them glue in the poem, and on the other side they traced an outline of one of their hands. They then filled their outlines with things they've held or touched that mattered to them. We hoped this listing activity would lead students to stories that were dormant in their thinking, and that Kay's masterful storytelling would inspire them to write those stories with an attention to word choice and rhythm. We modeled how to move from a list to a story by returning to our hand drawings, choosing objects to write about, and using sensory details to show, not tell, about moments in time connected to these objects. We then asked students to draft for eight minutes, and as they were writing, we wrote beside them.

CONSIDER This...

Early in the year students might correct punctuation or change a word or two when asked to revise a quick write, but as we model our thinking about revision, students begin to cut whole sentences and reorder ideas. We put a student's notebook under the document camera to celebrate when we find deeper-level revision. Attention to rereading and revision as a daily practice matters.

We wanted to dispel the notion that revision is something writers do only when the first draft is completed, so at the end of the quick write, we introduced the notion of "flash" revision. For two minutes, students watched us as we quickly reread and revised our drafts. We shared our thinking aloud about the four key "RADaR" moves writers make when revising—Replace, Add, Delete, and Rearrange—and then we asked students to use these moves to make their writing better. We gave them pens or colored pencils to mark their revisions so they (and we) could see them easily. We asked students to share some of the moves they made, and we collected this thinking on a class anchor chart titled "Making writing better means. . . . "

Teaching Clip

See Penny model one type of revision in "Cutting: An Essential Revision Skill"

Writing Connected to Events

Writers of narrative draw from deep wells of ideas, including places, objects, people, and events, and we wanted to make sure our work in this first lap had students working with this whole range of ideas. To that end, we watched the short video "Being 12: The Year Everything Changes" together and then opened our notebooks and listed ideas as they came to us. We narrated as we wrote in front of students: "I remember when I was twelve, riding my ten-speed with my best friends; I remember waiting for a tennis court at Mount Tabor Park; I remember trips to the library with my mom." (These are all events, although they connect with specific people and places.) We asked students to begin listing their memories. When we collected these we noticed that students had written primarily about people and places, so we steered some quick writes toward events. For example, we had students sketch outlines of their bodies and then map in the scars they have (see Figures 6.4 and 6.5). Students mapped their scars (both internal and external) after watching a few quick videos from the @Darwinawards Twitter feed.

Writing to Introduce Ourselves

To practice the skill of zooming in on a moment, we decided to have students draft 100-word memoirs to introduce themselves to their email partners in each other's classes. We asked them to show readers something, not just tell who they are. There are a number of websites dedicated to these memoirs, so mentor texts were easy to find. This invitation required students to shape a whole, albeit short, text and to focus at the word and sentence level because the word count is defined and limited.

First, students watched as we created our own memoirs in front of them. They learned new things about us as teachers, as they saw us struggle with what to say, how much to say, and how to compose a moment effectively in exactly one hundred words. As students began drafting, we

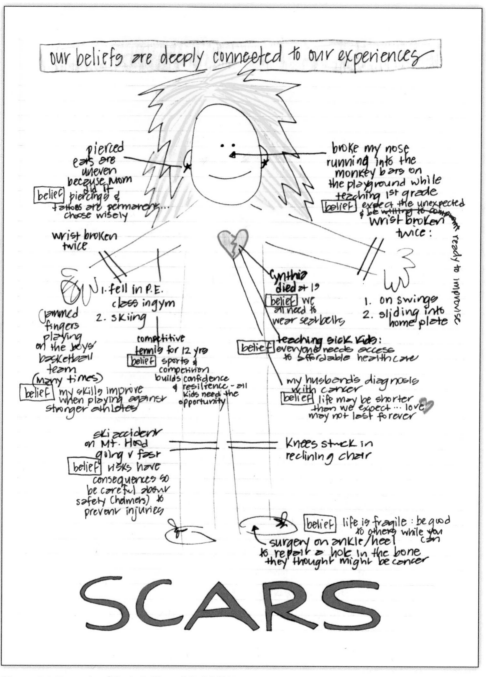

Figure 6.4 Example of Penny's "Scars" Quick Write

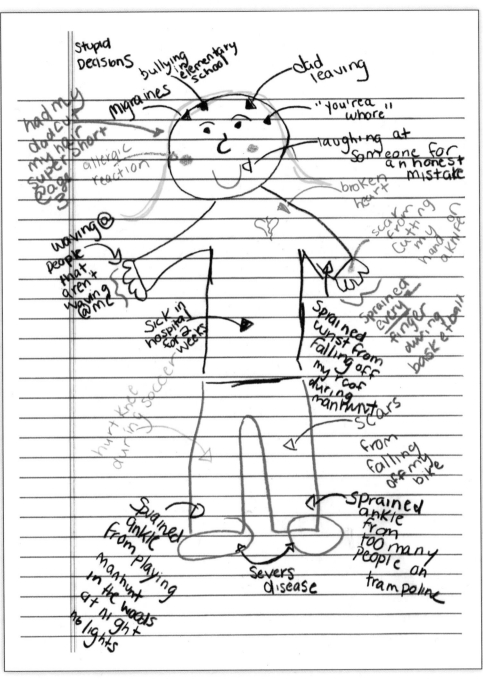

Figure 6.5 Student "Scars" Sketch and Quick Write

continues

Stupid Decisions

[margin note, vertical left: "what can I see inside window?"]

During the summer of 2013, I
decided to sit on a roof for hours.
As I sat on the red roof beside
my bedroom window I watched the stars
slowly appear one by one. I listened
to my friends below me running
and laughing. I could hear the twigs
and leaves snapping from people
below me. *[caret: their feet as they run around]*

As I continued to watch the stars
above me and stay as quiet as
possible, I heard a crack from
the stairs next to the roof I was
on. I try my hardest to move slowly
into the corner between the side
rail and the wall of the house.
"Come on, Kathryn, I know you're
over here," I hear my best friend, Jonny
whisper.

I try to hold in a giggle as I
continue to back up. She gets
closer and shines the flash light is directly
right into my eyes. I squint trying
to find the fastest way out
of here, so I dont lose the game.
I let out a giggle and then slowly
begin to lose my balance.
"Oh no," I think.
The world starts spinning
around me.

[margin annotations: "more descriptive of roof"; "more about stars"; "again, more about stars"; "describe stairs"; "Ddescribe house"; "painted at"; "finish"]*

Figure 6.5
Continued

moved from table to table learning about them as people and as writers. Although some wrote
one draft in their notebooks and were done—focusing more on getting to a hundred words
than shaping them—many students followed our model and reread and crafted these memories,
considering each word. However, when we told our students that their memoirs would be shared
with students across the country, almost every one of them circled back to revise, which reminds
us of the importance of having our students write to audiences outside their classrooms. Here
are examples from Melanie, a student in Kelly's class, and Rachel, a student in Penny's class:

Melanie's 100-Word Memoir

It was already seven o'clock and the annual party had just started. My face was painted sugar skull white. The backyard was purely lit with twinkling white lights hanging across the patio and swirling around the maple trees. The tables were filled with sweet Day-of-the-Dead treats: pan dulce, pan de muerto, tamales, champurrados, and buñuelos. An altar stood alone in the center of the party. Pictures of our past loved ones were displayed. Sugar skulls, tissue paper flowers and marigolds or flor de muerto scattered the tables. Instead of grieving their deaths, we spend our evening celebrating our loved ones.

Rachel's 100-Word Memoir

I sit on the edge of a moment, on a rock ledge that drops hundreds of feet below into an evergreen ravine. I'm halfway up the summit of Mt. Adams, my last peak in the Presidential range. My father stops me for a photo. I climb cautiously to a ledge that overlooks a glacier-carved canyon with cascades of emerald forest blanketing its walls. The summer heat casts a haze over the mountains in the background, yet visibility still reaches for miles and miles and miles. This moment is bliss. Each peak summited I call my own; these mountains are mine.

In the chart in Figure 6.6 you can see a few other prompts we used to get our students playing with story in their notebooks—learning to hear their voices; to use details to show, not tell; and to slow time down and focus on a moment. We paired these prompts with specific teacher actions we have taken in the past, but quick writing is always organic. We write in front of our students to demonstrate how we find stories as we write, and oftentimes we use these quick writes to also demonstrate the craft of narrative writing. We do not direct students to follow our writing. They can if they want, of course, or they can follow wherever their thinking leads them. This chart can help you consider the variety of moves you might model.

There is a direct relationship between the quality of the writing we put in front of students and the quality of writing they produce in their notebooks. When students write under the influence of beautifully crafted language, it shows. Students often say, "I didn't know I could write like this." It makes a difference that they write immediately after hearing beautiful language read aloud, while the phrases and sentences so carefully crafted still echo. Don't be tempted to give a lot of directions. Share the poem. Let them write.

Text	Teacher Demonstration
"An Origin Story" by Sarah Kay and Phil Kaye	We list key moments we've spent with best friends and the lessons learned in those moments.
"A Letter to the Girl I Used to Be" by Ethan Smith	The letter form leads to a close, confidential voice in storytelling. We might model a letter to our younger selves.
"On Turning Ten" by Billy Collins	We quick write memories connected to being ten, and develop one idea into a scene.
"For My Grandmother" by Phil Kaye	We write memories of grandparents using dialogue to reveal their voices.
"To the Boys Who May One Day Date My Daughter" by Jesse Parent	We might model the voice we use as parents of older children.
"The Revenant" by Billy Collins	We might model a shift in point of view by writing from the voice of a pet or sibling.
"Do You Love Me?" by Robert Wrigley	We might ask students to consider how dialogue reveals character.
"Lost Voices" by Darius Simpson and Scout Bostley	We might respond with an imitation of this poem, using the line, "You tell me you know what it's like to be . . ."
"After Second Shift" by Lowell Jaeger	We might ask students how authors create pivots to surprise the reader.
"Beethoven" by Shane Koyczan	We might respond to "He was not good enough" with times we have felt this way, or we might use a repeating phrase or line.

Figure 6.6 Notebook Seeds to Spur Daily Writing

Assessment in Lap One

Baseline Assessment

The habit of reading like a writer—intent on learning the moves writers make in a genre in order to imitate them—is a building block for all our units of study. We needed to know how skilled our students were at studying a text, so we administered a baseline assessment by giving them a passage from Gayle Forman's *If I Stay*. We asked students to closely annotate what they noticed about the crafting of the text. The assessment revealed that most students had forgotten lessons in writing craft from the year before, or may have never learned to unpack the craft of great writing. Our plan was to administer this assessment again at the end of the year to gauge how students had grown in their ability to read like writers.

We also needed a baseline assessment of students' ability to write and revise, so we asked them to revisit the floor plans of their homes and apartments (see "Writing Connected to Place") and select one memory. We directed students to "keep the camera on one moment" and to develop the story of that moment as best they could. We expected our students had been taught about slowing down time, zooming in on a moment, or stretching out a scene, but we wanted to know what they had retained. We told students we wanted to see what they already understood about writing, and then we gave them twenty minutes to write. Students chose to do this writing either on paper or on the computer, and after they drafted we invited them to reread their writing and revise.

We maintained a folder for each student where we collected surveys and closely studied these baseline assessments (we did not grade them). We kept all on-demand writing and best drafts on Google Docs for portfolio evaluation at the end of the school year.

Notebook Assessment

We also collected students' notebooks after they had written their first seven or eight quick writes, and we looked at the passages they marked with sticky notes for us to read. Our goals in these initial readings were to understand what our students needed, to encourage them to keep going, and to reinforce that their notebooks were a safe place to practice. We left sparse comments, little "footprints" of encouragement—"This piece has lots of potential. I hope you consider developing it." Or "This is a great story. Thanks for sharing." We underlined phrases or lines we found moving. Our feedback said, *We are interested in what you have to say. Good start! Keep going!*

Our first look at our students' notebooks gave us new insight into specific writers—a closer look into their skills and potential areas of growth. Here are three things we learned.

Many students saw the writing notebook as a school assignment.

There was little or no ownership of its contents. Many of our students wrote the bare minimum and told us that they would write only when they had to. There was little or no writing done outside class. This prompted us to discuss ways to connect students more completely to their notebooks.

Conversation Clip

See "Helping Students Take Ownership of Notebooks"

Some students had written bravely and well.

We were already finding writing that we could use as models for other students, writing that explored deep thinking about students' lives and the stories they carry. We selected a few entries to share with the class (with permission, of course) to try and lift the level of writing and the attention to notebook work.

There were whole-class issues that needed to be addressed.
We found issues that needed immediate attention. Some students were writing "too large" (their topics were too broad and they were not zooming in). Many students were not paragraphing. Most were not using dialogue. Seeing these deficiencies told us which minilessons needed to be moved to the front of the line in our next lap around the narrative track.

CONSIDER *This...*

It took Kelly more than four hours to read thirty-eight freshmen notebooks (even though he was only lightly commenting on them). This pace was much slower than expected, and, truth be told, induced a sense of panic. It was probably not a coincidence that later that evening Kelly had a nightmare in which he was driving a car at a high rate of speed before discovering it had no brakes. But we also knew that everything takes longer at the start of a school year. We were interested in learning about individual students within our large classes, and we were not yet facing the mountain of student writing to assess. We had time to linger on the moves students were making in writing and the stories they chose to tell. We kept a running list of what we needed to teach the entire class.

◆ Lap Two: Crafting One Scene

With lots of writing ideas collected in students' notebooks, we moved to the second lap, where the goal was for each student to craft a single scene through multiple drafts. We would build off the work we did in lap one, where we'd shown students how to slow down time and to use sensory details to both show and tell, and we would focus our teaching on these narrative features and conventions:

- using dialogue to reveal character
- using the conventions of punctuating dialogue
- revising sentences and words to develop the voice and tone of the piece
- balancing show and tell.

Notebook Writing

By the time we began our second lap in the narrative study, read-write-revise-talk had become a regular rhythm in our classrooms and a template for planning our instruction. As we thought about where our students needed more practice, we selected the quick write seed for the next day (see Figure 6.7 for examples of seeds we used). We hoped this habit of daily writing would lead students to think about writing when they are not in class—seeing story ideas as they drive to school, as they deal with difficult customers at work, or as they cook dinner for their siblings. We spoke of our own notebooks as a collecting place and showed students where we found story ideas in our daily lives.

Mentor Text Study

We selected mentor texts that reflected a diversity of experiences and cultures; we believed these would not only engage our students but also demonstrate the features and conventions we expected them to use. We wanted students to swim in models of what they would be writing—models that would invite them to more skillfully identify the features of narrative texts.

Our first mentor text was Sherman Alexie's "Indian Education," a work of fiction. In the story, Junior, a character in Alexie's National Book Award–winning novel *The Absolutely True Diary of a Part-Time Indian*, recounts small, intense memories from his K–12 school experiences (the piece has one memory per grade level).

We first read the piece aloud and modeled some of what we noticed Alexie doing to create images and to engage us with the first scene in the story. We then asked students to work in pairs and continue reading other scenes with the following question in mind: "What moves and techniques employed by the writer make this an effective scene?" In groups, students shared what they noticed, and then—to remind them of our learning that day—we charted these craft moves on an anchor chart that hung on butcher paper in our classrooms. We expected students

Text That Invites Storytelling

"Portraits of Grief" (*New York Times* web page)

Photographs That Invite Storytelling

"Best Photographs of the Year" by *National Geographic* and *Time* magazines

We encouraged students to write from their favorite photographs.

Spoken Word Poems That Invite Storytelling

"What You Will Need in Class Today" by Matthew Foley

"Knock Knock" by Daniel Beatty

"Montauk" by Sarah Kay

Poetry That Invites Storytelling

"Where I'm From" by George Ella Lyon

"The Gift" by Li-Young Lee

"Nothing Is Lost" by Noel Coward

Excerpts from *Poem, Revised: 54 Poems, Revisions, Discussions*, edited by Robert Hartwell Fiske and Laura Cherry

"September Twelfth, 2001" by X. J. Kennedy

"For the Falling Man" by Annie Farnsworth

"Photograph from September 11" by Wisława Szymborska

Videos That Invite Storytelling

Mini-documentaries from "Untold Stories" project from Georgetown University

Student samples of mini-documentaries from previous classes

"Humans of New York" video series on YouTube

Figure 6.7 Notebook Seeds for Crafting a Scene

to refer to these charts as they wrote, and we referred to them as we conferred. Here are some of the writer's moves we captured on the charts in our classrooms:

Craft Moves in "Indian Education"

- brutally honest voice

- uses attitude ("reared back and pitched a knuckle fastball")

- details ("symmetrical bruises like war paint," "dragged their braids across the desk," "outstretched hands")

- summarizes well: quick and short, but still tells a story

- not beginning-middle-end stories, but zooms in on one moment

- effective dialogue.

Notice that the examples next to the craft moves come directly from the text. When we asked, "What did you notice?" and a student answered, "Details," we followed up by asking, "Can you give me an example from this text of where they were effective?" We recorded the examples to reinforce what it means to use details well in a story.

Though our students noticed a number of techniques employed by Alexie, three writing moves in particular stood out—the author's use of dialogue, sensory detail, and the strong narrator's voice. After these elements were identified, we brainstormed school memories in our notebooks, picked one, and began drafting with emphasis on these same three moves.

For many of our students, studying these moves was an eye-opener. Before this lesson, their notebook writing was often devoid of all three of these elements: no dialogue, no sensory detail, no voice. As you can see in Kim's draft, inspired by Sarah Kay's spoken word poem "Hands," many of our students didn't even bother to paragraph, thus creating horrifically large chunks of writing. After studying Alexie's moves in the mentor text, however, Kim's writing markedly improved as he applied these moves.

Kim's Initial Narrative Draft "My Hands"

People have always complimented my "candle-like" fingers and the smoothness of my palms. Normally if you're Filipino you have stubby fingers and rough skin.

Kim's Narrative Writing After Studying Alexie

"Line up against the wall!" ordered Ms. Loper. "Who wrote this?"

Five sweaty hands shot up in the air, with mine being one of them.

However for me, my hands are the opposite which I take pride in. Throughout my life so far, my hands have held, high-fived, waved, touched and shook many things. They allowed me to start new passions and hobbies such as photography, cooking, and tennis. And yet, there was one time in my life that I had hated them. It was back in fifth grade, almost 3 more days until summer, when I had used my hands to hurt another person. One of my closest friends had been pestering me and chose to use his hands to draw on my shirt with a marker. My annoyance and rage had consumed my clear thought, thus influencing me to use them to draw on his jacket. This led to pushing, slaps, and then punches. I'm not proud of what my hands did that day as I had lost a friend who I had often shook hands with. Nevertheless, this incident has taught me to control my anger, as my anger usually results in controlling my body and hands. Hands should be used to make new friends, for pats of the back, thumbs wars, secret handshakes, and all the . . .

It was the last day until winter break, and the whole 6th grade class was allowed to have a "Game Day." This meant that we could bring our video games from home and have a carefree day full of fun, and most importantly, no schoolwork. Like the rest of my hyperactive classmates, drunk on the sugar running through their veins from the sodas and candies given to us, I had brought my very own Nintendo D.S.

"Kim hurry up! Join our chat room," said my friend Andres.

I could have said "no thanks" or "maybe later," but I quickly accepted his invitation, thus bounding my fate in having to make a terrifying trip into the vice principal's office. One word, four letters, is all it took for me to feel like a criminal. Had I not foolishly typed and sent one message, I could have escaped the clutches of disappointment and embarrassment. Have you guessed it yet? I'll give you a hint, it rhymes with the word duck.

Fast forward to lunch, and there I am in line trying to get my food. "Kim!" and several other names were called.

"Oh boy, what could possibly be happening now?" I thought.

"The students that I just called, drop what you're doing and go to the hallway. Now!" commanded Ms. Loper.

And there we were. Standing, Sweating. Terrified against the cold brick wall. 5 minutes. 10 minutes. This was taking forever.

Then finally, one of Ms. Loper's students walked into the hallway and handed her a sheet of paper. I could've filled buckets with the amount of sweat perspirating from me and my friends. In my opinion, it would have been enough to fix our drought in California right now. . . .

Passage Study

To help students begin to develop voice and tone, we studied how sentence boundaries and punctuation can be used to craft writing. We combined a book talk with passage study using this excerpt from Maria Dahvana Headley's *Magonia* as a mentor text.

> Adults want to talk about death way less than people my age do. Death is the Santa Claus of the adult world. Except Santa Claus in reverse. The guy who takes all the presents away. Big bag over the shoulder, climbing up the chimney carrying everything in a person's life, and taking off, eight-reindeered, from the roof. Sleigh loaded down with memories and wineglasses and pots and pans and sweaters and grilled cheese sandwiches and Kleenexes and text messages and ugly houseplants and calico cat fur and half-used lipstick and laundry that never got done and letters you went to the trouble of handwriting but never sent and birth certificates and broken necklaces and disposable socks with scuffs on the bottom from hospital visits.
>
> And notes you kept on the fridge.
>
> And pictures of boys you had crushes on.
>
> And a dress that got worn to a dance at which you danced by yourself, before you got too skinny and too breathless to dance.
>
> Along with, probably, though this isn't worthy of huge thinking, a soul or something.
>
> Anyway, adults don't believe in Santa Claus. They try hard not to believe in Santa Claus in Reverse either.
>
> At school, the whole rare-disease-impending-doom situation makes me freakishly intriguing. In the real world, it makes me a problem. Worried look, bang, nervous face, bang: "Maybe you should talk to someone about your feelings, Aza," along with a nasty side dish of what-about-God-what-about-therapy-what-about-antidepressants?
>
> Sometimes also what-about-faith-healers-what-about-herbs-what-about-crystals-what-about-yoga? Have you tried yoga, Aza, I mean have you, because it helped this friend of a friend who was supposedly dying but didn't, due to downward dog? (2016, 5–6)

We gave each student a copy of the passage and then we read it aloud so students would carry the memory of how it sounds. Next, we asked students to name the qualities of this character that we understand from her rant about dying. We explained that sometimes narrators interrupt the plot to say something about life, and this helps us understand the character more deeply.

Finally, we asked pairs of students to work together to examine two elements of punctuation in the passage—the intentional use of a run-on sentence and the use of a repeated hyphen—and to make theories about why the author chose these punctuation moves. We can't know the "answer" since the author is not in class, but making theories about an author's craft deepens our understanding of writing as well as our analytical skills.

We had students focus on punctuation as a craft move to help them see that all elements of a text are chosen to communicate with readers. We asked students to consider, "What happens when we read a run-on sentence?" Mentor text study is about inquiry, and although only a few students recognized that the sentence made them breathless and weary, all students focused on how and why authors choose punctuation to communicate meaning. When we ask, "Why would the author choose a run-on sentence here?" we lead our students to understand that punctuation tells readers how to read the text. Figure 6.8 reveals two students' close reading of the punctuation used in *Magonia*.

During this lap of the study of narrative writing, we studied both whole scenes and short passages from published texts, and we also chose student model texts from our classes to bridge the distance between published authors and student writers. Figure 6.9 lists short passages from professional mentor texts you might use to teach narrative features.

Modeling Process

As students drafted their scenes, we continued to tinker with our drafts in front of them, making our writing a bit better each day. We also introduced the idea of feedback and its important role in the process of writing. For example, to show his students how to use feedback in the midst of writing a story, Kelly shared a draft about the time in seventh grade when he was sent

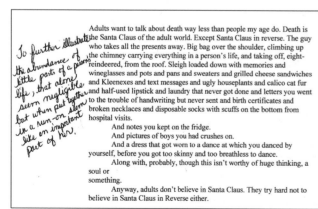

Figure 6.8 Student Notes on Passage from *Magonia*

What to Show Students	Text
How to use dialogue to develop characters	Passage from *Maybe a Fox* (Appelt and McGhee 2016, 13) "You and Dad," she said. "You're like a secret club." "What are you talking about?" "When the two of you get going about Mom. How do you think it makes me feel?" Sylvie looked puzzled. Jules kept going. "It's like you remember everything about her!" Jules rubbed her thumb along the smooth surface of the obsidian. "But me? I hardly remember anything. All I see when I try to picture her is her hair, which is exactly like . . . like . . ."
How to zoom in on one moment with sound details	Passage from *If I Stay* (Forman 2009, 15) And there was so much noise. A symphony of grinding, a chorus of popping, an aria of exploding, and finally, the sad clapping of hard metal cutting into soft trees. Then it went quiet, except for this: Beethoven's Cello Sonata no. 3, still playing. The car radio somehow still attached to a battery and so Beethoven is broadcasting into the once-again tranquil February morning.
How to slow down time	Passage from *LaRose* (Erdrich 2017, 160) They lifted their heads, dazzled, in the vast rumble of the engine. Their ears hurt. Occasionally bits of stone or gravel kicked up and stung like buckshot. Seams in the asphalt jarred their bones. Their bodies were pumped on adrenaline and a dreamlike terror also gripped them. On their stomachs, feet up, ankles curled around the bar, face-to-face, they clung fear-locked to their perch.
How to use humor in storytelling	Passage from *On Writing* (King 2010, 7) Eula-Beulah was prone to farts—the kind that are both loud and smelly. Sometimes when she was so afflicted, she would throw me on the couch, drop her wool-skirted butt on my face, and let loose. "Pow!" she'd cry in high glee. It was like being buried in marshgas fireworks. I remember the dark, the sense that I was suffocating, and I remember laughing.
How to use one-sided dialogue to show a conversation	Passage from *To Rise Again at a Decent Hour* (Ferris 2015, 23–24) She'd sniff at me like a bloodhound and then she'd say, "What exactly have you been doing?" I'd tell her, and she'd say, "Why do you feel the need to lie to me?" I'd tell her, and she'd say, "Scrutiny doesn't kill people. Smoking kills people. What kind of example do you think you're setting for your patients by sneaking off to smoke cigarettes?" I'd tell her, she'd say . . .
How to use details to create a setting	Passage from *Americanah* (Adichie 2014, 475) At first, Lago assaulted her; the sun-dazed haste, the yellow buses full of squashed limbs, the seating hawkers racing after cars, the advertisements on hulking billboards (others scrawled on walls—PLUMBER CALL 080177777) and the heaps of rubbish that rose on the roadsides like a taunt.

Figure 6.9 Mentor Text Passages for the Study of Narrative

continues

What to Show Students	Text
How to slow down time at a key moment	Passage from *All There Is: Love Stories from StoryCorps* (Isay 2012, 98) There was a building in flames underneath him, but Sean didn't even flinch. He stayed composed, talking to me, just talking to me the way he always did. I will always be in awe of the way he faced death. Not an ounce of fear: not when the windows around him were getting too hot to touch; not when the smoke was making it hard to breathe.
How to place one story in a larger history; the potential of a lead that engages a reader and focuses the story	Passage from *Caged Warrior* (Sitomer 2014, 4) Some kids have dads who raise them to be golfers. Others, quarterbacks. Still others to play tennis or soccer or baseball. I was raised to cage fight. Ever since I was three, my dad schooled me to brawl. Taught me to grapple, box, ground-and-pound, strike while standing up, and submit an opponent while lying down.
How to describe a character with a list	Passage from *Zac and Mia* (Betts 2016, 20) Mum's not a four-wall kind of woman. As long as I can remember, she's always had a straw hat and a sheen of sweat. She's hazel eyes and sun spots. She's greens and browns and oranges. She's a pair of pruning shears in hand. She's soil and pumpkins. She'd rather be picking pears or fertilizing olive trees than stuck in this room, with its pink reclining chair. More than anything, she's my dad's soul mate, though she won't go home when I ask her—even when I beg her.
How to open with setting details	Passage from the *New York Times* feature article "The Jockey" (Bearak 2013) Early mornings are a wondrous time on the backside of the racetrack. The shed rows are alive with pre-dawn activity, the stalls getting mucked out, the hay racks restocked, the feed tubs refilled. Floodlights partially sweep aside the darkness. Mist hangs in the heavy air. Seabirds swoop past in low arcs.

Figure 6.9 *Continued*

to the principal's office to get a swat (yes, corporal punishment was alive and well in the 1970s). Here is an excerpt from his first draft:

As I entered the principal's office I will admit I was nervous. I had never received a swat before (unlike my friend Kelly Worth, who received so many swats he began wearing multiple pairs of underwear to absorb the blows).

"You know why you are here," Mr. Large Principal said. "Turn and grab the table."

As I turned to grab the table, Mr. Large Principal reached up and grabbed his paddle, which was hanging on a hook on the wall behind his desk.

As Kelly's students read this passage, he asked them to flood his draft with questions. Students asked, "What was the principal's name? What was he like? What was the paddle like?" With these questions in mind, Kelly revised:

> As I entered the principal's office I will admit I was more than a bit nervous. I had never received a swat before (unlike my friend Kelly Worth, who received so many swats he began wearing three pairs of underwear daily to absorb any punishment that lay in his near future).
>
> "You know why you are here," said Mr. Patton, the principal. "Turn and grab the table." Mr. Patton was one of those principals who used to be a P.E. coach, and even though he was past his prime, he was one of those old dudes who really took pride in working out. By the looks of it, he was really into drinking Creatine shakes. The muscles bulging in his right arm told me this was going to hurt like hell.
>
> As I turned to grip the table, Mr. Patton reached for his paddle, which was hanging on a hook on the wall behind his desk. The paddle had an inscription in bright red letters: "The Board of Education."

Kelly put the two drafts of that passage side by side so students could easily see how their questions drove him to meaningful revision. The act of answering his students' questions helped him recall a detail he had forgotten (the name on the paddle).

We also exchanged drafts of scenes with one another, and we showed students what Penny learned from Kelly's reading of her work and vice versa, modeling how to respond to someone else's writing. Students were put in groups and asked to "question flood" their partners' papers. We asked them to trust each other as writers and to learn to give and receive feedback while in the process of shaping their writing.

Assessment in Lap Two

Each student turned in a "best draft" of the scene he or she had crafted. The timeline for work on this first scene was short for a reason. Although we had administered a baseline assessment of writing in the first lap, these scenes showed us what students understood about crafting a moment. We found numerous strengths in the drafts, but many students still told their stories superficially, skimming past details. Their first scenes showed us a need for additional direct teaching in order to empower them to craft a scene that invites readers to experience the moment.

Here are the evaluation descriptors we used to grade students' first scenes. These descriptors come from a schoolwide list of traits tied to the Common Core State Standards used at Penny's school, and we gave them to students before they started work on their best drafts.

Descriptors for Excellence in Narrative Scene Writing

The writing

- engages and orients the reader by setting out a problem, situation, or observation, establishing a point of view, and introducing a narrator

- uses dialogue, pacing, description, and reflection to develop experience, events, and/or characters

- creates a coherent whole with a smooth progression of events

- uses precise words and phrases, telling details, and sensory language to create a vivid picture

- polishes grammar and sentence structure.

CONSIDER This...

Daily reading and writing conferences proved invaluable for assessing student understanding, but we recognized a need to shorten them. Because it took longer than we had hoped to complete a full lap through all our students, we became conscious of trying to cut the length of our conferences. We studied Nancie Atwell's conferences shown in her *Writing in the Middle* DVD (2010), and we were struck by how focused and streamlined her conferences were. We wanted to confer with our students as often as possible, and to make this happen, we worked to shorten our conferences.

⤴ Lap Three: Crafting Several Scenes to Create a Story

By the time we started our third lap around the narrative track, students were more familiar with analyzing the structure of texts, so we selected more sophisticated writing for them to study. They would be expected to do more complex writing in this lap too, of course, crafting several scenes to tell a story. We planned to build on all the work we had done so far with individual scenes, but we would also turn more of our attention to planning the whole of a story. We planned to teach

- using a storyboard to plan the shape of a story
- recognizing the flexible structures in narrative writing (flashbacks and flash-forwards)
- rehearsing writing together (how it might go)
- reenvisioning a draft to imagine a different sequence of scenes
- tuning the narrator's voice with purpose: to draw a reader near or to keep the reader distant.

The hardest and most satisfying work in story writing often comes from playing with structure, and there are no formulas for how stories should go. The elementary idea of beginning-middle-end has been overused and we even read (with horror) about a program for middle and high school students in which they wrote *five-paragraph* stories. Instead of teaching a formula, we planned to explicitly teach the way stories are organized and to help students think through the options for their stories. These lessons would be clear and specific: identify how the story is introduced, how the author reveals the characters, what a flashback is and does in a story—not just where it occurs. We would present options and ask students to make decisions about their writing to increase ownership as well as to deepen critical thinking about the construction of their writing.

Mentor Text Study

For text study in this lap, we looked very closely at structure and how several scenes are woven together to create a story. On one day, we returned to Sherman Alexie as a mentor, studying a chapter from *The Absolutely True Diary of a Part-Time Indian*, "Why Chicken Means So Much to Me." We showed students how the chapter is structured—where scenes begin and end—and then put them in groups of three to study the text and make observations about writing-craft moves to add to our anchor chart. "Does this have the qualities of a great story?" we asked. When students study texts by the same author, they become familiar with the author's craft and can use that familiarity to go farther in their thinking. (It is similar to why a series of books deepens comprehension for students—they already know the characters and the setting, so they can think more deeply about plot and theme.)

We also used the text to study the narrative feature of character commentary, which is often used to develop a theme. If we map the plot of a story, these interruptions where characters speak about life do not advance the plot but rather deepen our understanding of the character. In this particular story, Alexie's narrator makes extended comments about living in poverty.

On another day we studied how a story is told in scenes in the opening chapter of Jeannette Walls' memoir, *The Glass Castle.* The writer moves from the taxi to her apartment and then to a restaurant. In each of these places, something happens. We had students identify where each of these scenes started and ended. We asked students to consider why the author told the three scenes in this order. What is the author trying to show here—and here—and here? (Walls is embarrassed when she sees her homeless mother rooting through a dumpster in the first scene, then feels guilty about it as she surveys her beautiful apartment in the second scene, and then invites her mother to a restaurant to show her concern and to offer help in the final scene.) The students underlined sensory details that helped them see and imagine the moment. We looked at how Walls uses dialogue in the final scene to develop the character of her mother—changing the reader's perception of her that was built in the first scene.

Modeling Process

How a writer determines the order of scenes in a story is complex and worthy of study, and the decision-making *process* is something we can't really learn from mentor texts where we only see the end result. We have to model this process for students, so we showed them how to take their scenes and consider their order. For example, Penny showed how, if she decided to write about the generosity of her father, she would imagine the scenes that show this throughout his life. Then she modeled by thinking out loud about the most effective order of those scenes to help maintain momentum and the interest of her readers.

After modeling the process, we had students create plans and then talk through "how the story

would go" in their writing groups. They explained the order of their scenes and asked others to give them feedback: "Is the order clear? Would another order of scenes be more effective?" Students learned about the flexibility of stories (there are many ways to tell the same story), but they also learned the importance of establishing a purpose for the whole of the story through the ordering of its parts. This is a transferable skill for all writing: we consider the whole of an essay as we write and revise it to create a through line that leads to our intended purpose.

Passage Study

As students began to work on their stories, we turned to passage study to deepen the earlier work we had done with punctuation and sentence structure as crafting tools. We showed students this passage from Kimberly Brubaker Bradley's *The War That Saved My Life* and asked them what they noticed:

> I slipped my hand into hers. A strange and unfamiliar feeling ran through me. It felt like the ocean, like sunlight, like horses. Like love. I searched my mind and found the name for it. Joy. (2016, 316)

We shared observations with the entire class, and we then asked students to imitate the structure and rhythm of sentences the author created—a process Tom Romano (2006) calls "copy change." To help them get started, we imagined possible sentence stems that corresponded to our students' lives—the fisherman, the skier, the band member:

> I slipped my hand around the fishing rod . . .
>
> I held the ski pole tight against me as I waited in the starting gate . . .
>
> I tightened my grip on the saxophone . . .

We created our own emulations in front of students. Penny wrote:

> My hand knit perfectly into his. A warm and familiar knowing ran through me. It felt like dawn in the dark of winter, like stars, like snow. Like silence. I rewound my life and found the name for it: contentment.

And in his classroom, Kelly wrote:

> I slipped my hand into the baseball glove. A nostalgic feeling ran through me. It felt like the early mornings on the Little League fields, like fall. Like childhood. I recalled the crack of the bat and found the name for it: innocence.

Our students followed:

> **Ramon:** *I slipped my body into a sousaphone. A lively feeling ran through my blood. I felt like energy, like sprinting, like electricity. Like Life. It ran through my body from my fingers to my mouth. That electrical charge, music.*

> **Ernesto:** *I pressed my palm against hers. Instantly, I surged with a new vibe. It felt wrong: like sleeping in someone else's bed. Like wearing someone else's shoes, like being far from home. Like distance. Searching, I found a name for it: moving on.*

> **Jonathan:** *I brushed my hand across her face. A new and frightening feeling crept through my veins. It felt like regret, like darkness, like a sinking ship. Like the goodbye you never got to say. Like the name for it: death.*

The process forced our students to reread, to study the punctuation and pay attention to the *sound* of the passage, and then to repeat the rhythm of short and long. It helped them experience the pleasure of tinkering with sentences.

⤴ Lap Four: Using Multiple Narrators to Craft a Story

Both of us play in our writing notebooks. It is a fail-free place where we think deeply about ideas and teaching practices, experiment with writing we'll share with students, and develop confidence as writers through regular practice. Because the writing notebook is a generative place, it leads us to the edge—to new thinking and possibilities. It is where we often find our best thinking.

One Saturday, Penny was playing in her notebook, planning a story from several points of view, and she knew instantly that the challenge of it was a perfect fit for her students, who were deeply engaged in this study of story. It would lift the level of her students' thinking—and in particular, their understanding of voice and point of view in writing. Many of them were reading the multinarrator stories so common in young adult fiction, and for students who were already navigating shifting points of view as readers, extending this narrative feature to their writing was a natural move.

There were other benefits as well. A multiple-narrator story confronts "the danger of a single story," a phrase used by Chimamanda Ngozi Adichie (2009) in her brilliant TED talk about the need for diverse books. Adichie explains, "It is impossible to talk about the single story without talking about power. How they are told, who tells them, when they are told, how many stories are told, are really dependent on power. . . . The single story creates stereotypes and the problem with stereotypes is not that they are untrue, but that they are incomplete. They make one story become the only story." We have all experienced this danger. We hear stories passed down that paint family members and friends in one way, when it is likely that if those people were given an opportunity to tell that same story, it would change. Our understanding would change. Imagine how deeply students will understand point of view if they *write* stories this way.

Penny could hear an echo of the essential question for the year: "How do others see the world differently than I do?" This helped her find a focus question for the unit: "How can multiple narrators deepen a reader's understanding of a story?"

CONSIDER This...

Penny sent pictures of her notebook thinking to Kelly and couldn't wait to plan this unit extension with him. Their conversation didn't go as she planned. After careful consideration, Kelly did not feel his students were ready for this extra lap through narrative. He felt writing multinarrator stories would confuse or frustrate his writers—many of whom were just achieving a tenuous confidence level for writing single-narrator stories. Kelly thought his students would be better served by continuing to hone their skills in writing single-narrator pieces, so we decided to parts ways for a couple of weeks.

As Penny planned, she considered all the skills and strategies she had taught her students in the three earlier laps, and then she mapped the new skills she planned to teach for multinarrator stories (see Figure 6.2). The unit was a risk, however. Penny had never written a story in which she gave several narrators a voice. There is an important energy in not knowing, however. We show students what we don't know and sometimes students find the solutions. They become the teachers. Willing to be vulnerable, Penny said to her students, "I'm not sure how to do this, but this is what I'm thinking." She invited them into the process of shaping her writing.

Penny began by modeling for her students. She brainstormed big ideas that could be worked out in fiction or memoir: coming-of-age, loss, friendship, betrayal, finding a passion,

Conversation Clip

See "Modeling the Struggle of Writing"

joy, persistence. Then she took one moment that happened when she was a child and used it to show the big idea at its core: her relationship with her older sister. She mapped out how different narrators would expand a reader's (and her own) understanding of the story/moment in time.

Penny planned quick writes to lead her students to ideas. She also planned to revisit some of her earlier minilessons, building understanding and a deeper retention of the skills or strategies she had taught, but this time with a specific focus on narrative voice (see Figure 6.10).

Penny's students spent several days gathering ideas for writing, and they moved forward in different ways. Some jumped right into writing scenes without having done much brainstorming. Others carefully crafted (and rearranged) storyboards before beginning their drafts. We believe writers can be productive when planning ahead and also when drafting without a plan. Both approaches work for us in our own writing, and we know many students who have written beautiful stories without having first created storyboards. We let students decide what kind of planning they need to do—as well as whether their narrative would be memoir or fiction. What's important is that they are writing as soon as possible.

As the first quarter ended, all of Penny's students had written multinarrator pieces. Some of them had finished best drafts while others were still in rough draft stages. Penny ran out of time to have her students polish this writing. If classrooms were true writing workshops, we would never run out of time, but most teachers live within the restrictions imposed by the school year and an insistence on regularly posting grades.

Quick Writes	Minilessons
Choose a person, and list moments with that person that had intense feelings for you. Write about one of these moments. Have "faith in a fragment" (Stafford 2003, 34).	In mentor texts with multiple narrators (*The Impossible Knife of Memory, Trash*), describe the differences in the qualities of the voices.
Consider objects that have mattered in your life; recall places you have loved—and how these objects or places might be seen differently by others.	Practice writing about the difference between what happened and what you (or another narrator) were thinking, using thoughtshots to develop internal dialogue.
Think about a big idea: jealousy, relationships, joy, love, loss. Put it on a timeline from your life and write about turning points.	In mentor texts, study movements forward and backward in time and then imitate the move between voices (a younger self and present day).
Flash draft with "show, don't tell" as a focus. Put the reader in that moment with you: show the difference between summarizing and storytelling. Write like a movie camera—zoom in—zoom past.	

Figure 6.10 Quick Writes and Minilessons for Multinarrator Stories

CONSIDER *This...*

Penny regretted cutting this unit short when the second quarter started—
and later in the year wondered if she had missed an important opportunity.
However, not every student was still completely engaged in writing these
stories. The yearlong clock was ticking, and there were still many units
waiting to be taught. The bottom line: Students need multiple opportunities
to understand the moves of a genre as complex as narrative. After reflecting
on the unit, we both decided to begin the next school year with a revised
guide to the study of story that included a final lap of multinarrator stories.

✈ Closing Thoughts: A Foundation of Trust

Beginning the year by teaching narrative writing not only provided our students with skills they used when writing in all genres but also eased them out of dormancy and into establishing a daily writing habit. It helped many of them begin to see themselves as writers again. It established the habits of writing.

But starting the year with narrative writing went deeper than that. When students wrote in a classroom that valued their stories—in a classroom that encouraged them to experiment, to take risks—something happened more than students simply developing their writing skills. They opened up to us. We opened up to them. As a result, we developed connections with them—connections that humanized our classrooms and helped our students find their voices as writers. When a student asks for help in shaping her piece about living in the shadow of her father's alcoholism, something happens that is bigger than simply teaching her to write better.

"Stories matter," Chimamanda Ngozi Adichie (2009) says. "Many stories matter. Stories have been used to dispose and to malign, but stories can also be used to empower and humanize. Stories can break the dignity of a people but they can also be used to repair that broken dignity."

Our stories and students' stories brought us together. Sharing them established a foundation of trust we would build upon as we moved from narrative writing and into the teaching of other discourses.

INFORMATIONAL

We are a culture hungry for information. We consume much of it online: a summary of the college football game we couldn't stay awake to watch, information on breeds of dogs we want to consider when we select our next puppy, details about a country we plan to visit for the first time. Our students are part of this culture, too. They read to understand the roots of a new band they've just discovered or to decide where to purchase a prom dress. We know before we ever start this unit that our students will recognize the moves of informational writing as readers. Over the course of the study, they will practice these moves regularly as writers.

Writing what we know and understand in order to inform others is deeply intellectual work. The proliferation of teacher blog posts that explain practices and beliefs has been a positive move for our profession in the last decade, not the least because all writers learn as they write. The writing process itself shapes our thinking and refines it. We understand planning and teaching better when we try to explain it to others. As we write, we wonder about our work and deepen our engagement with our own beliefs and ideas about teaching.

This unit of study is designed to foster an intellectual disposition toward texts, as best summarized by Tom Newkirk (2009), former director of writing programs for university students at the University of New Hampshire. We made a small chart with these habits listed on it (see Figure 7.1) and had students glue it into their notebooks. We referred to them often throughout the study.

For our college-bound students, writing to explain research and respond to ideas and information is a basic expectation regardless of major. Likewise, a person who is able to explain information well in writing is likely to move ahead in the workplace faster than someone who struggles to explain his thinking in clear and effective prose. No matter the career plans of our students, a study of informational writing is relevant.

Composing a unit of study of this genre *today*, however, stretches our thinking. Many informational texts are now composed with a combination of text and media. Our students rely primarily on visual images to share what they are thinking and experiencing, and most of us wouldn't dream of sending an email or posting news about a trip without attaching photos with

Habits of Mind

1. *The habit of observation.* What do you notice? This is the capacity to slow down, pay attention, notice the unusual detail, fact, or statistic—one that is not evident at first glance.

2. *The habit of generalization.* A key question is "What do you make of this?" What inferences, judgments, evaluations, conclusions, theses do you arrive at? It is to think in patterns, to make connections.

3. *The habit of evidence.* What is the basis of your generalizations? And what makes you think this evidence is solid, when there is so much suspicious information available?

4. *The habit of considering alternatives.* How could it be otherwise? What credible positions might differ from yours? What are the "rivals" to your own position?

Figure 7.1 Newkirk's Habits of Mind (2009, 142)

captions or hashtags. A new computer comes with a video tutorial instead of a printed guide. A doctor uses audio-to-text technology to take notes on a patient. The news is filled with info-graphics, so we consume a great deal of information in bite-size pieces. Today we all write in the form most engaging and easily consumed by those who need the information. Informational texts have moved far beyond the annual school research paper. Has our teaching?

Planning a Study in Informational Writing

Our journey through this unit echoed many of the features we introduced in our study of narrative texts. To help our students increase skills and understandings in this genre, we immersed them in expository texts, stopping frequently to notice the moves and techniques found in this discourse. We continued our daily book talks, but this time we included more books of nonfiction.

In any study we plan, we know that learning the features of a genre will help students as writers, but doing so will also change them as readers. This is especially important with infor-mational writing. We have both shared fake news stories with our students as if the news was real and been horrified when not a single student has questioned the article's source or validity.

Teaching Clip

See Kelly's book talk "*Thing Explainer*, by Randall Monroe"

With the amount of unreliable information in the world today, students need voluminous critical reading practice, so we frame all our teaching in this unit around a few critical questions about informational texts:

- Who wrote this?
- Who is the intended audience?
- What is the purpose of *this* information?
- Why is the information presented and organized in this way?
- What is said?
- What is not said?

We want our students to understand these questions deeply both as consumers and producers of informational texts, so in each lap of the study, we plan to teach skills for both reading and writing.

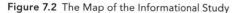 Time and Expectations

We planned four weeks for the study, with three distinct laps around the track of informational writing. The research and summary writing that stretches across the unit lays an important foundation for the argument unit that follows. We want students to infuse information into their arguments, so we intentionally teach them in this order. Figure 7.2 shows a map of our plan for practice in this genre.

The building block for narrative writing is a scene. The building block for texts that inform or explain is the summary. Just as we did with narrative, we plan to teach a progression of skills for composing texts in the genre. In the first lap, students will practice reading and summarizing information from a variety of increasingly complex infographics. In the second lap, they'll use that skill to write an engaging and effective review. The complexity of reviews will increase as students move from studying restaurant reviews to the *New York Times Book Review*. Finally, students will use digital tools to craft an informational movie. (The study of digital texts will move from book trailers and commercials in this unit to campaign ads in our next unit, argumentation). As

Week	Mapping the Writing Year: Informational Texts
1–4 Throughout the study	Notebook practice: read and write next to infographics, photo essays, informational videos, and a combination of texts; practice combining information into cohesive, clear summaries
2–3	Restaurant, book, or movie review and/or writing with research to inform and explain a complex idea in a feature article
3–4	Revisiting informational writing: a digital text

Figure 7.2 The Map of the Informational Study

projects increase in complexity, students are expected to compose effectively both individually and on a team: listening to others, sharing thinking, combining understandings, and prioritizing information into coherent, collaborative texts. Figure 7.3 shows the progression of skills across the three laps we planned.

Lap One: Interpret and Communicate Understanding of an Infographic in a Summary	**Lap Two:** Synthesize Information from a Variety of Sources to Write Accurate Summaries as Well as Fair and Effective Reviews	**Lap Three:** Synthesize Information About Your Community or Culture in a Digital Movie
Read like writers to develop an understanding of the craft and meaning of infographics.	Read like writers to notice effective writing craft in reviews of restaurants, movies, and books.	Read like writers and track your engagement to analyze what makes a digital text (book trailer, commercial) effective.
Read the scale and locate the key for understanding images or colors in infographics, charts, tables, and graphs.	Listen to informational podcasts and read articles that present complex information in a cohesive way, then summarize the key elements.	Analyze the balance and the impact of images (both still and in motion), voice-overs, music, and text in a digital composition.
Analyze headings and subheadings and the intentional order of information.	Recognize patterns of summarizing information.	Study how the pace of your movie affects engagement and understanding. Ask: What will the viewer be thinking here?
Locate the source of information, analyze the credibility, and incorporate an attribution in your summary.	Recognize how language informs and where it persuades.	Tighten elements of your movie for maximum impact. Cut to focus the whole of the text: leaner, clearer, stronger.
Consider multiple points of view on the information and their impact on understanding.	Identify the multiple sources of information used: first-person accounts, authors/owners, data on sales or statistics that compare things.	Tune your voice to inform with passion.
Summarize the big idea of the infographic in one sentence, then expand your thinking to question or respond with new ideas, using supporting evidence from the infographic.	Recognize what is withheld or minimized in a review and why.	Revise language to craft the tone of your piece.
Consider the order of the evidence in your summary: important first, less important next, most important last.	Engage readers with specificity of information.	Share your movie in a small group or with the whole class.
	Develop the review with significant examples and relevant information.	Listen to feedback and revise to clarify, develop, and extend your thinking about the subject.
	Adjust the order of information, elaborating or contracting the writing to improve clarity and engagement.	Proofread, edit, and polish.
	Use word choice appropriate for the domain and to engage your audience and to explain unfamiliar terms.	
	Listen to your writing at the sentence level and make it clearer and stronger.	
	Proofread, edit, and polish.	

Figure 7.3 The Laps We Planned for Informational Writing

✷ Lap One: Summarizing from Infographics

Writing next to infographics gives our students an opportunity to develop several important skills. First, we want them to be able to translate charts, tables, and graphs of information into clear, cohesive sentences that explain the information. We respond to the information in quick writing because infographics invite thinking. We connect the information to our experiences and beliefs, and we encourage students to use information presented in the infographics to spark thinking about their own ideas. Why? Making connections leads to deeper comprehension. Students write beside the infographic to explain their thinking (see Figure 7.4). As they write, we also have them practice crediting the source of the information.

We use the study of infographics to sharpen inference skills. When reading a new infographic, we ask two questions: (1) What does the graph say? and (2) What does the graph not say? This second question is key, as we want our students to understand that what is *not said* is often as important as what is said. The infographic is crafted with intention. *How* it is crafted is an essential understanding: writers select information to support an idea and omit information they feel is unnecessary or they want to conceal. Information might be omitted in hopes that readers or viewers will be distracted or impressed by other information and not notice its absence. When

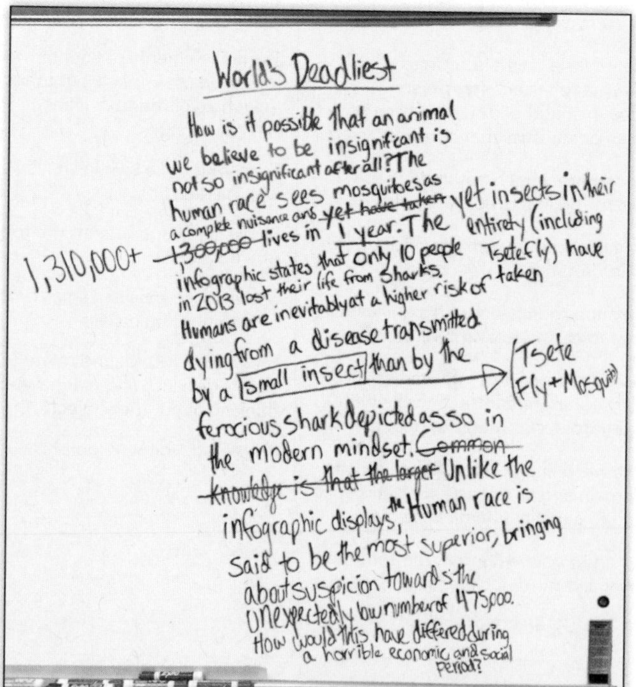

Teaching Clip
See "Writing Next to an Infographic"

Figure 7.4
Example of a Student's Quick Write Next to an Infographic

our students studied an infographic titled "Falsehood Face-Off," they created T-charts to answer both of these questions (see Figure 7.5). Demonstration writing is critical here. We both think out loud as we make our own charts, sometimes writing in prose and sometimes in lists.

Infographics raise all the critical questions that frame the study. We choose them carefully, however, as there are many inaccurate or distorted summaries of information. We choose from a wide array of sources (one example: the *New York Times*' "The Year in Visual Stories and Graphics"), and we often provide students with copies of *Upfront* magazine, a news magazine jointly published by Scholastic and the *New York Times*.

With copies of *Upfront* in hand, we asked our students to notice how information was conveyed through the use of text, graphics, photographs, and page design. We started anchor

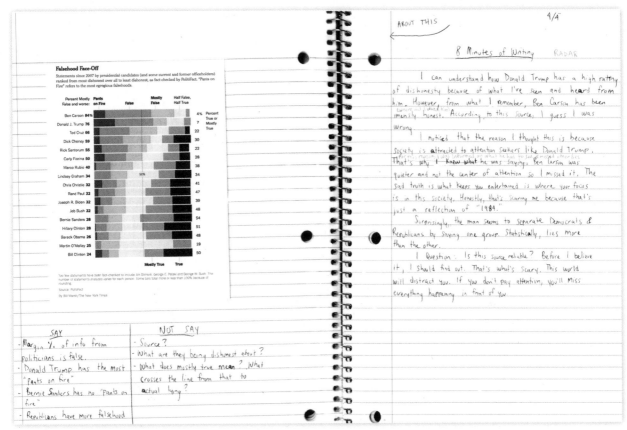

Figure 7.5 Example of Student T-Chart: What's Said / What's Not Said

Teaching Clip

See "Similarities
and Differences in
Narrative Writing"

charts to record the kinds of "moves" we noticed writers making in this genre, noting how these moves were similar to and different from those we had studied in narrative writing. We noted that writers

- lead with information

- establish a connection with a reader using a voice of authority or expertise

- establish their credibility

- organize information so it's easily readable

- use vivid details to define a problem

- pay attention to word choice so complex things are easier to understand.

After reading a number of *Upfront* articles, students chose "hot spots" from their reading and responded to these in brief entries in their notebooks.

Over the course of the week, we provided students with a number of other "seeds" to spur writing to inform others (see Figure 7.6). Approaches to this work varied, depending on the needs of the class. Sometimes we asked students to discuss the infographic in small groups first and to list observations together, then choose one fact or idea and write about it. At other times they wrote individual summaries first, then compared and discussed with a partner, then with a group of four students. Talk supports thinking and writing, so we encouraged a lot of it. While students were talking, we looked at their writing to see how well they understood the qualities of an effective summary. We looked for examples of lively language, cohesive thinking, and the use of facts to support ideas that we could share with the whole class. Once students had finished a number of quick writes over the course of a week, they each selected a seed to develop into a short, effective summary.

Notebook Seeds to Spur Daily Writing

"The Cost of Raising a Child" (USDA.gov)

"My Youth in 27 Records" by Questlove (Vulture.com)

"Cold Calculations: The Price of Being Wounded" (Washingtonpost.com)

"World's Deadliest Animals" (Gatesnotes.com)

Illustrated Interviews from the *New York Times Magazine* (Doppelt, nytimes.com)

"Deaths in Daycare" (Washingtonpost.com)

"The Boy-Band Blueprint" (visual.ly)

"How Lego Licensed the Universe, and Ended Up Ruling Us All" (Wired.com)

Figure 7.6 Infographics as Notebook Seeds

✒ Lap Two: Writing a Review

We believe the ability to summarize is a critical writing skill, and one that our students need to practice more, so in this second lap we expanded our summary writing to include short, everyday informational texts. We studied and summarized short Ted talks, podcasts such as *Left, Right, and Center,* as well as other texts. In doing so, we also showed students that summarizing could be done in different ways. For example, on one day we wrote next to "My Youth in 27 Records" by Questlove and thought about how to focus on a vivid summary of why one song matters to us. We looked at interviews in magazines to see how to summarize a person or an idea. We shared a column from *ESPN The Magazine* entitled "Six Things You Should Know About . . ." We shared variations of this idea, including "My Life in Numbers." We had students create glossaries of key terms for activities they love.

Teaching Clip
See "Writing About Meaningful Songs"

After studying these different possibilities, students selected topics, researched them, and then drafted a summary in a form they chose. Their topics varied greatly, from six things you should know about Taylor Swift to a glossary of strategies for the video game *Call of Duty.* For this middle lap assignment, students were asked to cite at least one source, and we conducted a minilesson on how to create both in-text citations and a works cited page.

In this lap, we also studied a variety of restaurant, movie, and book reviews. We showed students how to analyze the style of particular writers and publications over time: for example, Anthony Bourdain's *Parts Unknown,* the *New York Times Book Review, Thug Notes* (YouTube), and John Green's *Crash Course in Literature* (YouTube). Students chose a product and wrote a Yelp! review.

Like you, we have students who work at different rates and with different levels of understanding. We invited our students who needed a challenge in this lap to blend genres in order to create a multigenre feature article on a topic of choice. Each article had to center around a central topic and include at least four separate "pieces" that explored the topic in greater detail. Louis, for example, wrote his feature article about his favorite football player, Dez Bryant of the Dallas Cowboys. These were Louis' four pieces:

Piece 1: Bryant's biography

Piece 2: A closer look at the numerous obstacles Bryant had to overcome to reach the NFL

Piece 3: A retelling of Bryant's greatest game

Piece 4: Charts and graphs that recapped Bryant's career highlights.

Once the pieces were written, students were asked to format them into a feature article. They wrote headlines for each piece and inserted visuals (photos, charts, graphs, art).

⚡ Lap Three: Crafting a Digital Project

As a culmination to the information unit, we decided to push the boundaries of traditional school writing and have our students compose short, digital informational texts. This lap in informational writing occurred after a break in our schedules for Penny's midterm exams, allowing time for students to revise literary essays and write in cross-country book clubs.

Going into our planning, we knew that many of Kelly's students did not have computers at home, so time to create the projects would have to be built into the school day (and provided before and after school). We could have taken this work in a variety of directions, but we decided to use the project to connect our students across the country. First, we had our students read, analyze, and emulate George Ella Lyon's poem "Where I'm From," making lists to describe where they are from. We chose this poem because our students come from very different cultural backgrounds, and we wanted to provide them with an opportunity to open their worlds to one another. After the quick write, students shared ideas. Figure 7.7 shows the list Penny's students brainstormed about living in rural New Hampshire.

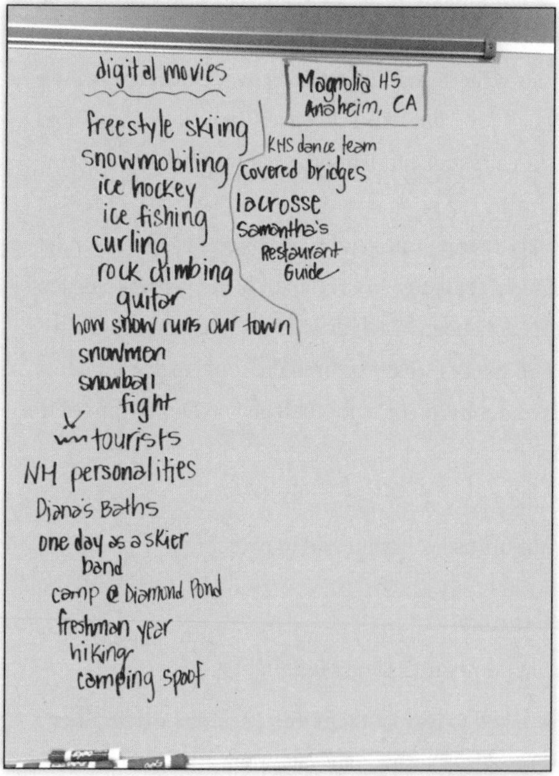

Figure 7.7 Ideas Brainstormed by Penny's Students About Life in Rural New Hampshire

Teaching Clip

See "Making an Informational Movie"

To help our students choose one topic for their digital projects, we explained that the question "Where am I from?" can be answered in many ways. Kelly, for example, is literally from Huntington Beach, California, but he is also from generations of baseball lovers, from Edison High School, and from years of visiting the public library. He could have focused his digital project on any of these things, but to try to include all would force him to treat each one superficially. We wanted these movies to explore one element in depth.

To help our students draft storyboards for a digital project, we created and shared storyboards of our own. We told our students that these storyboards were analogous to first draft essays—they would need to be revised as we moved closer to creating them. Students paired up to imagine their storyboards, and once they had them in place, we demonstrated how to turn storyboards into digital projects.

CONSIDER This...

We each polled our classes to see what expertise we had at hand. Some students knew how to create iMovies. Some were proficient in using Google Slides (with audio). Others possessed skills with other programs, like Movie Maker. Though there were a number of students who were not proficient in any of these programs, we decided there was enough expertise in our classrooms that students could learn from one another. And by devoting time to this work in class, we allowed those students to become teachers of their peers—and of *us*. Kelly, for example, did not know how to make an iMovie, but rather than hide his inexperience, he worked beside students who did, and they taught him how.

Conversation Clip

See "Modeling the Risk of Trying Something New"

We both created our own "Where I'm From" videos in iMovie, and we modeled revising our movies—adding here, deleting there, tinkering with the sequence—to show that the process of crafting a digital piece is very similar to the process of writing an essay. Penny, for example, first created a corn maze movie to highlight the October traditions in New England. She knew this tradition would be unfamiliar to California students. After a short bit of work on it, she became more interested in how bears come out of the woods and into town in the spring. She showed her students her thought process as she took a first draft of her movie, which included her own story of seeing bears in her yard, and then made it better in a second draft by including student stories of bear encounters. The audience is students, and her refinements were meant to better connect to that audience. Students evaluated her second draft as they were shaping their own films. (Both drafts are posted on Penny's YouTube channel.) In his classroom Kelly modeled his process as well, creating an "I'm from Huntington Beach" movie so that Penny's students could get a glimpse into Southern Californian surf culture (Kelly's video is posted on his website).

Our students' investment in making movies was intensified by the knowledge that they would be sharing their projects with students across the country. By this time the students had exchanged emails, had shared thinking about *Romeo and Juliet*, and had been in book clubs together. The connection between schools was a natural part of our work. Additionally, this cross-country sharing of projects produced a rich cultural exchange between our classes. When Penny's student ("I'm from a family of hunters") traded his video with Kelly's student ("I'm from a family that celebrates quinceañeras"), they stepped into unfamiliar worlds. In a time of deep polarization in this country, our students took strides toward learning from other cultures.

Upon completion, we had students self-evaluate their digital projects using the guidelines in Figure 7.8.

Category	Excellence in Digital Composition
Organization	A clear purpose is established early on and a focus is maintained throughout the movie. Images and video are organized to best engage a viewer. The ending brings closure to the subject.
Pacing	The pacing of photographs and video maintains audience interest. Voice-overs are paced well for easy listening and comprehension. There is adequate time to read text slides.
Images	The images are visually pleasing and communicate the tone of the piece. Thought went into the placement of the person being interviewed with the background of the setting.
Media	There is a combination of photographs and video (or recorded voice-over) as well as text slides when needed and music that matches the topic appropriately. Music and video are adjusted to maintain a comfortable sound level for the audience.
Editing	All spelling and punctuation is correct on text slides. Transitions are creative and do not distract viewers between sections of the video.

Figure 7.8 Descriptors for Excellence in Digital Composition

CONSIDER *This...*

Once we show students who have never attempted to compose digitally the basics in design and thinking, they run with it. Digital work is intoxicating. We find students will spend hours composing movies, public service announcements, and book trailers, far beyond what we assign them to do. For example, when we showed models of book trailers in class, several groups of students crafted their own to add to our classroom websites.

The digital work we received from our students ranged from awful to brilliant, but even the students who produced substandard work gained value from their initial forays into digital composition. How do we know this? As this is being written, the ninth graders we describe in this book are now tenth graders, and Kelly has looped with his class. As part of a recent inform/ explain unit, Kelly selected the topic of "Magnolia High School" and asked students to create digital projects. Under this topic, students were allowed to choose what they wanted to showcase. Here were some of the topics they created:

- a "Humans of Magnolia" project (based on Brandon Stanton's popular *Humans of New York*)
- an MHS campus tour
- a day in the life of an MHS student
- "Ten Things You Should Know About MHS"
- a specific program at MHS (e.g., band, football)
- a specific person at MHS (e.g., the principal, a faculty member)
- a look at the history of MHS
- famous alumni

Many of those freshman students who once created poor digital projects had now morphed into sophomores whose skills had flourished. Penny noticed the same impressive growth with the students she had again as sophomores as well. Students in both schools submitted projects that were leaps and bounds better than the ones they had created the year before. They did a much better job weaving in graphics and music. They were more aware of capturing proper lighting and sound. Their editing was cleaner, crisper. Their progress in one short year was truly stunning.

But why? We had not taught them anything new, so why did our students improve so much in one year's time? We think it comes down to this: doing something well often means we begin by doing it poorly. Rarely is a complex task learned instantly. Instead, learning something like how to make a movie involves a large learning curve—one filled with numerous trials and errors. Although many of our students' initial forays into digital work resulted in poor products, they learned a lot from the process—learning they built upon when asked to do it again.

CONSIDER *This...*

In our year together, our students used Google Docs to share their writing with one another across the country, they created public service announcements, they recorded dramatic readings, they exchanged "Where I'm From" movies. We liked how these technologies deepened our students' thinking. And though we were pleased with these projects, we realized that there was room in our curriculum to weave in more digital work.

This year, we are using Padlet and TodaysMeet so that students can interact within and between classes. We are using Flipgrid so students can post digital book reviews, article-of-the-week reflections, and poetry readings. We also connected our seniors in cross-country book clubs to sophomores at Miami University using both Flipgrid and Google Docs to extend their thinking about books they read together. We know our students swim in digital texts outside class, so we bring them and study them, expanding an understanding of composition for our young writers.

✒ Using Texts as Mentors Across the Study

Engaging texts packed with information are the key to inquiry in this unit. We find it is most effective to use current news articles (the *New York Times* multimedia feature articles are favorites of ours) or to pull from journals and magazines that align with the interests of our students. We study some texts as a whole class, of course, but we can also gather several texts on a variety of topics and let students form groups based on interest in the subject. A *Sports Illustrated* article on Tom Brady will engage Penny's football fans, but she'll engage more students in the reading and analysis of informational writing if she provides other options for those who don't love football. A collection of six articles in a class of thirty is bound to align with the interests of most students. The other bonus to this approach is that when students study different texts in small groups, they do not rely as easily on the thinking of a few students in class. Engagement and talk increases within smaller groups of students. It is harder to hide or to "hitchhike" in a small-group setting.

Sentence Study

We value sentence study practice because all students can lift their writing by focusing on just one skill at a time, but sentence study becomes even more empowering when we link the skills writers use across genres. Informational texts often persuade and narrate as well. We want students to see the way text types blend, so we name the skills we have learned in our study of narrative that transfer to texts than inform or explain. Sometimes we even return to the same sentences and passages we have studied in other genres. For example, specific detail is important to both narrative and informational writing, so students in Penny's class studied and imitated the following mentor sentence from the first page of Paul Fleischman's *Seedfolks* (2004) in both units: "I stared at my father's photograph—his thin face stern, lips latched tight, his eyes peering permanently to the right." In notebooks, her students practiced using the dash to give specific information.

In the narrative unit, Penny spoke aloud as she wrote an imitation in front of her class: "I watched Yukari drive while I rode shotgun—her dark hair . . ." She stopped midsentence and told the class, "Wait a minute. I need to put *Yukari* directly before the dash so the reader knows all of the description that follows is connected to her." When used skillfully, the dash should immediately follow the subject of elaboration. Penny then corrected her imitation: "I rode shotgun and watched Yukari—her dark hair lit by the streetlights, eyes squinting through the rain, the window cracked so she could flick the ash from her cigarette onto the pavement." This deliberate modeling helps students avoid practice that reinforces bad habits.

While writing restaurant reviews during the informational unit, Penny went back to this same mentor sentence from Paul Fleischman and had students imitate it once again to describe a meal at a favorite local restaurant. Penny modeled her imitation first: "At Delaney's I ordered the Sicilian bruschetta—a crusty French loaf brushed with garlic basil butter, a heap of sun-dried tomatoes, and Parmesan cheese, finished with a dunk into homemade marinara." And her student

Matt followed with his own: "My mouth waters for Delaney's hickory burger—cheddar cheese from Sherman Farms, sizzling applewood-smoked bacon, and a slab of meat brushed with maple jalapeno BBQ sauce. Grab an extra napkin to mop the juicy slime off your cheek between bites."

CONSIDER This...

Even our best demonstrations sometimes leave students needing more support. When Penny walked by Robert's desk the first time he practiced using a dash to elaborate, she saw that he had written in his notebook: "I studied the defensive lineman while we waited for the snap—his neon green mouthguard. . . ." She stopped him before he went further and said, "I love this image of you at the scrimmage line, but it looks like you made the same mistake I did." Robert glanced up to the whiteboard and Penny's model sentence, still with its cross-outs and improvements. He then corrected his writing: "While we waited for the snap, I studied the defensive lineman—his neon green mouthguard, eyes gray and angry, his sweaty forehead pinned beneath his helmet."

This in-time feedback was important for Robert and for other students who were seated nearby. Looking at students' work while they are writing helps us see how well students understand what they are imitating. It saves us from making notes in notebooks later, and it prevents students from practicing incorrectly.

Passage Study

For passage study, we looked for mentors who showed students how to lift writing beyond the simple delivery of information to an engaging, must-read piece. For example, we studied these opening two paragraphs from David Grann's *New Yorker* piece "Trial by Fire: Did Texas Execute an Innocent Man?" (2009):

> The fire moved quickly through the house, a one-story wood-frame structure in a working-class neighborhood of Corsicana, in northeast Texas. Flames spread along the walls, bursting through doorways, blistering paint and tiles and furniture. Smoke pressed against the ceiling, then banked downward, seeping into each room and through crevices in the windows, staining the morning sky.
>
> Buffie Barbee, who was eleven years old and lived two houses down, was playing in her backyard when she smelled the smoke. She ran inside and told her mother, Diane, and they hurried up the street; that's when they saw the smoldering house and Cameron Todd Willingham standing on the front porch, wearing only a pair of jeans, his chest blackened with soot, his hair and eyelids singed. He was screaming, "My babies are burning up!" His children—Karmon and Kameron, who were one-year-old twin girls, and two-year-old Amber—were trapped inside.

Students shared what they noticed in small groups first, and then we came together to chart the specific writing tools the author used to craft facts into hauntingly beautiful prose. Look at all they highlighted in just two paragraphs:

- a lead that engages readers by creating an image with sensory details and dialogue
- a dependent clause that delivers information in the first sentence of each paragraph
- active verbs: *bursting, blistering, pressed, banked, seeping, staining*
- the use of the dash to signal elaboration.

Sentence Templates

Many students benefit from standing next to mentor sentence frames that help them enter an existing academic conversation. Penny has used *They Say/I Say: The Moves That Matter in Academic Writing* (Graff and Birkenstein 2014) as a core text in her research writing course for seniors for years, and the book is used by hundreds of colleges and universities to guide freshmen composition courses. The "They Say / I Say" templates help students move beyond simply citing a source to writing effectively using the source combined with their own thinking. She had students paste the templates (see Figure 7.9) into their writing notebooks to use during the informational study and then again later in the argument study.

time / MODELING NOTEBOOK

Why Templates?

Academic writing requires presenting your sources and your ideas effectively to readers. According to Gerald Graff and Cathy Birkenstein (2014), the first element in the process involves "entering a conversation about ideas between you—the writer—and your sources to reflect your critical thinking" (ix). The templates allow you, the writer, to organize your ideas in relationship to your thesis, supporting evidence, opposing evidence, and conclusion of the argument.

The Most Important Templates

On the one hand, _____. On the other hand, _____.

Author X contradicts herself. At the same time that she argues _____, she also implies _____.
I agree that _____.
She argues _____, and I agree because _____.
Her argument that _____ is supported by new research showing that _____.
In recent discussions of _____, a controversial issue has been whether _____. On the one hand, some argue that _____. On the other hand, others argue that _____.

Introducing Standard Views

Americans today tend to believe that _____.
Conventional wisdom has it that _____.
My whole life I have heard it said that _____.

Making Those Views Something You Say

I have always believed that _____.
When I was a child, I used to think that _____.

Writing a Summary

She demonstrates that _____.
In fact, they celebrate the fact that _____.

Introducing a Quote

X insists, " _____. "
As the prominent philosopher X puts it, " _____. "
According to X, " _____. "
In her *Book Title*, X maintains that " _____. "
X complicates matters further when she writes that " _____. "

Disagreeing

I think that X is mistaken because she overlooks _____.

I disagree with X's view that _____ because, as recent research has shown, _____.

Introducing Your Point of View

X overlooks what I consider an important point about _____.
I wholeheartedly endorse what X calls _____.
My discussion of X is in fact addressing the larger issue of _____.
These conclusions will have significant applications in _____ as well as in _____.

Source: Graff and Birkenstein 2014

Figure 7.9 "They Say / I Say" Templates

✈ Modeling the Process of Crafting Informational Texts

In all three laps of the study, we modeled for our students how we read and write informational texts. We showed them how we do not just consume facts but rather hold them next to our experiences and consider their validity. We question what we know and have experienced. We shared our natural curiosity and built relationships with our students in unscripted moments.

When we wrote next to infographics with our students, we changed our teaching based on the needs of the class. Sometimes we modeled our first thinking in one class and then extended the writing in the next class to show how thinking develops over time. And when students in a class needed more or less support, we were more or less explicit in our demonstrations.

Students need to see demonstrations of how people compose differently—from first-draft thinking to complicated revisions— so we also invited students to model for each other. Penny often had a student serve as a quick-writer-of-the-day and model thinking and writing alongside her on the whiteboard. When this is a regular practice, over the course of the school year many examples of the writing process are shared.

When some students struggled to get started, we kept writing, careful not to swoop in when things got difficult. We gave students time and space to write without the pressure of being watched. In the preface to the twentieth-anniversary edition of Don Graves' seminal work *Writing: Teachers and Children at Work* (2003) Don wrote about the importance of a room of writers all struggling together and how it affects student initiative. "Good teachers conduct their lessons using either their or their students' texts. Students acquire much of their learning by observing their teacher or their peers share their work in process" (xiv). We demonstrated our engagement and struggle to find words, and this encouraged our students to seek the "right" words to match their ideas.

✈ Minilessons to Support Informational Writing

Throughout the unit, we read student work to determine the skills students needed in whole-class instruction or in reteaching in small groups. We also studied the lists of observations students made about mentor texts to see where they needed additional practice. From this assessment, we designed minilessons around these ideas:

- creative ways to list several elements of information
- organizational frames (images, ideas, questions)

- transitional phrases and sentences

- strong leads and endings

- combining big ideas to compare or contrast them to improve a reader's understanding of the information

- breaking down a complex idea into parts

- asking questions of your writing as a reader might

- tracking the moves of the piece: introducing the subject, elaborating on the idea, igniting an interest in the topic, and in some cases, making a call to action.

✦ Closing Thoughts: Literacy in an Information-Rich World

There is an old joke: 73.6 percent of all statistics are made up.

That joke would be funny if we did not live in a world in which more data have been created in the last two years than in the entire previous history of the human race—data that are often less than reliable (Marr 2015). We are now swimming—some would say drowning—in oceans of information. On Google alone, people query more than forty thousand times per second. This year, people will purchase more than 1.4 million smartphones, each capable of collecting all kinds of information. By 2020, 6.1 billion people will possess smartphones (Marr 2015). We are approaching global smartphone market saturation.

Having tools (smartphones and computers) that enable us to access unlimited information at lightning speed is good, but having these tools brings to mind an old expression often used in the IT world: "A fool with a tool is still a fool." Being able to access information is one thing. But being able to read, question, and deeply analyze information is another. And if we may take this to another level: being able to clearly *write* to convey information to others is a skill that will only be increasingly valued in an information-rich world.

ARGUMENT

Today we are awash in argument. Unfortunately, reasoned argument is often drowned out by unsubstantiated sound bytes, by fake news, and by people talking (yelling!) past one another. In an age when we are asked to accept "alternative facts," it is more important than ever that we teach our students how to critically examine evidence, how to question a source, how to clearly reason, how to support their thinking. We are reminded of the words of Mike Schmoker and Gerald Graff (2011), who note:

> If we want record numbers of students to succeed in postsecondary studies and careers, an ancient, accessible concept needs to be restored to its rightful place at the center of schooling: argument. In its various forms, it includes the ability to analyze and assess facts and evidence, support our solutions, and defend our interpretations and recommendations with clarity and precision—in every subject area. Argument is the primary skill essential to our success as citizens, students, and workers. (1)

This last line bears repeating: "Argument is the primary skill essential to our success as citizens, students, and workers." As such, we believe argumentation should be woven into every classroom, into every subject, into every grade level, into every school year. Teaching students the conventions of argument helps them develop a schema foundational to being critical thinkers.

⚜ Planning a Study in Argument

The argument unit is designed to help our students enter a conversation that already exists in the world, and we pointedly direct them to write about issues that are broiling in their communities. We want them to gather evidence, explain, interpret, and look beyond the surface of the arguments swirling around them and to enter the ones they find compelling. Studying the structure and content of argument exposes our students to the diversity of experiences and beliefs in our classrooms, in our towns, and in our world.

CONSIDER *This...*

In many English classes the literary analysis essay counts as an argument. This is not what we mean by teaching students the structures and conventions of argument. Crafting an effective argument is different from identifying and analyzing the central theme in a whole-class novel.

Before the study began, we developed a notebook-sized anchor chart based on the essential elements of argument we planned to teach. We had students paste the charts into their notebooks to use as a reference throughout the study. The elements included how to

- recognize the following skills of argument necessary to create a cohesive text around a central claim:
  - reason with clarity
  - use credible evidence
  - craft anecdotes to create empathy
  - address the reader's preconceived notions
  - anticipate and refute counterarguments
  - use a moderate tone and reasoned voice to persuade, rather than to complain, irritate, or blame
  - (often) include a call to action.
- unpack a text (editorial, commercial, essay) to understand a writer's decisions and the effective organization of content
- research multiple perspectives
- recognize different ways of developing an argument to sustain the reader's engagement: blending craft moves from other discourses (e.g., dialogue, flashbacks, sensory detail).

In planning to teach these essential elements, we pay particular attention to the organization of ideas to counter the overreliance on formulaic writing our students have experienced in school.

✦ Time and Expectations

The year we taught together, we planned for five weeks of study. Figure 8.1 shows the map of the laps we took through argument.

Writing a strong argument is complex, so we planned our unit as a progression of skills: we started simply and then had our students write increasingly complicated arguments. In constructing the map for the study, we planned for much of the student thinking to arise from inquiry into important issues (see Figure 8.2).

Week	Mapping the Writing Year: Argument Study
1	Reading and writing next to infographics and short reviews
2	Reading and writing next to "The Ethicist"
3–4	Writing to presidential candidates
5	Creating a digital public service announcement

Figure 8.1 The Map of the Argument Study

Lap One: Reading and Writing Next to Infographics and Short Reviews	**Lap Two: Reading and Writing Next to "The Ethicist"**	**Lap Three: Writing to Presidential Candidates**	**Lap Four: Creating a Digital Public Service Announcement**
Daily analytical reading of arguments (essays, editorials, infographics, reviews, YouTube, TED talks).	Consider central argument points, anticipate counterarguments, refute counterarguments.	Make an argument about one topic.	Convert a written argument (letter to a candidate) into a one-minute digital text.
Recognize what is said and not said.	Use a "small" example to make a large point.	Engage readers with a dynamic lead (e.g., story, striking facts).	Select what to keep from your letter and what to leave out.
Identify how tone is created through word choice, graphic design, and visuals and how information is organized and presented.	Infuse skills learned in other discourses (e.g., support your argument with narrative, use all your senses to describe people, places, and events).	Consider central argument points, anticipate counterarguments, and refute counterarguments.	Organize images, facts, and tone to create momentum and to best develop the purpose of your text for readers. (e.g., transition effects, use of black screen for facts, size of font, voice-overs, and music).
Identify the use of evidence to support ideas.	Read like a writer. You'll see elements of argument in everything you read.	Organize a letter to create momentum and to best develop a convincing case. Create effective transitions to link major points and to bring cohesion to the argument.	Create an effective ending to reflect on why this argument matters.

Figure 8.2 The Laps We Planned for Argument Study

continues

Lap One: Reading and Writing Next to Infographics and Short Reviews	Lap Two: Reading and Writing Next to "The Ethicist"	Lap Three: Writing to Presidential Candidates	Lap Four: Creating a Digital Public Service Announcement
Identify the author's claim and analyze where and how it occurs in the text.	Use word choice intentionally to create a believable, consistent argument.	Create an effective ending to reflect on why your argument should be heeded.	Craft word choice to create authority in the voice-overs.
Write shorter arguments daily, practicing argumentative voices.	Polish your writing for an audience by proofreading line by line.	Craft word choice to create a respectful and intellectual tone for the piece.	
Generate a lot of argument possibilities to write about in notebooks.		Proofread, edit, and polish as you write.	

Figure 8.2 *Continued*

This map also reflects our understanding that persuasive skills and argument skills are not the same thing. When someone is trying to persuade you, they may lie to you. They may use propaganda. Argument, on the other hand, should be based in reason, in facts, in logic. It should be "above board." We like George Hillocks Jr.'s (2011) notion that there are two kinds of argument our students should be practicing: arguments of judgment (e.g., a book review) and arguments of policy (e.g., "Do you support the president's position on immigration?"). With this map of study, our students practiced both kinds of argument.

⚑ Lap One: Reading and Writing Next to Infographics and Short Reviews

We spent one week on this first lap through argumentation with time for students to build on their experience in the information unit and to quick write next to infographics and other texts. We believe our students like to write when given provocative information, so we were on constant lookout for timely and controversial ideas that would stir their passions. In daily, ungraded practice, students read and discussed these texts, and then, instead of summaries, they were asked to write brief arguments that could be supported from the information. Along the way, we demonstrated rereading our quick writing to find ideas—highlighting the places where arguments might arise.

On one day, our students analyzed an infographic explaining the events surrounding the killing of Michael Brown, an unarmed teenager in Ferguson, Missouri. Brown, an African

American, was shot by a white officer, Darren Wilson. When a grand jury decided not to indict Wilson, protests erupted around the country. We gave our students an infographic from *USA Today* that included a timeline of key events, and we also gave them a number of other articles written from various perspectives. We nudged our students to move beyond summary and into argument: "What other information do you need before deciding if the grand jury made the proper decision? What other questions and/or issues are raised when you read 'between the lines'? What is not said in the infographic and in the articles? When you carefully consider this information, what is worth arguing about?"

CONSIDER *This...*

We saw that students needed more practice reading charts and graphs of information. Much of their reading remained superficial, stuck at the *What does it say?* level. They needed help moving into the other deeper levels of reading—*What does it not say? How is it said?* and *What influence does this have on the reader?*—so they could uncover arguments embedded in the organization or selection of information.

With our quick-writing practice, we also showed students how information can bloom into a number of different arguments. The infographic "The World as 100 People" (visual.ly), for example, includes a number of facts about what the world would look like if the planet's population was encapsulated in one hundred people. Here's an example:

> If the world had 100 people, 30 of them would have internet access; 70 of them would not.

This is one simple fact, but thinking about it closely lends itself to various arguments that might be inferred from the information. We asked, "What arguments can be inferred from this?" We then brainstormed the following possible arguments with our students:

- Internet access should be a right, not a privilege.
- As long as there is this gap between who has internet access and who doesn't, there will be injustice in this world.
- Closing the internet gap is this generation's civil rights movement.

- Some governments do not want their citizens to have internet access—and what we can do about it.

- Closing the internet gap in our city is an achievable goal.

- All public buildings should have free internet access.

- All students should have free internet access.

- Having internet access is critical, but students still need to apply critical reading skills when reading online.

- The internet might be making us dumber.

Students chose other facts from the infographic and brainstormed arguments that might arise from this data. From there, they wrote in many directions, generating their own questions from their inquiry and curiosity. Students are much more invested in writing arguments if they are encouraged to organize and support arguments they believe are critically important in their world.

From reading infographics, we revisited the writing of short reviews. As you may recall from the previous chapter on informational writing, our students wrote reviews in that unit as well. A review not only informs but, in doing so, makes a central argument: Should you buy this product? Is this restaurant worthy of the price? The nature of reviewing invites students to blend discourses, often including their own experiences as evidence to support their thinking. Revisiting the genre would help our students see this important connection, so we spent a couple of days analyzing and drafting short Yelp!, Amazon, and Goodreads reviews. We showed students reviews we'd already written, and we wrote new reviews alongside them.

After students had drafted several short reviews, they each selected one to revise. Figure 8.3 includes other seeds we have used to launch argument writing.

Notebook Seeds for Writing Argument
(a Google search will lead you right to these)

Text That Invites Argument

"Our Insanity Over Guns Claims More Victims" and other essays by Leonard Pitts Jr.

Editorials

Screenshots of tweets

Figure 8.3 Notebook Seeds for Writing Argument

Infographics That Invite Argument

"Homicides per 100,000 in G-8 Countries" (gunwatch.blogspot)

"The 100 Best Infographics" series

Graphs found at fivethirtyeight.com and informationisbeautiful.net

The Best American Infographics book series

Spoken Word Poems That Invite Argument

"Why I Hate School but Love Education" by Suli Breaks

"19 Mexicans" by Joaquin Zihuatanejo

"Can We Auto-Correct Humanity?" by Prince Ea

Poetry That Invites Argument

"How to Live" by Charles Harper Webb

YouTube Videos That Invite Argument

"20 Things We Should Say More Often" by Kid President

Figure 8.3 *Continued*

✒ Lap Two: Reading and Writing Next to "The Ethicist"

One of our favorite columns is "The Ethicist," which runs every Sunday in the *New York Times Magazine*. Every week, readers write in with ethical dilemmas, and Kwame Anthony Appiah ("the Ethicist") shares his thinking about the ethical dilemmas at hand.

To introduce "The Ethicist" to our students, we placed them in small groups and gave each group a different question that had been submitted to the columnist. Before drafting their own thinking in their notebooks, students were asked to read and debate questions such as "Should I tell my friend that I had a fling with her ex?" or "Should a nephew be told who his real father is?" After talking and writing, we gave them the "answer" provided by the columnist, which, in turn, spawned more debate, as students sometimes disagreed with the Ethicist's response.

Teaching Clip

See Penny
confer with Ryan
as he explores
this topic in his
multigenre project

On the second day, we chose one question for the entire class to ponder: Is it wrong to watch football? This question was prompted by the following letter submitted to the Ethicist (Klosterman 2014):

> I've recently begun to question my support for the N.F.L. I suspect that the recent discoveries about concussions and the prevalence of early-onset dementia among players are just the tip of the iceberg. Is it unethical to support a league that seems to know it is detrimental to the health of its participants? And if so, what should my response be? Don't go to games? Don't buy merchandise? Don't watch on television? Start actively opposing the N.F.L? Write letters?

> —Darren Williams, Dallas

To help shape their thinking on this issue, students were provided with a number of articles both supporting and condemning the NFL. They spent a full period reading both sides of the argument, highlighting key points, recognizing and marking counterarguments, and paying close attention to the refutations of the counterarguments. Students were asked to take a stand on the issue, and they spent the next three days drafting, revising, and editing their arguments.

This argument was graded, receiving more weight than the review, and before they started writing, we gave students descriptors of what we would be looking for (see Figure 8.4).

Category	Excellence in Argument Writing
Scope	The writing exhibits a thoughtful treatment of a substantive topic. The claim is supported from relevant sources and shows an understanding of counterclaims. The writer addresses the audience's expectations, concerns, possible misunderstandings, and/or biases.
Sequence	The writing maintains a strong, overall focus. A strong lead introduces the claim and moves it forward; the conclusion inspires thought and/or action. The evidence is arranged in logical order and the elements work together. Transitional phrases connect evidence strands to one another and to the central argument.
Development	The claim is supported well with credible reasons and evidence. Explanations clarify the relationship among claims, counterclaims, reasons, and evidence.
Craft	The writing is clear and focused. The writer exhibits a strong voice that holds the reader's attention and shows a command of the subject. The tone is appropriate for audience and purpose. Strong word choice is evident and the writing contains original, ear-catching phrases. The writing also contains mature, varied sentence structures that advance the argument.
Editing	Spelling and punctuation are strong throughout.

Figure 8.4 Descriptors for Excellence in Argument Writing

To wrap up this lap of the argument study, we dedicated a class period to having students debate the issue. Students from both sides selected representatives to participate in the debate, while the rest of the class watched and took notes. Because the students were properly prepped for the debates, they were quite lively. Students were still debating as they walked out the door at the end of the period.

This assessment gave us clear direction for planning minilessons for the second half of the unit. From reading students' essays, we learned.

Argumentative writing brought out more student voice. *Our students' passions surfaced when they were given opportunities to generate their own arguments. For some, this was the first time we heard their distinct voices emerge.*

Some students were stuck in the "three reasons approach" to argument. Students were listing instead of arguing. They needed to see more authentic arguments and how argument is elevated when formula is abandoned. In response, we revised arguments in front of them, dabbling with different approaches, showing them options so they could make better decisions about the construction of their arguments.

There were unity and alignment problems. *Many students' essays were "jumpy." They sometimes wrote paragraphs that did not support their topic sentences. Or sometimes their essays bunched up—they blended too many reasons into a single paragraph. We needed to show them how to give their arguments some breathing room by separating big ideas that could be elaborated in different paragraphs.*

Arguments were shallow. Sometimes students had clear claims, but they supported them with weak or irrelevant evidence. They often had trouble explaining why their reasons were good reasons. Or they would cite dubious sources to support their arguments. Some students completely ignored or glossed over valid counterarguments.

There were citation problems. Students were unclear about how to infuse in-text citations into their arguments. Information was often dropped into their essays cold, uncited. When students attempted to include citations, they were often improperly used, and many had trouble "handing over the microphone" to outside sources without losing their voice.

✦ Lap Three: Writing to Presidential Candidates

When making an argument in a letter, a writer must think very specifically about both purpose and audience, so letter writing is a good lap to take in any school year.

It was an especially good lap to take the year we planned together.

As we started around the track for the third time in the argument unit, the country was in the midst of a presidential race. We decided this was an opportunity for our students to become versed in the candidates and their stances on key issues, and to build on the critical reading skills they developed in the informational study. We introduced them to the ProCon.org website as well as the *Left, Right, and Center* podcast. There are more than forty issues on the website, and after students swam around in them a bit, we asked each student to pick one key issue to study more deeply and to practice his or her reading skills by considering the three essential questions in Figure 8.5.

Three Key Questions	Things to Consider
1. What does the candidate say?	What is the candidate's stance on this issue? What reasons are given to support this stance? Does the candidate address counterarguments? Does the candidate refute these counterarguments?
2. What does the candidate not say?	What issues are raised that are not addressed? If an opponent were to rebut the candidate's stance, what would the opponent say? What does the candidate ignore or leave out?
3. How does the candidate say it?	What moves and techniques are employed by the candidate to try to influence your thinking? What do you notice about how the argument is constructed? How does this construction affect the reader's thinking?

Figure 8.5 Essential Questions for Close Reading

Our goal was to have students write letters to a candidate about the issue they had studied. When it came time to draft the letters, we went first. In a minilesson, we showed students the proper formatting (which included proper headings and salutations) and how to adopt and maintain a respectful tone with someone who has a different opinion. We explained that a candidate (or more likely, a candidate's staffer) would not take the time to read long letters, so we needed to keep our letters short.

To demonstrate how to take crummy first drafts and make them better, we gave students our first drafts and had them color-code each of the following elements:

- the central claim

- the reasons that support the central argument

- the explanation as to why these reasons are good reasons

- the counterarguments

- the response to the counterarguments

- a conclusion that does not simply restate what was already said.

After students had drafted, they met in small writing groups and color-coded these same elements in each other's papers.

Once we had revised our letters, we placed our first and second drafts alongside one another in T-charts and highlighted the improvements we had made based on their feedback. We discussed where our papers had moved, noting both surface-level and deeper-level revisions. Students then repeated this process, highlighting the moves they had made from their first to second drafts, and then shared these moves with one another.

When students had completed a second draft, we exchanged these drafts between our two classes and had our students conduct peer response with one another. We asked them to complete "I noticed . . ." and "I wonder . . ." statements on their partners' papers, and once they had received this feedback, they were directed to take their drafts through another round of revision. We analyzed well-written letters from each other's classrooms, and in addition to seeing good models, our students also heard voices on issues they were unlikely to hear in their own worlds. Even if they weren't seeking understanding, they heard different points of view and their horizons were broadened.

With students' final drafts, we went "old school" by printing their letters and sending them via traditional snail mail. We found many of our students did not know how to address an envelope, so we modeled this skill as well. Finally, we graded students' letters using the same descriptors we'd given them for their first piece of argument writing (see Figure 8.4).

Teaching Clip

See Kelly's students use the *I noticed/ I wonder* lens to study a college admissions essay

CONSIDER This...

Looking back, we should have given more consideration to the idea that Latino students living in Southern California might have very different political leanings than Anglo students living in northern New Hampshire. To say that things got really interesting on the day our classes exchanged their letters would be an understatement. One of Kelly's students, for example, began his letter with the following line: "Dear Mr. Trump, If you want to make America great again, drop out of the race." This essay was opened and read by a student in Penny's class, a staunch Trump supporter who had said in his letter that we could not build a wall fast enough.

As students on each side of the country opened and read letters they disagreed with, our worst fears were realized. Swirls of angry talk and derisive laughter swept through our classes. Students began huddling around letters and started mocking the writers: "Listen to how stupid this guy is . . . Can you believe what he wrote?"

These letters were grenades, and the pins had been pulled.

After taking a few deep breaths, we reminded our students that it is important to respect what a writer is trying to do, even if we disagree with the writer's position. That's why it is called an "argument"—a good argument will elicit strong contrary opinions. We were not trying to change our students' political viewpoints, but we recognized this as an opportunity to teach them to listen with kindness and sensitivity to others—especially to those who think differently than they do. We wanted them to understand why someone who grew up in a different culture on the other side of the country might hold different beliefs.

In retrospect, we should have anticipated this and spent time preparing our students *before* they opened the letters. But we didn't, and as a result, we had an I'm-going-to-need-a-glass-of-wine-this-evening day in the classroom.

CONSIDER *This...*

Our students mailed nearly eighty letters to presidential candidates and
not a single student received a response. What did this teach our students
about a participatory democracy?

✈ Lap Four: Creating a Digital Public Service Announcement

Once students had written to candidates on issues they cared about, we asked them to shrink
their multipage letters into one-minute digital public service announcements (PSAs). We began
by analyzing professionally produced PSAs (easily available on YouTube) and paying close attention to how they were constructed. We studied one on the dangers of texting while driving and
another that showed what happens to your body when you smoke. We then took our letters and
planned our PSAs in front of our students, mapping them out on a storyboard.

After seeing our process, students took their letters and, pulling the central issues from
them, created storyboards of their PSAs. We gave them a couple of days to craft PSAs in class
and an additional week to finish them at home. And just as we had with both argument essays,
we gave students a set of descriptors we would use to grade their PSAs (see Figure 8.6).

Category	Excellence in Digital PSAs
Organization	A clear argument is established and a focus is maintained throughout the digital text. Images and video are organized to draw the viewer into the argument.
Pacing	The pacing of photographs and video fits the argument and maintains audience interest. The video has just the "right amount" of detail. It does not seem too long or too short.
Images	The images are visually pleasing and help make the argument. Thought went into the placement of the person or place featured within the background and/or setting.
Media	There is a combination of photographs and video (or recorded voice-over), as well as text slides when needed and music, that appropriately matches the tone of the argument. Music and video are adjusted to maintain a comfortable sound level for the audience.
Editing	Spelling and punctuation are correct on all text used in the movie. Transitions are smooth and do not distract viewers between sections of the video.

Figure 8.6 Descriptors for Excellence in Public Service Announcements

✈ Using Texts as Mentors Across the Study

Each time we studied a piece of argumentative writing, we returned to our favorite question: "What do you notice?" We kept anchor charts in our classrooms to post the moves and techniques we saw writers using in this discourse. Some of these moves overlapped those we'd studied in earlier units (use of dialogue, strong verbs, metaphor), while others were more specific to this discourse (recognizing counterarguments, refutation of these counterarguments).

We planned ahead to call attention to some features in texts we knew students needed to see:

- the difference between arguments of judgment and arguments of policy

- the flexible structures of argument writing: use of data, charts, graphs, statistics, and the infusion of narrative elements

- the development of a claim and the way writers move it to a deeper, more focused place.

We also knew from the start that studying the structure of arguments and the organization of ideas would be important to help our students move beyond formulaic writing. We turned to mentors to help us with this teaching. We studied the structure of Sir Ken Robinson's TED talk "Do Schools Kill Creativity?" (2006) and Rick Reilly's essay "Gamers to the End" (2007) to point out how writers break free of formulas in writing arguments. With each mentor text we studied, we assessed students' annotations to see what they understood about the conventions of argument.

We knew we wanted our students to see how critical word and sentence crafting is to making a compelling argument, so we also turned to a Pulitzer Prize–winning mentor, Leonard Pitts Jr., to show students the way. We zoomed in for two rounds of passage study with two of Pitts' columns. The first passage was from "Some Harsh Sentences Prove Unjust" (2012), where he argues that draconian prison sentences have violated the Eighth Amendment. Here is the section we studied:

> From now on, judges would be severely limited in the sentences they could hand down for certain crimes, required to impose certain punishments whether or not they thought those punishments fit the circumstances at hand. From now on, there was a new mantra in American justice. From now on, we would be "tough on crime."
>
> We got tough on Jerry DeWayne Williams, a small-time criminal who stole a slice of pizza from a group of children. He got 25 years.

We got tough on Duane Silva, a guy with an IQ of 71 who stole a VCR and a coin collection. He got 30 to life.

We got tough on Dixie Shanahan, who shot and killed the husband who had beaten her for three days straight, punching her in the face, pounding her in the stomach, dragging her by the hair, because she refused to have an abortion. She got 50 years.

We got tough on Jeff Berryhill, who got drunk one night, kicked in an apartment door and punched a guy who was inside with Berryhill's girlfriend. He got 25 years.

Studying the passage, students noticed the use of narrative to strengthen the argument and how Pitts is "writing small" with very specific examples to make a big point. They were also struck by the intentional repetition, and we decided to emulate this structure to practice in our notebooks. Here is Kelly's emulation:

From now on, the Rams told us, things would be better. From now on, they would be energized by their relocation. From now on, the Rams would become a winning franchise. From now on, it was "Time to Win."

They tried to get better by drafting Greg Robinson, a left tackle out of Auburn University who was taken second overall in the draft. He got benched.

They tried to get better by starting Case Keenum as their quarterback, but under his leadership they scored the fewest points in the league. He got benched.

They tried to get better by trading a slew of draft picks so they could draft Jared Goff, who ended up having the lowest passer rating in the league. He got benched.

They tried to get better by extending the contract of their coach, Jeff Fisher, who has lost more games than any other coach in NFL history. He got fired.

And here's an example from one of Kelly's students, Celeste:

From now on, our band director told us things would be different. From now on, he said, we are going to properly play the second movement, LaBelle. From now on, we will not be adding any extra notes during the grand pause.

We tried to get better the first time and the trumpets accidentally played an extra measure. We had to start over.

We tried to get better the second time, but the flute player accidentally added three extra notes. We had to start over.

We tried to get better a third time, and a freshman forgot to cut off (stop). We had to start over.

We tried to get better a fourth time, but Ricardo, our xylophone player, missed his cue. We had to start over.

The band director was so angry he threw his baton and slammed his fist on the podium.

We should note here that Celeste's passage is not an argument. It is a narrative. But as we have stated elsewhere in this book, narrative strengthens arguments. Pitts, for example, uses a number of small stories to argue that some prison sentences are too harsh. When Celeste emulates this passage, she is learning to sharpen her narrative skills, but she is also acquiring a universal writing skill that is transferable to argumentative writing.

Passage study is also a means to cultivate an interest in the study of punctuation—to have our students examine the many ways writers craft sentences. We had that in mind when we chose this second excerpt, from "Sometimes, the Earth Is Cruel" (2010), where Pitts is trying to capture the repeated devastation in Haiti brought on by a series of hurricanes.

Sometimes, though, you have to wonder if the planet itself is not conspiring against this humble little nation. After 1994, when Tropical Storm Gordon killed several hundred people, after 1998, when Hurricane Georges swept away more than 500 lives, after 2004, when the rains of Tropical Storm Jeanne claimed more than 2,000 souls, after 2005, when Hurricane Dennis took 25 lives in July and Tropical Storm Alpha snatched 17 in October, followed by Hurricane Wilma, which stole 11 more, after the double whammy of Hurricanes Fay and Gustav in 2008 killed more than 130 people and destroyed 3,100 homes, after all that, comes this latest insult—and a death toll officials cannot begin to even imagine. Perhaps as many as 100,000, they were saying on Wednesday.

We want our students to understand that punctuation is rooted in the author's expectation for how the passage should be read. We asked them: "Why would the author punctuate this passage in this way? What effect was he trying to achieve? How does he want you to read this piece? Pitts certainly knows he has written a lengthy run-on sentence. Why did he do it?"

After studying the sentence, students created their own intentional run-on sentences in the passage study sections of their notebooks. Why have students emulate run-on sentences when so many of them already struggle with sentence boundaries? Because we want them to understand that sometimes rules are broken for effect (in this case, creating an intentional run-on sentence can create a breathless effect on the reader). When it comes to making punctuation decisions, we want our students to move beyond simplistic "right versus wrong" thinking. We want them to read their writing aloud, to listen to it, to consider how *they* want the reader to hear it. In Figure 8.7, you will find a sampling of some of the other sentences we chose for close study.

Intentional fragment example(s)	Five athletes. Five futures. All gone. Five of 84 Americans killed from New Year's Day through Sunday. Five of 3,084 Americans killed since the war began. ("Gamers to the End" by Rick Reilly [2007])
Sentence variety example(s)	Picture riding the lid of a turkey roaster pan down a roller coaster rail after an ice storm. Picture it at almost 80 miles an hour, with wicked turns, at G-forces so powerful that you cannot raise your helmet from the ice, which glitters just an inch away. Now picture making that ride face first. ("Skeleton Plunges Face-First Back into the Winter Games" by Rick Bragg [2002])
Parallel structure	Some look for scapegoats, others look for conspiracies, but this much is clear: violence breeds violence, repression brings retaliation, and only a cleansing of our whole society can remove this sickness from our soul. (Remarks to the Cleveland City Club by Robert Kennedy [1968])
Hyphenated adjectives	They are honest people who do honest work—crack-the-bones work; lift-it, chop-it, empty-it, glide-it-in-smooth work; feel-the-flames-up-close work; crawl-down-in-there work—things that no one wants to do but that someone must. ("They, Too, Sing America" by Charles M. Blow [2011])
Use of dashes to add emphasis	When I asked Gene Wilhoit, executive director of the Council of Chief State School Officers—which, along with the National Governors Association, created the Common Core—he told me that CEOs and university professors championed the shift to nonfiction. Only a small, vocal group objected. ("How I Replaced Shakespeare" by Joel Stein [2012])

Figure 8.7 Sentence Study Possibilities

continues

Use of dashes to include an aside	Think of all the nasty notes you wrote—or, if you're more like me, that were written about you—in middle school. Then imagine the ability to cut and paste them and send them to your 10 closest buddies. The Internet facilitates and expands the ability of kids to do the dumbest things.
	("IMs: What's a Mother to Do?" by Ruth Marcus [2006])
Strong verbs	I have broken my wrists, fingers, a tibia, a fibula, chipped a handful of teeth, cracked a vertebra and snapped a collarbone. I have concussed myself in Tallahassee, Fla., and Portland, Ore. I've skittered across the sooty hoods of New York cabs and bombed down many of San Francisco's steepest avenues.
	("All Parents Are Cowards" by Michael Christie [2015])

Figure 8.7 *Continued*

Conversation Clip

See "The Hows and Whys of Grammar and Editing"

With passage study, we balance between choosing sentences that teach how to make a specific, conventional punctuation move (e.g., punctuating dialogue properly) and sentences where writers are taking interesting risks. We seek a balance between editing and craft moves. Both matter. We want our students to know more about punctuation after spending a year in our classrooms, but we also want them to be awake to the study of craft at the sentence level. We want them to recognize that when Leonard Pitts writes a run-on sentence, he is doing more than conveying information. He is making the reader begin to feel the collective impact of a series of disasters.

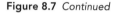 Modeling the Process of Crafting Argument

Mentor text study taught our students a lot about the craft of argument writing, but they needed us to teach them about the process of argument writing. Across the four laps of study, we showed them how to generate ideas, find topics inside those ideas, rehearse how writing might go, use a storyboard or outline to plan the arc of an argument, and draft, revise, and polish a finished piece.

In minilessons and in the one-to-one teaching we did in conferences, we also zoomed in and taught our students a lot of the process and decision-making that is *specific* to argument writing. As we stated earlier, argumentative writing brought out a strong voice in our students' writing, and these lessons helped them effectively channel their passions.

Invite Your Reader into Your Argument

We taught our students that if they began their letters by going into attack mode, they ran the risk of losing their reader(s). The wrong word choice or tone can derail an argument before it gets started. Arguments often begin by establishing a reasonable tone, easing the reader into the argument.

Establish Your Credibility or "Ethos" as a Writer

In an argument, it is helpful for the writer to establish credibility with the audience. We taught our students to consider the following question when crafting their arguments: "Why should the reader pay attention to what I am saying?" For example, if a student writes a letter to a political candidate challenging his stance on immigration, he might begin by saying, "As the son of parents who immigrated from Mexico . . ." Of course, establishing credibility is also rooted in using appropriate word choice and in making sure grammar is correct.

Establish an Emotional Connection or "Pathos" with Your Reader

Often, people make an emotional connection to an argument. As this is being written, President Trump has closed the borders to refugees from select countries. In a letter to the president, one could outline reasons to oppose this policy, but this approach might not carry the same impact as telling the story of a Syrian child who narrowly survived a bombing. Sometimes a "small" story helps the audience understand the bigger picture. Though most arguments are designed to appeal to people's logic, sometimes it is better to touch a nerve—to compel people to listen. We encouraged our students to weave anecdotes into their arguments as a way to connect with and to influence their readers.

Establish the Logic or "Logos" of Your Argument

Though students were able to develop reasons for their arguments, the logic behind these reasons was often weak or unsubstantiated and their writing lacked unity. At times, they had trouble explaining how the evidence supported their claims. To address this, we intentionally drafted paragraphs that had these problems and then demonstrated how to revise these problem areas. We color-coded places where we supported our main points and places where the argument "jumped the tracks."

Include a Call for Action

Not all arguments include calls to action—this decision often hinges on careful consideration of audience and purpose. But when our students wrote to presidential candidates, we encouraged this practice. We modeled sentence stems that helped students include this feature (e.g., "Dear Candidate X, I am writing you today to ask you to reconsider your position on _____.").

Conclude with a "Hooking" Strategy

Students are often taught to use "hooking" strategies (e.g., a quotation, an unusual statement, a question, an interesting anecdote, a statistic) to start a paper, and we teach our students to consider ending their essays with one or more of these moves. What we do not want is for our students to simply summarize what they have already written. Instead, we want an ending that has a punch—an ending that makes the reader think, "Hmm . . . I need to reconsider this."

✦ Closing Thoughts: Argument in a Changing World

The presidential race made this a compelling argument unit, but, of course, we will not be repeating it. The world changes. The year following the election, for example, Kelly's students argued whether building a wall was an effective immigration measure.

What key issues will emerge this year? As this is being written, arguments continue to swirl around us: Is the government's response to the flooding in Houston and the hurricanes in Puerto Rico and Florida adequate? Is the president making the right move in removing immigration protection from undocumented students? What should be done about the threat of North Korea? What can be done to solve the health care crisis? Is Taylor Swift's new album worth buying? These are in-the-moment issues.

We are still three months away from this year's argument unit, and though we don't know yet where this will take us, we do know one thing: getting our students to read and write critically in argumentation will again stake a central place in our writing year.

9

MULTIGENRE Research Projects

We feel a tension in teaching writing.

There is the life we have as writers and then there are the units we plan for students. At home we write, revise, rethink, and resist temptations to walk away because we are driven to explain or share something we've experienced. We want to write well, and it energizes us to discover and sharpen our thinking in words. We decide how we work and what we work on.

We want our students to think this expansively about writing, and yet, we give our students assignments. We narrow their vision. We ask students to write stories, editorials, arguments, and reviews and to create movies and poems. We segment our school year into units of study and set due dates.

Why don't we allow our students more freedom since it means so much in our own writing lives? There are three reasons: One, we both teach students who believe writing is a formula; our units will give them opportunities to experience new ways to create meaning. Two, we have *a lot* of students. Three, many states have adopted standards that dictate specific kinds of writing, and this leads districts to mandate certain kinds of writing (ours both do).

Our writing map for the year is a compromise between our ideals for writers and the realities of teaching diverse students who need a lot of support. We target our minilessons to demonstrate writerly thinking and to invite practice with skills. We study the writing craft that differentiates genres to deepen student understanding of the structure and design of texts as well as to build students' confidence. We work all year toward this multigenre unit: a place where we set students completely free.

✦ Planning a Study in Multigenre Writing

In multigenre research projects, our students synthesize the many skills they've learned over the year. They choose topics they are interested in exploring, but they also choose the way they work (some in partners, some alone) and, as always, have the choice to abandon one idea and start on

Conversation Clip

See "An
Experiment with
Blended Genre"

another, even in the midst of this unit. We believe teaching students to write well means teaching them a process for discovering and working with the ideas they have. Throughout the school year, we have worked in every unit to give students practice in this process. With this project, students will feel the freedom and assume the responsibility of making *all* the decisions about their work.

To understand multigenre writing, it's important to remember that genres evolve and tools for writing change over time. Most of us can remember when we had never heard of a podcast or a Twitter chat. The Wikipedia definition of *genre* captures the natural evolution of writing forms over time and the borrowing and recombining of conventions as new genres are invented:

> Genre is the term for any category of literature or other forms of art or entertainment, e.g. music, whether written or spoken, audio or visual, based on some set of stylistic criteria. Genres are formed by conventions that change over time as new genres are invented and the use of old ones are discontinued. Often, works fit into multiple genres by way of borrowing and recombining these conventions.

The process of standing next to mentors (both writers and texts) and learning to emulate and create—a process we've nurtured all year long—will serve students both now and as they encounter new genres throughout their lives.

Tom Romano (2000) has written extensively about the many benefits of having students write about the same topic across genres. He defines a multigenre project as something that

> arises from research, experience, and imagination. It is not an uninterrupted, expository monolog nor a seamless narrative nor a collection of poems. A multigenre paper is composed of many genres and subgenres, each piece self-contained, making a point of its own, yet connected by theme or topic and sometimes by language, images, and content. In addition to many genres, a multigenre paper may also contain many voices, not just the author's. The trick is to make such a paper hang together. (x–xi)

With multigenre projects, we want students to think expansively about possibilities for writing, so we do not tell them what or how to write—the only requirement is that they include at least four different genres. The year we planned this unit together, all our students used research in their projects, but then they went in many different directions with their writing. Some wrote stories like the novel *Where'd You Go, Bernadette*, told in many genres and/or with multiple narrators, while others wrote to convey information about a period of history or an important place. Some students wrote layered arguments and others did all three—they blended discourses to create rich, textured papers that told stories, informed readers, and argued in poetry, song, and other media.

Multigenre projects generate rich and rigorous thinking. When we ask students to imagine ways to organize and frame their ideas, investment rises. You can see and hear this in the conferences we had with students as they shaped their projects. You can feel *our* energy as well. When students think expansively, we feel the power of engaging their creative minds; it fuels our engagement with teaching at a difficult time of year. The wider we open up opportunities for students to create texts, the more engaged they become in the act of composition.

Teaching Clip

See multiple conferences with writers working on multigenre projects

◁ Time and Expectations

We planned for five weeks of multigenre writing as the last formal study of the year. We knew students would move forward at different paces, so our plans for different kinds of work overlapped across the weeks. Figure 9.1 shows the map of our plan for the project.

Week	Mapping the Writing Year: Multigenre Project
1–2	Playing with ideas and imagining genres (notebook work)
2–3	Creating initial drafts
3–4	Meeting in writing groups; developing and revising drafts
5	Polishing, shaping, revising, editing, evaluating, and sharing projects

Figure 9.1 The Map of the Multigenre Project Study

CONSIDER This...

We soon learned that the five weeks we had planned was not enough time. Engagement was high—even at the very end of the school year—and the vision students had for their work was not quite realized for too many. It is a classic teacher mistake: we rush. We build a school year toward something important and then run out of time to allow it the space needed. Spring rushes toward summer and assemblies, field days, standardized tests, student absences, and preparing for final exams; it disrupts our days. We planned for five weeks, but most students would have remained engaged though six or seven.

Because students were directing all their own work, there wasn't really a need for us to plan for a ramped-up progression of skills in our teaching, as we had done in other units. Instead, we planned for a single lap around the multigenre track, which would result in one final project.

To help them understand the expectations for their projects, we invited our students to first study projects from years past. They selected four or five to closely study, and we asked them to consider the genres the writer chose and how those genres worked together. Students then discussed the effectiveness of the three parts of the project they were expected to include.

Part 1: A "Dear Reader" Letter

This letter serves as an invitation to explore the rest of the project: it is lively, enticing, and brief. It introduces the focus of the writing, which can be centered on "a person, idea, topic, era, cultural phenomenon, movement, thing, or place" (Romano 2006, 1). The writer may also explain the purpose of the project. Is it to inform? To tell a story? To make an argument? When written with courage, zest, and insight, the letter will cause readers to turn the page.

Part 2: Four (or More) Elements

Students must use at least four genres to offer insight into the big ideas they want to communicate. We suggest that one of these genres be visual (e.g., artwork, a collage, photographs, a movie). Although students may plan these before they begin working, as they draft one idea, another idea and often another way to express that idea will arise. We expect students to follow their thinking—not their plans—while writing this project. It is an essential part of the writing process: following language to meaning. We know that one gift of writing is surprise. We appreciate how the act of writing leads us to new thinking, and we hope our students will experience this in this project.

Once students have drafts of genres, the challenge is to connect the parts together. What "glue" can the writer put between the genres to bring unity and flow to the project? Students have written definitions, used quotations and excerpts from songs, designed word graphics and mock yearbook entries. Students find that "glue" is a genre that requires more thinking than they expect. Because of this, we encourage them to focus on the possibilities for this early in the drafting process.

Part 3: Works Cited and Endnotes

This section may be best described as a narrated works cited page. Regardless of topic, some type of research is required for the multigenre project. Students should properly cite multiple sources and then comment on why each genre was chosen and how it is intended to shape the reader's understanding of the subject. Kelly's student Andrew, for example, took a close look at the decade of the 1960s for his project. His first piece consisted of imagined journal entries written by John F. Kennedy during the Cuban Missile Crisis, and here is how he discussed it in his endnotes:

> **The World at Its Brink:** I wanted this piece to be like a sort of journal for all the major things that happened during the Kennedy administration. I wanted to make it sound like it was made at that moment in time and I tried to capture the anxiety and urgency in the writing to make it seem more realistic and believable. My research for this piece came from the Kennedy library. (JFKLibrary.org)

✦ Modeling the Process of Planning Multigenre Projects

To help students envision how a suite of genres can communicate the complexity of an idea, we both imagined our own multigenre projects alongside our students. Kelly wanted to capture the Anaheim Angels' 2002 World Series championship (sadly, at least for Kelly, the only championship in that franchise's history). Kelly imagined the following elements: a recipe for winning a championship, a straight game-by-game recounting of the seven-game series, a firsthand narrative of attending the clinching game, an analysis of why the Angels won the series, a commentary explaining what the victory meant to his family, and a photo album of the series. For his glue, Kelly planned to weave quotations from reporting on the 2002 World Series between each of his genres. Kelly told his students that he would begin with this plan, knowing that as he wrote he might discover other ideas or artifacts he might decide to include.

For her project, Penny wanted to create a celebration of her long friendship with her mentor Don Graves. She told her students she settled on the idea when she walked out of her house and heard the sound of a black-capped chickadee, which always heralds the arrival of dawn in the spring. Penny remembered sharing her love of its call with Don and always thinks of him when she hears it. She recorded the bird's song on her phone and decided that the recording would have to be incorporated into her project, possibly as part of a podcast. Penny planned to

Teaching Clip
See "Organizing a Multigenre Project"

Teaching Clip
See "Finding a Direction for a Multigenre Project"

write about the day Don taught all her eighth-grade classes and to present a series of scenes of his work with children: She wanted to depict his keen attention when conferring with young writers; his exasperation one morning while they were coteaching Sunday School; and his playful delight in Penny's own young children. Her research plan was to focus on the aging of the human brain, and she would use photos of her and Don as the glue for her project. She told students that she had written a eulogy and had delivered it at Don's funeral, but that she wanted this project to be a celebration, not filled with sadness and loss, so she would not include it.

Penny told students of her intentions to share her project with Don's wife, Betty. We believe it is important to tell students why we write and our hopes for the work our writing can do in the world. When you share your thinking and plans for writing with students, you model joy and struggle. Engagement—the teacher's love of words—is contagious. We don't write beside students merely like mechanics changing oil to demonstrate technique. We live the satisfaction that words bring to us.

CONSIDER This...

We think it is important to mention that neither of us wrote final drafts of our projects. We planned them with our students and demonstrated first-draft thinking throughout the unit, but we did not write best drafts of all the parts of our projects. Students don't need us to always finish drafts and share them: they need to see our process and our first attempts more than they need to see polished work.

Teaching Clip

See Sully's conference about his multigenre project

✒ Notebook Work

First, we asked students to skim their year of notebook entries looking for threads that repeat: people, ideas, interests, and passions. It quickly became evident to students that they had a lot of good (unfinished) writing in their notebooks that they had forgotten about. We weren't surprised. We had worked all year to have the notebooks contain mostly blasts of rich writing that connects our students to ideas and experiences they want to develop, just as our notebooks hold those things for us.

We began notebook practice in different forms on the second day of the unit, immersing our students in possibility and play, and we continued the practice of writing quickly next to a text (poem, video, photograph, short passage of writing) throughout this unit. However, we also used notebook time to explore new genres. Each day we presented a different possibility: a menu, a recipe, creative definitions, a blackout poem—and we encouraged students to share genres we hadn't studied in class. To open up possibilities, we practiced our thinking in different genres. For example, after watching the spoken word poems "A Love Letter from a Toothbrush to a Bicycle Tire" by Sarah Kay, "Why Am I Not Good Enough?" by seventh grader Olivia, and "What I Wish I Could Have Told My Mom" by Brittany, we asked students to write letters in their notebooks—trying on the sound of a love letter or a thank you or an apology in letter form—imagining this genre's fit with the big idea of their project. This directed practice in genres was balanced with freewriting as we had practiced it all year.

Teaching Clip

See "Researching and Planning for a Multigenre Project"

After a year of practice, quick writes can do two kinds of work in our classrooms. When our students looked at a recipe from *A Little Bit Wicked: Life, Love, and Faith in Stages* by Kristin Chenoweth with Joni Rodgers (2010), they first discussed how the word choice created the voice and tone of the piece and then wrote their own creative recipes for their projects.

The Top Secret Recipe for Kristi Dawn's No Calorie Left Behind Butterfinger Pie

- Crunch up six king-size Butterfinger bars. Smash them up in a plastic bag or beat them with a rolling pin while they're still in the wrapper. Exercise your aggressions. Very therapeutic.

- Take a twelve-ounce deal of Cool Whip and mix it up with the candy-bar shrapnel.

- Plop all that into one of those graham-cracker crusts. (Just get over yourself and buy the premade kind. Don't be all Barefoot Contessa about it.)

- Freeze! No, not you, the pie. I mean freeze in the freezer, not in the theatrical sense. This is important. If you skip this step, people will assume it's French onion dip and stick their potato chips in it.

- Serve with a smile on paper plates. The kind with the rippled edges, whenever possible. (40)

Although some students took several days to settle on a clear focus for their projects, others knew almost right away what they wanted to explore. In Figure 9.2 we share other "seeds" we used to help our students to consider the possibilities within a multigenre project.

Spoken word "Common Ground" by A Muslim Girl and a Jewish Girl (YouTube)

Serial podcast by *This American Life* (we listened to the opening three minutes of the first episode of season 1)

"How We Move," a digital poem by student Serena McHugh (pennykittle.net)

"Teeth" by Phil Kaye (YouTube) plus Holocaust survivor obituaries on Legacy.com

"Interesting Uses of Drones" infographic (personal-drones.net)

"Blood and Bravery," a multigenre project on Bram Stoker's *Dracula* from Miami University of Ohio (www.users.miamioh.edu/romanots/pdf/bloodandbravery .pdf) (in particular, we studied the concrete poem with the image of a cross)

"How to Overcome Our Biases? Walk Boldly Toward Them," a TED talk by Vernā Myers (ted.com)

"Poem for an Inked Daughter" by Jean Wyrick

"Good Bones" by Maggie Smith

Excerpts from *The Lover's Dictionary* by David Levithan and *Encyclopedia of an Ordinary Life* by Amy Krouse Rosenthal

"The Encyclopedia of Gear: 187 Amazing Stories About Everything We Use" from *Outside* magazine (www.outsideonline.com/2111576/encyclopedia-gear)

Examples from *The Book of Qualities* by J. Ruth Gendler, in which emotions are personified

Figure 9.2 A Few Notebook Prompts for Multigenre Writing

✴ Minilessons to Support Multigenre Projects

Teaching Clip
See Celeste's conference about her multigenre project

We provided students with extensive lists of possible genres during the launch. These lists are cocreated with students and include everything from Wikipedia entries to radio scripts. They evolve each year with new tools for composing and new forms to share thinking. As we confer and listen to students' ideas, we refer to these lists and often suggest new genre possibilities students haven't considered. For example, when Penny conferred with Celeste, she had written a pledge of allegiance to band. Celeste imagined it as a speech she would deliver on the final night of her reign as drum major, but Penny suggested Celeste record the delivery as a podcast.

Early in the process, we have students share plans for projects—storyboards, lists, out-lines. We encourage them to consider the arc of the project and how it will move a reader. These minilessons can be accessed by other students throughout the unit if you create a gathering place for student thinking. We have used Flipgrid for this purpose. Each student's vision allows other students to imagine their own plans differently. We especially hope students will expand digital work to include voice recordings, documentaries, interactive maps, and TED-style talks and to share those plans with all students to raise expectations and suggest possibilities.

CONSIDER *This...*

In a digital age, students should also be reading, writing, listening, and speaking to others outside their classroom. We found, for example, that when our classes read *Romeo and Juliet* together, when they shared drafts of their writing with one another, when they participated in cross-country book clubs, and when they shared movies they had made, their motivation increased and their thinking deepened. There is something really good that happens when one's audience is expanded, and, recognizing this, we will continue to explore ways to have our classes interact with students outside our schools.

✈ Using Texts as Mentors Across the Study

Depending on the genres they decide to use in their projects, students select their own mentor texts to support their vision for writing. However, we still plan for some whole-class text study to support students' thinking and help them consider possibilities. The year we planned together, we studied obituaries and podcasts.

Obituaries

Obituaries have many forms and are relevant since students often choose to memorialize a person or an animal in their final projects. We had looked at "Portraits of Grief" from the *New York Times* during our first-quarter narrative unit, and we reminded students of those obituaries as we studied multiparagraph summaries of a life. For example, we looked at these eight information-packed sentences from an obituary for Biggie Smalls in the *Independent*. Notice how in such a short space, the writer, Pierre Perrone (1997), gives voice and life to this man:

> Born Christopher Wallace 24 years ago, B.I.G. grew up in the Bedford Stuyvesant area, one of the toughest neighbourhoods in Brooklyn, New York. His childhood was bleak, surrounded by crackheads and drug dealers. Indeed, by his teens, Notorious B.I.G. had fallen for the life style that was all around him. "Hustlers were my heroes," he later admitted. "Everything happened on the strip I grew up in. It didn't matter where you went, it was all in your face." The rapper did it all: hanging around street corners, acting as a look-out, making deals. Soon, the fun and games took a darker turn. The police and rival gangs were after him and several of his friends got shot and ended up in coffins.

Choosing obituaries to study is an opportunity for responsive mentor text selection: Have you read an obituary for a local person in your community or a person of interest to your students that was well crafted? Keep it. You want a collection of four to six obituaries, so that after the initial practice with the form, students have a stack of texts to study if they choose to write one. Figure 9.3 shows a few obituaries and teaching points we have used with our students.

"Arthur Ashe, Tennis Star, Is Dead at 49" from the *New York Times*, February 8, 1993	The organization of events in this obituary is worthy of study.
"Glenn Frey, Eagles Guitarist, Dies at 67" from *Billboard* magazine, January 18, 2016	The narrow focus of this obituary and extended quotes from Don Henley show the relationship between the audience for this publication and the content.
"James Dean Dies in a Car Accident" on the History Channel's *This Day in History* for September 30, 1955	Use this text to study the difference between reporting on a death and an obituary.
"Tupac Shakur, 25, Rap Performer Who Personified Violence, Dies" from the *New York Times*, September 14, 1996	Consider the title of this one.
"Leslie Ray Charping" from Carnes Funeral Home, 2017	This is obituary as revenge, an interesting balance between tone and word choice.
"The Aspirations of an Athlete, Businessman Cut Short" from the *Minneapolis Star Tribune*, June 29, 2016 "David Robert Forster, Jr." from the *Minneapolis Star Tribune*, June 28, 2016	Two obituaries from two perspectives: one as news, and then the same story told by the family.

Figure 9.3 Obituary Text Study Possibilities

Podcasts

In the last few years, podcasts have become increasingly sophisticated and diverse. With a free voice recorder app, students can easily record and edit their own, and some text study of podcasts will give them the support they need to try out this new genre. We invited our students to analyze the structure of several different podcasts. We posed questions such as

- What is the balance between interviews and commentary by the host?

- What kinds of sound effects add to the development of the setting of the podcast?

- How are empty spaces or pauses in the podcast utilized? What purpose do they serve?

- How many voices are included, and what is the impact on you, the listener, of having a number of voices to remember and attend to?

We had our students listen to a *Longform* interview in which Brian Reed, the creator of *S-Town*, discusses how the seven episodes were organized to follow a novel's construction. We then listened to a short segment from episode 5 that illustrates the complex composition of podcasts. The narrator uses a section of opera at the moment of crescendo to intersect with the central character's extensive rant on the state of our world. His rant demonstrates his passion and his intelligence as well as his frantic energy, and opera lends sophistication as well as intensity. His rant coincides with the last notes of the opera. You hear him sigh and then say, "I gotta have me some tea." There is a pause and a bit of silence—breathing room for listeners—followed by a slow acoustic guitar and then a return to narration.

When we show students how complex the construction of a podcast is, they are more likely to weave interviews and the sound of the street or the woods, bits of their favorite songs, and dramatic pauses to create a performance that delivers a story differently than writing does. Composing experiences is complex regardless of medium, and students who create podcasts will think about organization and pace and word choice just as all writers do.

Here is a list of a few podcasts we have shared with students. We encourage them to find podcasts they admire to add to our list. You can store links to these on your Google Classroom page.

- "The Kittle Classroom—Exposed!" (which was created during the school year when we wrote this book and includes three ninth graders) from season 1 of the *Book Love Foundation* podcast

- *Revisionist History* by Malcolm Gladwell ("Carlos Doesn't Remember," which tells the story of a young, talented student is particularly compelling)

- *Serial*, season 1, from *This American Life*

- *S-Town* from *This American Life*
- *Longform*, which interviews writers about their processes

✦ Assessment of Multigenre Projects

Once students had ideas and were working to develop them, we gave them a description of an excellent multigenre project Penny adapted from Tom Romano's (2006) lively definition.

> An excellent project knocks readers off their feet, bowls them over, so informative and emotionally moving is the paper. Throughout there is evidence of original thinking, depth, *specificity of detail*, delights of language or insight. The multigenre project is rife with excellent writing that includes attention to a pleasing visage of the page, *action* verbs, varied sentence length, effective word choice, skilled placement of payoff information, strong leads and endings, visual and other sensory imagery. Research is interesting, surprising, and deftly and creatively incorporated into the paper.

As students were drafting, we had them highlight a few descriptors (specificity of detail, delights of language or insight) in their writing and look for places where adding elements specified in the description would improve their projects.

The final multigenre projects were as individual as our students. Figure 9.4 shows an example from each of our classes of the elements two students chose to include.

Andrew's Topic: The 1960s	Jacob's Topic: Broha (short for *brother*)
"Dear Reader" letter	**"Dear Reader" letter**
Glue: Quote from JFK	**Glue:** (Student-created) definition: brotherhood
Piece 1: Imagined JFK journal entries	**Piece 1:** "What Has Changed?," a poem
Glue: Quote from JFK	**Glue:** Definition: arrogance
Piece 2: A mock newspaper of the Kennedy assassination	**Piece 2:** "Area Man Forgets Arrogance to Bond with Brother," a parody in the style of the *Onion*
Glue: Quote from JFK	**Glue:** Definition: inspire
Piece 3: The British Invasion, a collage and brief commentary	**Piece 3:** "The American Trail," a map with a plan for a cross-country trip
Glue: Quote from JFK	**Glue:** Definition: hero

Figure 9.4 Two Sample Multigenre Project Outlines

Andrew's Topic: The 1960s	Jacob's Topic: Broha (short for *brother*)
Piece 4: An imagined speech from Martin Luther King Jr. announcing the upcoming Selma Freedom March	**Piece 4:** "I Choose Heroic," a narrative scene of a moment when he had a seizure
Glue: Quote from JFK	**Glue:** Definition: legacy
Piece 5: An argument claiming that the television age was born from the Nixon/Kennedy debate	**Piece 5:** A poem
Glue: Quote from JFK	**Glue:** Definition: rivalry
Piece 6: A speech written for a civil rights rally	**Piece 6:** "Sibling Order," a research article
Endnotes	Endnotes
Works cited	Works cited

Figure 9.4 Continued

✈ Closing Thoughts: The Value of Multigenre Writing

We want to inspire our students to write novels, poetry, music, or the next wildly successful Broadway musical. We want writers who can comfort others, who can deliver a wedding speech, who can write into the world. We want writers whose editorials carry influence and inspire action. We want writers who generate and discover their own thinking. The multigenre project invites students to practice writing they will use later in life. To move beyond traditional school boundaries into writing they will create long after high school. Most importantly, we want students to find joy in writing.

We are English teachers. What power lies in our hands. In every classroom and every school there is the possibility for rich, sustained reading and writing that engages, empowers, and opens up the potential to be both academic and creative. To make this happen, we need to inspire our students' imaginations. We need to wake them from their academic stupor to help them rediscover their individual voices and creative spirits. If you're looking to take one step toward that vision, the multigenre research project can help you get there.

Afterword

A late afternoon in September. We are all writing in notebooks when the whir of the printer splits the silence. Penny lifts the pages from the tray and finds an essay from Jack, a former student. He chose the wrong printer while working down the hall. She scans it: first, second, third—yep, count those five paragraphs. She reads voiceless transitions between a handful of sentences that tell this, tell that. The young writer followed directions, stacking paragraphs like blocks.

This gap between what could be and what is on the page is magnified because Penny knows this writer. When he was in ninth grade, she struggled to channel his tangled but sophisticated ideas for constructing stories. He was reading complex novels with multiple plot lines, so how could she use his deep engagement with independent reading to fuel his writing? She nudged him to grow his understanding of how narratives are built and developed. He did.

Jack raced through *Romeo and Juliet* the first weekend after we began it in class and was hungry for talk—for thinking about the layers of relationships outside the one at the center of the play. Jack analyzed the dynamics between Romeo and his parents and friends because the fantasy series he was reading, *Eragon*, ignited his thinking about the purpose of minor characters in the central narrative. Jack's regular, sustained practice in reading fantasy helped him imagine the ways Shakespeare's classic play *could have been written*. He then compared it with the way *it was written*. His analysis generated a lot of "What if?" thinking. Conferences with Jack (far too few) left Penny dazzled.

So why does it matter that now he writes the lifeless, no-one-but-a-high-school-English-teacher-reads-it, five-paragraph essay in grade ten? Because it is devoid of Jack. It is a task (grocery shopping, laundry) and Jack will complete it, but he won't light up inside it. He won't stretch. He won't corral all the ideas that flood his mind at once. He'll just write the essay he's been assigned to write, another lap around a formulaic, mindless track. Perhaps this one writing experience won't hurt him, but the relentless repetition of this form will. Standardized thinking stifles what we most value in writers: insight, courage, creativity, and joy.

We think a lot about the Jacks out there. They are held back by stifling standardization, and we've made the case in this book that there are more effective ways to elevate the literacy skills of young readers and writers. It begins with volume—the *daily* practice (reading, writing, and revising)—which leads all students to gain confidence and skill. Students will engage in reading when they are given time to read, choice in what they read, and access to the best books we can get our hands on. Students will approach writing with greater ease when they've practiced generating their own thinking instead of being restricted by the teacher's questions. When students write next to poetry and images and ideas, it builds curiosity—an interest in language, in words, and in analyzing the moves writers make to create sentences that hold our attention. Curiosity matters.

These practices create a deep understanding of what is possible.

Conversely, the habit of not thinking, just doing, is dangerous. Bad habits kill love. Kill joy. Kill confidence and interest. Evidence abounds. Too many students are fake reading. Too many students follow a formula and stop composing their ideas. Too many students believe a rubric can define excellent writing. They are reluctant to vary the formula because they are rewarded for following it. We treat formula as necessary when it is instead incendiary. It consumes the creativity, the voice, and the originality that students are capable of bringing to their writing.

Limiting the imaginations of readers and writers comes with consequences. If current practices were effective, more students would love to read and write outside school. When given the open road, they'd take it. We know how increasingly rare this is. Young writers must be given time to tackle issues they are struggling with, time to listen closely to their first drafts and imagine how to deepen the images their words create—to re-see, rework, struggle, and create something new. There is so much more to reading and writing than ordering paragraphs to answer a teacher's question. Our students live in a world filled with conflicts and discoveries, disappointments and revelations. We must get out of the way and let students read, write, and talk about those experiences or we risk losing them. We risk losing the power of each student's brilliant individuality, which can teach us all.

We've closely studied our decision-making and teaching practices for two years—one as we co-planned and taught a year together and one as we wrote this book. Writing helped us ask questions about what we taught. About what we believed. About our decisions. About our mistakes. We also wrote this book to push back against those practices that are stubbornly persistent in our schools—practices that have proven to be ineffective in producing independent and empowered readers and writers. We wrote this book because we want more for our students and because we expect more of ourselves.

We have made ourselves vulnerable to you, our colleagues, because we believe that you'll give this work a charitable read—that you'll view it with kindness and generosity instead of scorn. We are not proposing that what we do is the answer for you, or that we can presume to map your curriculum for your students in your particular setting. We share this book with you because we hope it will launch your own good ideas. We believe all teachers struggle to learn every year, as what we know shifts and new insights are gained. We struggle because we are told we must do it all. We've been bombarded with hundreds of strategies with no plan for when, where, and how to use them. We've been given pacing guides and curriculum maps that are presented as mandates instead of the aspirational, sometimes blind-to-our-kids documents they are. The endless list of what we "must" do presses on us, and the demands are not going away. What is important is how teachers respond to these demands.

How did we respond? We named our values and beliefs about teaching, and we aligned our practices to that vision. We took time to stop, to step out of the rush of our classrooms, and to examine our practices. We looked back on our teaching year much like we asked our students to look back on their year in our classrooms. In compiling portfolios, our students were asked to collect, select, and reflect. We did the same. We have collected a year of teaching in detail, we have selected the experiences we felt were most important to share with you and to think deeply about, and we have reflected on why our decisions mattered. We have shared some successes, as well as some mistakes, because we want to hold our teaching up to the light. We want to get better at what we do. Teaching is art—creation—and a curriculum map is only as good as the teacher who considers it, who questions it, and who revises it to meet the needs of each year's students.

We are reminded of a conversation Kelly had with an administrator who had taught for seven years before becoming an assistant principal. When Kelly asked her why she had left teaching, she replied, "I felt that after seven years of teaching I sort of had it down. I was ready for a new challenge." We find this response baffling, as we have each taught for thirty-three years and we still do not believe we "have it down." As Tom Newkirk (2009) has aptly noted, "Teaching is profoundly situational" (142). You know this already—what works in your second-period class may not work in your third-period class. Different kids, different tone, different pace. One size does not fit all. And while "group comparison research may suggest patterns for large populations, . . . teachers must make decisions in complex and individual human situations. Consequently, there is an inevitable mismatch between the guidance research can provide—and the decisions teachers must make" (Newkirk 2009, 148). We will never "have it down" because the "it" is in constant flux. Each year—each day— is a living, breathing thing, as we continue to meet students with different and ever-changing abilities, interests, and needs.

We believe our profession needs just what our students need: less standardization and more teacher creativity. Less common ground and more radical transformations—beginning with the smart thinking and professionalism of each of you. Let us recapture the spirit of innovation that is the central ingredient in great, passionate teaching. Let us make decisions that lead to increased student engagement with reading, writing, listening, and speaking. Let us slow down and go deeper—even if this means the entire curriculum is not covered. We can regain ownership of our craft, of our profession. And in doing so, we should never forget that the pathway to great teaching is a long one. Excellence happens incrementally. Let's work on one thing, and when we feel good about our progress, let's pick the next thing to work on. And then let's multiply this by thirty years.

As we close this book, we return to the question that started our project: "How do you fit it all in?" Answering this question has led us into a slow collaboration over time—into sustained engagement with hard thinking. We found that reading and writing about teaching pushed us to new places. There was no flinching from hard conversations; we spent our time together trying to figure things out. We responded to each other as learners, as colleagues, as friends, and we hope this book ignites similar conversations among you and your colleagues. It is easy to remain in silos, but that is where teaching stagnates. We hope you discover motivated peers and students who will question you, who will challenge you, and who will validate you.

And as you read this, we are already responding to the needs of this year's students and to the politics, economics, and history of our time. We remain committed to students. To reading, to writing, to student talk. To volume. To feedback. To conferences. To learning new tools and using them. To teacher expertise and decision-making. To responsive, alive teaching. Given the challenges in front of us, this will not be easy. We know that teaching well can feel like an act of rebellion, and we take comfort in the words of Frederick Douglass, who said, "The thing worse than rebellion is the thing that causes rebellion" (2012, 196). May you find the strength to rebel when rebellion is called for—to find a way through the storms of teaching. And may you emerge stronger, filled with joy, and alive to the possibilities in your work.

Conversation Clip

See "The Power of Teacher Collaboration"

Acknowledgments

There is a famous Red Wedding scene in *Game of Thrones* where an unexpected massacre occurs. In a flash, violence erupts. No prisoners are taken. The devastation leaves nothing but blood-red silence.

That scene reminds us of us.

Well, specifically, that scene reminds us of a moment that occurred early in the writing of this book. We were just getting started, and we were trying to find that delicate balance between our distinctly different voices. We did not want this to be too much of a "Penny book," and we did not want this to be too much of a "Kelly book." We wanted this to be *our* book, but finding that voice is tricky. Early on, we were still tiptoeing around each other's writing, trying not to inflict pain.

Until our Red Wedding day.

Penny had written a passage in her writer's notebook and she was excited to share it with Kelly. She sent it to him, along with the following note:

> It feels like I've hit on something important here that we need to think about. I've figured out how to explain something I haven't explained well before. I know I have more to say about this. It is *important* and clear to me, so I'm kind of jumping up and down in my chair right now.
>
> And it's truly a shitty first draft right now, so just try to get the gist of my ideas and ignore the crap of the writing.

Kelly's response is shown in Figure A.1.

Unlike what happened in *Game of Thrones*, Penny did not die. Somehow she found the strength to overcome the "bloodshed" of Kelly's jumping into pink-pen editing when she had asked only for a response to her thinking. We were both reminded that feedback on writing must be given delicately. We have to listen to a writer before we cover her work with corrections. On this day Penny did not want to work on the writing—or even read Kelly's corrections—because he wasn't listening to her.

Fortunately, our writing partnership not only survived but flourished. And we are thankful it did, for we have written a book we think you will find thought-provoking. We are deeply grateful to those who helped us get that work done.

However, crafting beautiful writing ~~craft~~ is not important in most writing for tasks in school. Functional, clear writing is 'good enough' for tests and assignments. Because of the pressure of time, ~~I see~~ writing in middle and high school has become factory-like—one task after another—and these assignments remain ~~becoming a factory to practice Writing~~ writing ~~that~~ is unimportant to the student. ~~—one task after another—and~~ There is little or no emphasis on ~~rarely about naming and~~ exploring the beauty and conflict that is coursing through each of our students ~~in our rooms.~~

We feel conflicted by how much time we spend on the necessary, often mind-numbing writing of explaining, answering, providing information, or in the case of our students, of proving that they remember or know something that been told to them—in orderly, complete sentences that can be outlined into paragraphs and turned into coherent essays. ~~But we are making a critical error We make critical errors in teaching writing when we focus it on writing for tasks only. We feel conflicted, I'm sure, by how much time we spend on the necessary, often mind-numbing writing of explaining, answering, providing information, or in the case of our students, of proving that they remember or know something that has been told to them—in orderly, complete sentences that can be outlined into paragraphs and turned into coherent essays.~~ This is the writing of reports on science experiments the students had no interest in conducting, the writing of essays on wars they see dimly, and still find no purpose in understanding, and often, the writing of essays on books they didn't read and have no interest in thinking about. This is the writing for school that we believe we have been hired to do. But we are making a critical error when we focus on writing for tasks only.

Figure A.1 Kelly Butchers the Passage

Four people deserve special mention:

✦ Katie Wood Ray, our editor at Heinemann, who had immeasurable influence on this book. To simply call Katie our editor does not do justice to the extent of her influence on these pages. She was much more than an editor. She was an engineer—exhibiting a skill set that proved invaluable when our original manuscript came in at 135,000 words and needed to be trimmed to 80,000 words. Katie's ability to rearrange, to cut, to tighten—to see new possibilities for this book—was amazing. We are in awe and deeply grateful.

✦ Tom Newkirk, who gave us advice after reading an early version of this manuscript. Tom's thinking challenged our own thinking, and it was instrumental in helping us make numerous positive changes in this book. We have always deeply admired Tom's books, and it was critical to have him offer insight into ours.

✦ Our spouses, Kristin and Pat, who endured two years of sacrifice while this book was being written. We do not use the word *sacrifice* lightly here. We wrote this book while teaching and traveling, which meant we were too often absent (both physically and mentally). We recognize how hard this was on you. Thank you for your strength and your patience. We hope this book does justice to what you had to endure.

We thank everyone at Heinemann who worked on this book. Shout-outs to Kim Cahill, for her oversight as marketing product manager; Vicki Kasabian and Patty Adams, for their production contributions; Suzanne Heiser, for her exquisite design; Edie Davis Quinn, for her work as editorial coordinator; Jennifer Greenstein for her sharp copyediting skills; and Brett Whitmarsh and Lauren Audet, for getting the word out via social media. Huge thanks to Vicki Boyd for her inspired, focused leadership of Heinemann. Penny also sends thanks to Michelle Flynn for helping to manage her travel life.

This book is better because it is augmented by the work of the best film crew possible. Thank you to Sherry Day, video wizard, for her coordination of people, snacks, and technicalities on our filming days; and Michael Grover, for being a skilled videographer and photographer, as well as for trying to surf the worst day of the year in Newport Beach. We love you both and look forward to the blooper reel of our mishaps. Two additional cameramen, David Stirling and Michael McEachern, helped us capture the intelligence and beauty of our students, and Keith McManus and Alan Chow's talent with sound is evident in every clip.

Thank you to the students in our ninth- and twelfth-grade classes at Magnolia High School and Kennett High School. You made it a joy to go to work every day. We like to think you learned from us; we know we learned from you. We believe in you.

Kelly would also like to thank those in the Anaheim Union High School District who did so much to support him over the course of this project. Thanks to Michael Matsuda, Jaron Fried, Manuel Colon, Jackie Counts, and Mike Switzer. Thank you as well to Jessica Uvalle and Jessica Russo, Kelly's student teachers over the course of the writing of this book. And thanks, as always, to the lunch table crew (Michelle, Robin, Lindsay, Kalli, Katrina, and Dana) for helping him to cope with the craziness of the Big M.

Penny would like to thank Kennett High School principal Neal Moylan and Conway School District superintendent Kevin Richards for continued support of her career in education. Huge thanks to her writing group colleagues: Ed Fayle, Ryan Mahan, Melissa Cyr, and Taylor Kanzler. They read sections of this book with kindness and good sense. They helped her unpack thinking from rambling and always made her want to get back to writing. Gratitude to her hall duty partner, John Weitz, who sees the joy in teaching and helps her stay focused on what matters. And love to her Boothbay and Pac-Lit colleagues Kylene Beers, Bob Probst, Linda Rief, and Chris Crutcher.

Lastly, we send deep appreciation to all the teachers we meet who understand that effective teaching sometimes springs from acts of rebellion. From the courage to change. From standing up. This book was written to honor you and your willingness to imagine what is possible.

REFERENCES

Adichie, Chimamanda Ngozi. 2009. "The Danger of a Single Story." TED talk. July. www.ted.com/talks
/chimamanda_adichie_the_danger_of_a_single_story/transcript#t-727788.

———. 2014. *Americanah*. New York: Anchor Books.

Alexie, Sherman. 2011. "Why the Best Kids Books Are Written in Blood." *Speakeasy* (blog), *Wall Street Journal*, June 9. blogs.wsj.com/speakeasy/2011/06/09/why-the-best-kids-books-are-written-in-blood/.

Anderson, Carl. 2000. *How's It Going? A Practical Guide to Conferring with Student Writers*. Portsmouth, NH: Heinemann.

Appelt, Kathi, and Alison McGhee. 2016. *Maybe a Fox*. New York: Simon and Schuster.

Atwell, Nancie. 2002. *Lessons That Change Writers*. Portsmouth, NH: Heinemann.

———. 2010. *Writing in the Middle*. DVD. Portsmouth, NH: Heinemann.

———. 2015. *In the Middle: A Lifetime of Learning About Writing, Reading, and Adolescents*. 4th edition. Portsmouth, NH: Heinemann.

Atwell, Nancie, and Anne Atwell Merkel. 2016. *The Reading Zone: How to Help Kids Become Passionate, Skilled, Habitual, Critical Readers*. 2nd ed. New York: Scholastic.

Bearak, Barry. 2013. "The Jockey." Article and narration (video). *New York Times*, August 14. www
.nytimes.com/projects/2013/the-jockey.

Beers, Kylene, and Robert E. Probst. 2017. *Disrupting Thinking: Why* How *We Read Matters*. New York: Scholastic.

Betts, A. J. 2016. *Zac and Mia*. Boston: HMH Books for Young Readers.

Blow, Charles M. 2011. "They, Too, Sing America." *New York Times*, July 15. www.nytimes.com/2011/07
/16/opinion/16blow.html.

Bradley, Kimberly Brubaker. 2016. *The War That Saved My Life*. New York: Penguin Putnam.

Bragg, Rick. 2002. "Skeleton Plunges Face-First Back into the Winter Games." *New York Times*, February 18. www.nytimes.com/2002/02/18/sports/olympics-skeleton-skeleton-plunges-face-first-back-into-the
-winter-games.html.

Burkins, Jan Miller, and Kim Yaris. 2014. *Reading Wellness: Lessons in Independence and Proficiency*. Portland, ME: Stenhouse.

Carnegie Mellon University. 2017. "What Is the Difference Between Assessment and Grading?" Carnegie Mellon University. Accessed October 25. www.cmu.edu/teaching/assessment/basics/grading
-assessment.html.

Chenoweth, Kristin, with Joni Rodgers. 2010. *A Little Bit Wicked: Life, Love, and Faith in Stages*. New York: Touchstone.

Christie, Michael. 2015. "All Parents Are Cowards." *Opinionator* (blog), *New York Times*, February 12. https://opinionator.blogs.nytimes.com/2015/02/12/all-parents-are-cowards/.

Council of Writing Program Administrators, National Council of Teachers of English, and National Writing Project. 2011. *Framework for Success in Postsecondary Writing*. Council of Writing Program Administrators. www.ncte.org/positions/statements/collwritingframework.

Danielson, Charlotte. 1996. *Enhancing Professional Practice: A Framework for Teaching*. Alexandria, VA: Association for Supervision and Curriculum Development.

Darwin Center for Biogeology. 2009. *Darwin Center for Biogeology*. www.darwincenter.nl/Content /Downloads/def%20binnenwerkdarwin08%E2%80%A2%E2%80%A2%E2%80%A2.pdf.

Douglass, Frederick. 2012. *In the Words of Frederick Douglass: Quotations from Liberty's Champion*, edited by John R. McKivigan and Heather L. Kaufman. Ithaca, NY: Cornell University Press.

Duckworth, Angela. 2016. *Grit: The Power of Passion and Perseverance*. New York: Scribner.

Education Reform Now. 2016. "Americans Spending at Least $1.5 Billion in College Remediation Courses: Middle Class Pays the Most." Press release. Education Reform Now. April 6. https://edreformnow.org /release-americans-spending-at-least-1-5-billion-in-college-remediation-courses-middle-class-pays -the-most/.

Erdrich, Louise. 2017. *LaRose*. New York: Harper Perennial.

Ferris, Joshua. 2015. *To Rise Again at a Decent Hour*. New York: Back Bay Books.

Fleischman, Paul. 2004. *Seedfolks*. New York: HarperTrophy.

Fletcher, Ralph. 2016. "Power and Possibility for the Reading and Writing Classroom." Keynote address at the New England Reading Association Conference, Portland, ME, May 20.

Forman, Gayle. 2009. *If I Stay*. New York: Speak.

Gallagher, Kelly. 2009. *Readicide: How Schools Are Killing Reading and What You Can Do About It*. Portland, ME: Stenhouse.

Glover, Matt, and Mary Alice Berry. 2012. *Projecting Possibilities for Writers: The How, What, and Why of Designing Units of Study, K–5*. Portsmouth, NH: Heinemann.

Glover, Matt, and Ellin Oliver Keene, eds. 2015. *The Teacher You Want to Be: Essays About Children, Learning, and Teaching*. Portsmouth, NH: Heinemann.

Goldberg, Mark. 1990. "Portrait of Madeline Hunter." *Educational Leadership* 47 (5): 41–43.

Graff, Gerald, and Cathy Birkenstein. 2014. *They Say/I Say: The Moves That Matter in Academic Writing*. 3rd high school ed. New York: W. W. Norton.

Graham, Steve, and Dolores Perin. 2007. *Writing Next: Effective Strategies to Improve Writing of Adolescents in Middle and High Schools*. Alliance for Excellent Education. https://all4ed.org/reports -factsheets/writing-next-effective-strategies-to-improve-writing-of-adolescents-in-middle-and -high-schools/.

Grann, David. 2009. "Trial by Fire: Did Texas Execute an Innocent Man?" *New Yorker*, September 7. www .newyorker.com/magazine/2009/09/07/trial-by-fire.

Grant, Adam M. 2017. *Originals: How Non-conformists Move the World*. New York: Penguin.

Graves, Donald H. 1985. "All Children Can Write." *Learning Disabilities Focus* 1 (1): 36–43. http://www .ldonline.org/article/6204.

———. 2003. *Writing: Teachers and Children at Work*. Portsmouth, NH: Heinemann.

Hargreaves, Andy, and Michael Fullan. 2012. *Professional Capital: Transforming Teaching in Every School.* New York: Teachers College Press.

Hattie, John. 2013. "Think of Feedback That Is Received Not Given." Interview. Visible Learning. https://visible-learning.org/2013/01/john-hattie-visible-learning-interview/.

Headley, Maria Dahvana. 2016. *Magonia.* New York: Harper.

Hillocks, George, Jr. 2011. *Teaching Argument Writing, Grades 6–12: Supporting Claims with Relevant Evidence and Clear Reasoning.* Portsmouth, NH: Heinemann.

Isay, David. 2012. *All There Is: Love Stories from StoryCorps.* New York: Penguin.

Ivey, Gay, and Peter H. Johnston. 2013. "Engagement with Young Adult Literature: Outcomes and Processes." *Reading Research Quarterly* 48 (3): 355–75.

Jago, Carol. 2004. *Classics in the Classroom: Designing Accessible Literature Lessons.* Portsmouth, NH: Heinemann.

Jamison, Leslie, and Francine Prose. 2015. "What Early Job Later Informed Your Work as a Writer?" *New York Times Book Review,* November 17.

Johnston, Peter H. 2004. *Choice Words: How Our Language Affects Children's Learning.* Portland, ME: Stenhouse.

Johnston, Peter H., and Gay Ivey. 2015. "Engagement: A Hub of Human Development." In *The Teacher You Want to Be: Essays About Children, Learning, and Teaching,* edited by Matt Glover and Ellin Oliver Keene, 50–63. Portsmouth, NH: Heinemann.

Kennedy, Robert. 1968. Remarks to the Cleveland City Club, April 5. "Robert F. Kennedy Speeches." John F. Kennedy Presidential Library and Museum. www.jfklibrary.org/Research/Research-Aids/Ready-Reference/RFK-Speeches/Remarks-of-Senator-Robert-F-Kennedy-to-the-Cleveland-City-Club-Cleveland-Ohio-April-5-1968.aspx.

King, Stephen. 2010. *On Writing: A Memoir of the Craft.* 10th anniversary ed. New York: Scribner.

Kittle, Penny. 2008. *Write Beside Them: Risk, Voice, and Clarity in High School Writing.* Portsmouth, NH: Heinemann.

———. 2013. *Book Love: Developing Depth, Stamina, and Passion in Adolescent Readers.* Portsmouth, NH: Heinemann.

Klosterman, Chuck. 2014. "Is It Wrong to Watch Football?" "The Ethicist," *New York Times Magazine,* September 5.

Konnikova, Maria. 2014. "What's Lost as Handwriting Fades." *New York Times,* June 2. www.nytimes.com/2014/06/03/science/whats-lost-as-handwriting-fades.html.

Langer, Judith A., and Arthur N. Applebee. 1987. *How Writing Shapes Thinking: A Study of Teaching and Learning.* Urbana, IL: National Council of Teachers of English.

Lessing, Doris. 2007. "Doris Lessing—Nobel Lecture." Nobelprize.org. December 7. www.nobelprize.org/nobel_prizes/literature/laureates/2007/lessing-lecture_en.html.

Marcus, Ruth. 2006. "IMs: What's a Mother to Do?" *Washington Post,* March 7. www.washingtonpost.com/wp-dyn/content/article/2006/03/06/AR2006030601238.html.

Marr, Bernard. 2015. "Big Data: 20 Mind-Boggling Facts Everyone Must Read." *Forbes,* September 30. www.forbes.com/sites/bernardmarr/2015/09/30/big-data-20-mind-boggling-facts-everyone-must-read/#2a2aca0b17b1.

Murphy, James S. 2016. "How a Teacher Bombed the SATs." *Boston Globe*, July 14. www.bostonglobe.com /ideas/2016/07/13/murphy-sat/y8pJbuv1ZTNXkMl6ZyZSHN/story.html.

NAEP. 2012. *Trends in Academic Progress: Executive Summary*. National Center for Education Statistics. https://nces.ed.gov/nationsreportcard/subject/publications/main2012/pdf/2013456.pdf.

Newkirk, Thomas. 2009. *Holding On to Good Ideas in a Time of Bad Ones: Six Literacy Principles Worth Fighting For*. Portsmouth, NH: Heinemann.

———. 2014. *Minds Made for Stories: How We Really Read and Write Informational and Persuasive Texts*. Portsmouth, NH: Heinemann.

Orlean, Susan. 2005. Introduction to *The Best American Essays, 2005*, edited by Lauren Slater and Robert Atwan, xv–xviii. New York: Mariner.

Palmer, Parker J. 1997. *The Courage to Teach: Exploring the Inner Landscape of a Teacher's Life*. San Francisco: John Wiley and Sons.

Paul, Annie Murphy. 2013. "How the Power of Interest Drives Learning." *MindShift*, November 4. ww2 .kqed.org/mindshift/2013/11/04/how-the-power-of-interest-drives-learning/.

Perrone, Pierre. 1997. "Obituary: Notorious B.I.G." *Independent*, March 10. www.independent.co.uk/news /people/obituary-notorious-big-1272140.html.

Pitts, Leonard, Jr. 2010. "Sometimes, the Earth Is Cruel." *Dallas News*, January 14.

———. 2012. "Some Harsh Sentences Prove Unjust." *Miami Herald*, May 19.

———. 2013. "Our Insanity Over Guns Claims More Victims." *Miami Herald*, September 17.

Popova, Maria. 2017. "Rebecca Solnit on Hope in Dark Times, Resisting the Defeatism of Easy Despair, and What Victory Really Means for Movements of Social Change." Brain Pickings. Accessed October 25. www.brainpickings.org/2016/03/16/rebecca-solnit-hope-in-the-dark-2/.

Reeves, Douglas. 2006. "Five Top Tips to Improve Student Engagement." *Center for Performance Assessment*. www.edutopia.org/pdfs/resources/reeves-five-tips-improve-stu-engagement.pdf.

Reilly, Rick. 2007. "Gamers to the End." *Sports Illustrated*, October 13. www.si.com/vault/2007/02/05 /8399843/gamers-to-the-end.

Robinson, Ken. 2006. "Do Schools Kill Creativity?" TED talk. February. www.ted.com/talks/ken_robinson _says_schools_kill_creativity.

———. 2013. "How to Escape Education's Death Valley." TED talk. April. www.ted.com/talks/ken _robinson_how_to_escape_education_s_death_valley.

Romano, Tom. 2000. *Blending Genre, Altering Style: Writing Multigenre Papers*. Portsmouth, NH: Heinemann.

———. 2006. "The Multigenre Paper." Student handout. https://binged.it/2iHXyO4.

Rosenblatt, Louise M. 1956. "The Acid Test for Literature Teaching." *English Journal* 45 (2): 66–74. www .ncte.org/library/NCTEFiles/Resources/Journals/EJ/1956/RosenblattAcidTest.pdf.

Sacks, Ariel. 2014. *Whole Novels for the Whole Class: A Student-Centered Approach*. San Francisco: Jossey-Bass.

Schmoker, Mike, and Gerald Graff. 2011. "More Argument, Fewer Standards." *Education Week*, April 19. www.edweek.org/ew/articles/2011/04/20/28schmoker.h30.html.

Schwalbe, Will. 2016. *Books for Living*. New York: Alfred A. Knopf.

Sitomer, Alan Lawrence. 2014. *Caged Warrior*. New York: Hyperion.